Pike

 3

HEAT WAVE

Pike

A SOCIAL AUTOPSY OF
DISASTER IN CHICAGO

HEAT WAVE

Eric Klinenberg

THE UNIVERSITY OF CHICAGO PRESS   CHICAGO AND LONDON

The University of Chicago Press, Chicago 60637
The University of Chicago Press, Ltd., London
© 2002 by The University of Chicago
All rights reserved. Published 2002
Paperback edition 2003
Printed in the United States of America

12 11 10 09 08 07 06 05 04   4 5
ISBN: 0-226-44321-3 (cloth)
ISBN: 0-226-44322-1 (paperback)

Library of Congress Cataloging-in-Publication Data

Klinenberg, Eric.
    Heat wave : a social autopsy of disaster in Chicago / Eric Klinenberg.
        p. cm.
    Includes bibliographical references and index.
    ISBN 0-226-44321-3 (cloth : alk. paper)
    1. Sociology—Urban.   2. Chicago (Ill.)—Social conditions.   3. Disasters—
Social aspects—Illinois—Chicago.   4. Heat waves (Meteorology)—Illinois—
Chicago.   5. Social problems.   6. Social science.   7. Aged—Services for—
Illinois—Chicago.   8. Aged—Services for.   9. Aged—Illinois—Chicago—Social
conditions.   I. Title.
    HV1471.C38 K585 2002
    363.34′921—dc21

                                                                    2001043724

♾ The paper used in this publication meets the minimum requirements of the
American National Standard for Information Sciences—Permanence of Paper for
Printed Library Materials, ANSI Z39.48-1992.

For my parents, Rona Talcott and Edward Klinenberg.
And for Herbert J. Davis, whose incisive mind and generous spirit will always provide inspiration.

Contents

Illustrations

TABLES

Acknowledgments

I did not intend to study Chicago when I moved to Berkeley in 1995, but once I recognized my habit of writing about the metropolis from afar I understood that the city I had always claimed as my home had also made a claim on me. I am fortunate that so many other Chicagoans are similarly bound to the city. Their attachment is the basis for an unusually strong collective conscience, and I suspect that it is also the condition that makes conducting social research in Chicago such a meaningful experience. I have many people to thank for their contributions to this book, and none deserve more credit than those who actively participated in the research: the senior citizens, block club participants, community activists, political officials, city employees, medical workers, social service providers, and journalists who opened their doors to me and shared either memories of the heat wave or personal accounts of their everyday experiences in the city.

Sociology is better suited for explaining and understanding social processes and events than for denigrating or celebrating particular individuals or groups, so although many complex personalities and difficult social problems appear in this account, no singular heroes or villains come to light in the analysis I offer here. If the social autopsy of the 1995 heat wave uncovers some of Chicago's hidden blights, it does so not to impugn or embarrass any people or institutions but to make sense of and call attention to emerging forms of isolation, deprivation, and vulnerability that deserve critical scrutiny. This book is both an invitation to consider the ways we live and die in the cities of today, and a challenge to imagine how we will transform and inhabit the cities of tomorrow.

It would have been impossible to conceive of this project—let alone to conduct the research for it—without the training I received as a graduate student in sociology at the University of California, Berkeley. I would like to thank my dissertation committee, Loïc

Wacquant, Manuel Castells, Michael Rogin, Martín Sánchez-Jankowksi, and Margaret Weir, as well as two readers, Claude Fischer and Nancy Scheper-Hughes, who acted as full-fledged committee members even though they were not formal participants. Lawrence Cohen, Gil Eyal, Neil Fligstein, Arlie Hochschild, Mike Hout, Tom Laqueur, and Sam Lucas added insight and support.

Fellow graduate students at Berkeley created an exciting intellectual environment. In particular, my thanks go to Kimberly McClain DaCosta, Daniel Dohan, Rodney Benson, Jeff Juris, Shai Lavi, Andrew Perrin, Onesimo Sandoval, Jessica Sewell, and Matt Wray for knowing how to mix criticism with compassion and companionship so that we could make it through our dissertations and live well in the process. Colleagues I got to know before arriving in California, especially Barbara Epstein, Sam Kaplan, David Lewis, and Louise Jezierski, provided wise counsel and friendship. The members of SAGS kept me on my toes while the rest of Berkeley rested, and made my small jumps forward feel like giant leaps.

Several institutions provided me with resources and the time, space, and critical attention that make scholarship possible. The early research and writing for this project were funded by fellowships from the Jacob Javits graduate fellowship program and the National Science Foundation, as well as small grants from the Berkeley Humanities Division and Phi Beta Kappa. An Individual Projects Fellowship from the Open Society Institute offered the final boost that I needed to continue my research and craft this book. I am grateful to OSI administrators Gail Goodman, Joanna Cohen, Gara LaMarche, JoAnn Mort, and Pamela Sohn for their support, and to OSI Fellows Jamie Kalven, Eyal Press, Jonathan Schorr, and Elaine Sciolino for helping me engage with the world outside of academe.

When I did my fieldwork in Chicago, Edward Lawlor welcomed me as a visiting scholar at the University of Chicago's Center for Health Administration Studies and introduced me to a network of local organizations concerned with health and aging. I spent six months in Paris at the Center for European Sociology of the École des Hautes Études en Sciences Sociales, where I learned new approaches to the study of politics, culture, and the media through seminars and discussions with Patrick Champagne, Remi Lenoir, Dominique Marchetti, and Pierre Bourdieu. I spent my last year in Berkeley working in ideal conditions at the Center for Urban Ethnography. I received excellent feedback from scholarly audiences at many academic events, including colloquia at the sociology departments of the University of California, Los

Angeles, the University of Chicago, New York University, Northwestern University, and the University of Lyon-Lumiere II; conference presentations at the American Anthropological Association meetings in 1997 and the American Sociological Association meetings in 1998; and a public lecture in the Medicine, Markets, and Bodies series at the University of California, Berkeley, in 1999. The influences of these institutions are apparent throughout this book.

I wrote the final version of the manuscript at Northwestern University, where colleagues in the Department of Sociology and the Institute for Policy Research offered fresh perspectives that allowed me to see beyond the parameters of my initial work. Soon after I returned to Chicago in 2000, Arthur Stinchcombe gave me useful suggestions for strengthening the theoretical apparatus that holds the book together—sometimes, indeed, less is more. Jeff Manza delivered on his promise to read each chapter that I dropped at his office door and convinced me that the best days of public sociology might still be ahead of us. And although Mary Pattillo likes to say that I would have finished the book months earlier had we not gotten caught up in so many long conversations and debates, the final product is better because of what I learned during our exchanges. Other colleagues at Northwestern have provided valuable feedback on portions of the manuscript. Thanks go to Nicola Beisel, Fay Cook, Gary Alan Fine, Benjamin Frommer, Jennifer Light, Ann Shola Orloff, Ethan Shagan, and Wes Skogan for their many contributions, and to Ellen Berrey, Liz Raap, Scott Leon Washington, and Pete Ziemkiewicz for their expert research assistance.

A number of friends and colleagues outside Chicago have also given me trenchant criticism and advice. Jack Katz and Richard Sennett read the entire manuscript and helped me refine various arguments and ideas. Evelyn Brodkin, Jodi Cantor, Dalton Conley, David Grazian, Doug Guthrie, and Sudhir Venkatesh offered suggestions on individual chapters. Paul Dimaggio, Serge Halimi, and Paul Willis provided sharp editorial comments and substantive feedback in reviews of journal articles about the heat wave that I previously had published in *Theory and Society* 28 (1999), *Ethnography* 2 (2001), and *Le Monde Diplomatique* (1997). Alane Salierno Mason played a crucial role in sustaining this project by expressing interest in a book about the heat wave while I struggled through the early stages of the research.

My gratitude also extends to the people whose willingness to share data on the heat wave and Chicago helped me build the empirical foundations of this project. Foremost among them are Steve Whitman, former director of the Epidemiology Program at the Chicago Department of Public Health and now the director of the Urban Health Institute at Mount Sinai Hospital; and Edmund Donoghue, the Chief Medical Examiner of Cook County. These two men have done more than anyone to explain the events of July 1995, and their generosity enabled me to explore the social dimensions of the disaster. Other local scholars and institutions helped as well. The Office of the Cook County Public Administrator accommodated my requests for information and gave me access to materials uncovered in investigations of heat wave decedents. Celia Berdes and Madelyn Iris of the Buehler Center on Aging at Northwestern University facilitated my access to a database of elderly people living alone who wished to participate in research studies. Robert Sampson shared data on neighborhood collective efficacy from the Harvard School of Public Health's Project on Human Development in Chicago Neighborhoods, and provided useful suggestions for thinking about community-level vulnerability. Jan Semenza offered data as well as an engaging account of how the U.S. Centers for Disease Control and Prevention carried out its research on the heat wave. Ron Theel and Trina Cieply at the *Chicago Sun-Times* helped assemble photographs from the newspaper archives; Neal Weisenberg and Fran Preston took time out from their busy jobs at ABC7 Chicago to make still images from ABC's television news broadcasts. Abigail Silva and Suzanne Lagershausen worked with me to map the heat wave mortality and to trace spatial patterns with geographical software that I could not handle alone. I thank them for their assistance.

It has been a pleasure to work with the University of Chicago Press. Doug Mitchell, whose daughter was married in Chicago during the week of the heat wave, was fated to edit this book. Doug had an intuitive feel for this project from the moment I explained it to him, and his suggestions for how a social autopsy could "take the temperature of the city" were always productive. Robert Devens and Sandy Hazel deserve special thanks for their many literary interventions.

Finally, I would like to thank the close friends and family members who supported me throughout this project. Danielle Klinenberg, Edward Klinenberg, Rona Talcott, Herb Davis, Anne McCune, Matt Brown, Katerina Christopolous, Brickson Diamond, Adam Gross, Colin Hall, Giev Kashkooli, Tamar Kelber, Sheryl Kelber, Ronald Lieber, Barbara Messing, Melanie Nutter, Marquez Pope, and Audrey Prins-Patt have led a genuinely communal effort to see this book into print. Esther Bishop, Florence Klinenberg, and my late grandparents, Jerome and Muriel Klinenberg, Irving Bishop, and Martin Talcott, provided inspiration. Caitlin Zaloom, who in the course of living with me has developed her own first-hand knowledge of the pleasures and perils of Chicago and urbanism, has been a consistent source of encouragement, advice, inspiration, and love. Caitlin has been a collaborator on this project from the moment she arrived in the city, and her influence is evident on every page. During my work on this book, my friends and family have taught me a lesson that my research in Chicago has only reinforced: there is nothing more valuable than good company.

It is conventional among social scientists to assign pseudonyms to the participants in their research projects; I have followed that convention in identifying people whose statements and experiences were not matters of public record, such as seniors living alone, residents of the neighborhoods and hotel residences where I conducted fieldwork, and social service providers. The people named in this book—political officials and activists, published journalists and scientists, heat wave victims, and medical officials—were impossible to disguise, either because the significance of their accounts is related to the roles they played during the heat wave, or because they are already on record for their involvement in the event.

The Urban Inferno

On Wednesday morning, 12 July 1995, the *Chicago Sun-Times* reported that a heat wave was heading for the city. An article proclaiming "Heat Wave on the Way—And It Can Be a Killer" ran on page 3 of the news section instead of on the weather page. Forecasters were predicting that the temperature would reach the mid-nineties that afternoon and stay near one hundred degrees Fahrenheit for the next two days. The humidity and ozone levels also would be high, making the air feel tropical, as if Chicago were in Fiji or Guam. The heat index, which measures the temperature that a typical person would feel, could top 120 degrees.

On Thursday the temperature hit 106 degrees and the heat index climbed to 126. Brick houses and apartment buildings baked like ovens, and indoor thermometers in high-rises topped 120 degrees even when windows were open. Thousands of cars broke down in the streets. Several roads buckled. City workers watered bridges spanning the Chicago River to prevent them from locking when their plates expanded (fig. 1). Train rails detached from their moorings and commuters endured long delays.

In the newspapers and on television, meteorologists recommended that Chicago residents use air conditioners, drink plenty of water each day, and relax: "Stake out your turf at the nearest beach, pool, or air-conditioned store. Slow down. . . . Think cool thoughts." Appliance stores throughout the city sold out their air conditioners and home pools. "This is the kind of weather we pray for," remarked one spokesperson for a regional supplier. Nearly one hundred thousand people crowded into a small downtown beach (fig. 2). Others took boat trips onto Lake Michigan, only to return when passengers became dehydrated and ill. Hundreds of children riding in school buses developed heat exhaustion when they got stuck in mid-day traffic. Adults carried

Figure 1. City workers hose down the Kinzie Street Bridge to prevent it from locking. Source: *Chicago Sun-Times;* photographer: John White. Reprinted with special permission from the Chicago Sun-Times, Inc. © 2002.

Figure 2. Tens of thousands swarm to the North Avenue Beach, seeking relief from the heat. Source: *Chicago Sun-Times;* photographer: Andre Chung. Reprinted with special permission from the Chicago Sun-Times, Inc. © 2002.

Figure 3. Makeshift public health: Fire Department personnel hose down children in a city park. Source: ABC7. Courtesy of WLS-TV.

many of the children out of the vehicles, firefighters hosed them down, and paramedics provided emergency assistance (figs. 3, 4). Those with the worst illnesses were hospitalized.

The city soon experienced scattered power outages as a result of unprecedented electrical use. As lights, air conditioners, radios, and television sets were rendered useless, news, weather updates, and health advice were hard to get. Elevators stopped, making it necessary for members of the Police and Fire Departments to carry elderly high-rise residents down from the stifling heat of their apartments. Many people with no power or simply no air-conditioning packed bags and stayed with family or friends. On Friday three power transformers failed at the Northwest Substation of Commonwealth Edison, the city's primary electric delivery services company, causing forty-nine thousand customers to lose power—some for as long as two days.

In neighborhoods with few air-conditioned public spaces, young residents opened fire hydrants and showered themselves in the spray to keep cool. At one point more than three thousand hydrants spouted freely, contributing to an expenditure of almost two billion gallons of water, double Chicago's consumption on a typical summer day. Water pressure

Figure 4. Children receive emergency care for dehydration. Source: ABC7. Courtesy of WLS-TV.

Figure 5. Commonwealth Edison crew sprays power generators to prevent overheating. Source: ABC7. Courtesy of WLS-TV.

Figure 6. "Water Wars": City workers attempt to seal one of the three thousand hydrants illegally opened during the heat wave. Source: ABC7. Courtesy of WLS-TV.

fell. Neighborhoods where several hydrants were open lost all pressure for hours; malfunctioning pumps left buildings without water for days. Police announced that anyone found tampering with hydrants would be arrested and fined, and the city dispatched one hundred field crews to seal these emergency water sources (fig. 6). In some places people saw the crews coming and threw bricks and rocks to keep them away. Some shot at the trucks, and four workers received minor injuries.

On Friday, 14 July, the heat index exceeded one hundred degrees for the third consecutive day, and temperatures remained high at night. Because the body's defenses can take only about forty-eight hours of uninterrupted exposure to such heat before they break down, city residents were becoming ill. Many more people than usual grew sick enough to be hospitalized: between 13 and 19 July ambulance services received several thousand transport requests above the norm. In thirty-nine hundred cases, no vehicles were available, so the city sent fire trucks to handle the calls. Although the average response time for Chicago's emergency health services had been less than seven minutes that year, now the paramedics were often delayed. Some residents who phoned for ambulances were told that that they would have to wait because the vehicles were all booked. Fifty-five emergency callers were left unattended for thirty minutes or longer; some endured a two-hour wait. In a few cases of heat stress the victims waited so long for medical attention that they died.

Hospitals and other health-care providers also had trouble meeting the demand for their services. The number of people admitted to emergency rooms and inpatient units began to rise on Wednesday and continued to increase through the weekend. Some emergency rooms ran out of beds and their staffs could not handle more work. More than twenty hospitals, most on the South and Southeast Sides of the city, went on bypass status, closing the doors of their emergency facilities and refusing to accept new admissions. There was no reliable way for citizens or paramedics to learn which emergency rooms were still open, so ambulances and private cars continued to arrive at the hospital ports. Often their passengers required urgent treatment, but facilities on bypass could not tell drivers where such care was available. Some hospitals reported that patients had traveled more than ten miles before finding a facility that could treat them. Medical workers grew anxious. What would happen to the diverted cases? Where could they go?

Many heat victims were not discovered or taken to hospitals until it was too late for doctors to help. On Friday, for example, Margaret Ortiz, the owner of a small day-care service that she operated from her home, took a group of ten small children to an air-conditioned movie theater in her Ford Bronco. After the movie ended, Ortiz took the children back to the center and brought them indoors. Everyone was exhausted and the toddlers napped. An hour and a half passed before Ortiz went to her Bronco on her way to picking up more children. When she reached her vehicle, she discovered that two boys had been left inside. Ortiz carried the children indoors and called 911. The boys were already dead, though, and when the paramedics arrived, they determined that the body temperatures were 107 and 108 degrees. Chicago newspapers and television news programs featured stories of the children's deaths prominently in their heat wave coverage. The Cook County Medical Examiner scheduled autopsies on the children for the next morning, but there was little question about the cause of death.

As the day wore on, more Chicagoans succumbed to the heat. By comparison, on Wednesday, 12 July, and Thursday 13 July, 74 and 82 people, respectively, lost their lives, figures that are only slightly above the July norm of about 72 deaths per day. When the effects of the continuous heat began to accumulate, however, the death toll increased substantially (figs. 7, 8). On Friday, 14 July, 188 Chicago resi-

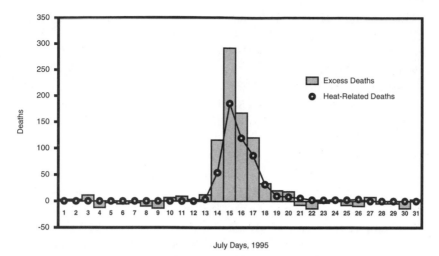

Figure 7. Excess and heat-related mortality in Chicago, July 1995. Source: City of Chicago, Department of Public Health.

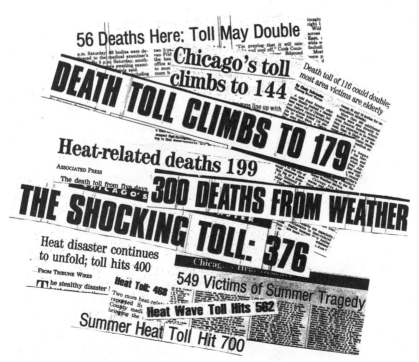

Figure 8. Newspaper headlines track the death toll.

dents perished. On Saturday the reported mortality was 365, five times the typical rate. Two hundred forty-one people died on Sunday, 193 on Monday, and 106 on Tuesday. On Wednesday, 19 July, citywide deaths dropped to 92, then to 91 on Thursday. City agencies, already scrambling to manage the crisis, searched for a place that could hold the dead. According to emergency workers, the task was equivalent to handling one fatal jetliner crash per day for three consecutive days.

THE CITY OF DEATH

Police officers took hundreds of the dead bodies to the Cook County Medical Examiners Office, a modern concrete building across from the county hospital and a few miles west of the Loop. The discreetly housed morgue there typically receives about seventeen bodies per day, but the staff can usually process more. Now they were receiving more corpses than they could handle, and the clinical staff of fourteen pathologists worked marathon shifts to keep up. The Chief Medical Examiner recruited forensic dental workers and students from a nearby school of mortuary science to assist in identifying and examining the cadavers. Moreover, he asked police officers to cart bodies from the parking lot to the office and city workers to clear space for the pathologists to work. But even this amount of help was not enough. Consequently, Cook County corrections officials offered people on probation two days of credit for each day that they worked at the morgue; some of them accepted this proposal. Nonetheless, a long line of police vehicles carrying dead bodies formed outside the Medical Examiners Office building, with some waiting as long as three hours for an available worker to receive the body. "It's like an assembly line in there," one officer said. In many cases police delivered decomposed bodies to the morgue several days after the date of death because no one had noticed that the person had not been seen in a while. It was impossible to know how many more victims remained in their homes, undiscovered.

By Saturday the number of bodies coming in to the morgue exceeded its 222-bay holding capacity by hundreds. Incoming bodies were scattered around the office, and many of the examined corpses remained unclaimed because there were no next of kin. The owner of a local meat-packing firm volunteered to bring his fleet of refrigerated trucks to the morgue for storing the excess bodies. The first group of red and yellow vehicles, each about forty-eight feet long, arrived on Friday, but they filled up quickly and dozens of bodies remained. The crew brought more trucks through the weekend, and ultimately there were nine altogether. Parked in the morgue's lot, the trucks were sur-

Figure 9. At the Cook County Medical Examiners Office, refrigerated trucks stored bodies when the bays at the morgue filled to capacity. Source: *Chicago Sun-Times;* photographer: Robert Davis. Reprinted with special permission from the Chicago Sun-Times, Inc. © 2002.

rounded by police wagons, radio and television vans, hearses, and private cars. Images of the scene appeared on television screens and newspapers around the world (fig. 9).

In the end, the city reported that between 14 and 20 July, 485 Chicago residents died directly from heat-related causes, bringing the total mortalities for the month to 521.[1] (These numbers were based on medical autopsies and police examinations that officially established causes of death for each case.) More than one thousand people in excess of the July norm were admitted to inpatient units in local hospitals because of heatstroke, dehydration, heat exhaustion, renal failure, and electrolytic imbalances. Those who developed heatstroke suffered permanent damage, such as loss of independent function and multisystem organ failures. Thousands of other stricken by heat-related illnesses were treated in emergency rooms.

After the heat had subsided, epidemiologists compiled statistics on the mortality patterns during July, taking into account the deaths of people who had not been taken to the Medical Examiners Office. They determined that the death count based solely on the medical autopsies had underestimated the damage. Between 14 and 20 July, 739 more Chicago residents died than in a typical week for that month. In fact, public health scholars have established that the proportional death toll from the heat wave in Chicago has no equal in the record of U.S. heat disasters.

Comparisons with other historic catastrophes help to establish the magnitude of the trauma. More than twice as many people died in the heat wave than in the Great Chicago Fire of 1871, when approximately three hundred people perished. More recent U.S. environmental disasters, such as California's Northridge earthquake of 1994 and Florida's Hurricane Andrew in 1992, caused the deaths of one-tenth and one-twentieth the heat wave total, respectively. The Oklahoma City bombing in April 1995, which killed 168, and the crash of TWA Flight 800 in 1996, which killed 230, were several times less fatal. Reporters, public officials, and scientific authorities have developed compelling and straightforward accounts of the reasons that so many people died in these other environmental or technological disasters. In the Chicago heat tragedy, however, the causes of the mortality are more elusive and complex.

In recent years, a number of meteorological studies and journalistic reports have examined the reasons for the historic mortality figures. According to the National Oceanic and Atmospheric Administration, "The principal cause of the July 1995 heat wave was a slow-moving, hot, and humid air mass produced by the chance occurrence at the same time of an unusually strong upper-level ridge of high pressure and un- usually moist ground conditions."[2] The geographer Laurence Kalkstein provided a deeper analysis of the weather. Using a new air mass–based synoptic procedure to pinpoint the meteorological conditions that im- pose serious health hazards, Kalkstein found that a moist tropical sys- tem, with high humidity, low winds, and high minimum temperatures, created an unusually dangerous July climate.

But does the severe weather fully account for Chicago's human catas- trophe? According to the meteorologists and epidemiologists who have studied the event, the answer is decidedly no. In an article published by the *American Journal of Public Health*, a group of scholars headed by the former epidemiology director of the Chicago Department of Public Health reported that it had "examined some weather variables but failed to detect relationships between the weather and mortality that would explain what happened in July 1995 in Chicago." Even the most sophisticated meteorological analyses "still leave a fair amount of vari- ance in the mortality measure unexplained."[3] The weather, in other words, accounts for only part of the human devastation that arose from the Chicago heat wave. The disaster also has a social etiology, which no meteorological study, medical autopsy, or epidemiological report can uncover. The human dimensions of the catastrophe remain unexplored.

This book is organized around a social autopsy of the 1995 Chicago heat wave. Just as the medical autopsy opens the body to determine the proximate physiological causes of mortality, this inquiry aims to examine the social organs of the city and identify the conditions that contributed to the deaths of so many Chicago residents that July. If the idea of conducting a social autopsy sounds peculiar, this is largely because modern political and medical institutions have attained monopolistic roles in officially explaining, defining, and classifying life and death, in establishing the terms and categories that structure the way we see and do not see the world. As Gaston Bachelard has written, "It quite often happens that a phenomenon is insignificant only because one fails to take it into account."[4] The missing dimension in our current understanding of the heat wave stems precisely from this kind of diagnostic failure.

What happened in Chicago was more than a natural disaster, and its story is more than a catalogue of urban horrors. The 1995 heat wave was a social drama that played out and made visible a series of conditions that are always present but difficult to perceive. Investigating the people, places, and institutions most affected by the heat wave—the homes of the decedents, the neighborhoods and buildings where death was concentrated or prevented, the city agencies that forged an emergency response system, the Medical Examiners Office and scientific research centers that searched for causes of death, and the newsrooms where reporters and editors symbolically reconstructed the event—helps to reveal the social order of a city in crisis. This study establishes that the heat wave deaths represent what Paul Farmer calls "biological reflections of social fault lines"[5] for which we, and not nature, are responsible. We have collectively created the conditions that made it possible for so many Chicago residents to die in the summer of 1995, as well as the conditions that make these deaths so easy to overlook and forget. We can collectively unmake them, too, but only once we recognize and scrutinize the cracks in our social foundations that we customarily take for granted and put out of sight.

I first learned about the outbreak of deaths in Chicago from an international newspaper I was reading during the week of the heat wave. I was twenty-four years old at the time, living in Europe and preparing to enter a graduate program in sociology at Berkeley the next month.

It had been uncomfortably hot in Europe, too, that summer, with temperatures in the high nineties and low hundreds from Paris to Madrid. But I had heard nothing about heat wave deaths there. The headline caught my eye not only because of the contrast between Europe and the United States; more important, I was one of Chicago's native sons, one of the many who had grown up navigating the physical and moral geography of the famously divided city, tiptoeing along or across the borders which separated regions and the groups that, in University of Chicago sociologist Robert Park's famous words, "touch but do not interpenetrate."[6] Chicago was, and still is, my home. The story of its heat epidemic captivated me, suddenly bringing into focus my blurry morning survey of the world's events. I wanted to learn what happened, but the article, rich with fine journalistic detail of scandal, death, and political and scientific debate, failed to offer the clues I needed. The events in Chicago, I guessed, were even more intriguing than the account suggested.

It was hardly the first time I had been puzzled by Chicago. Growing up in the center of the city, I had always been fascinated by the stark and storied contrast between its opulent Gold Coast and lakefront highrises and its ghettos and slums; by the legends of colorful political leaders and insider deals that, to my child's eyes, made the city seem like a sprawling kingdom divided into small fiefdoms and governed by fanciful rulers whose personalities and connections carried more weight than the scales of justice or the balance of reason; by the mysterious underground roads, abandoned railways, and empty factories that haunted the city; by the rushing crowds on Michigan Avenue and the solitary men and women who sat nearby and watched them pass. When I decided to pursue a doctorate in urban sociology, it was, in part, based on my hope that my studies in Berkeley would help me make sense of what I had experienced in Chicago.

When I reached northern California in August of 1995, few people had thought about or even remembered what had happened in the Midwest just a few weeks before. The booming region, fantastically wealthy and economically confident, had little time for such a story. It was easy to dismiss the West Coast reaction as a mark of the vast cultural and physical distance between California and Chicago, a sign that, though I was closer to home than I had been in Europe, I was once again living in another country. But a few weeks later I went to Chicago and discovered that many of my oldest friends and relatives responded to queries about the catastrophe with analogous forms of detachment and disavowal. Paradoxically, people who had lived through the heat wave had both absorbed the magnitude of the disaster and blocked out its significance and implications. Something about the event had rendered it unintelligible or inexplicable; people in the city were apparently having trouble engaging it; the human side of the disaster was elusive, beyond words.

Everyone, of course, remembered the heavy air and the interminable heat, and several people I knew gave elaborate accounts of what they did when their power was out for hours or days. Yet I was confused by the frequent references my friends made to the possibility that the heat wave deaths were not, to use the phrase that recurred in their accounts, "really real"—in other words, as several political officials suggested, that the massive mortality figures from the week had somehow been fabricated, or that the deaths were simply not related to the heat. How could such ideas have grown so popular?

What made the question all the more intriguing was that many of the Chicagoans I spoke with also had strong, vivid memories of the scene at the coroner's office, of the incredible spectacle of hundreds of dead bodies and dozens of workers that every news outlet in the city had put on display. I knew of several human rights investigations in which the discovery of a mass grave had settled questions about whether a reputed massacre or a history of violent repression had actually taken place. Yet in Chicago, it seemed, the very opposite process was at work: rather than clarifying the conditions or causes of death, attention to and examination of the victims had somehow obfuscated their status. The dead bodies were so visible that almost no one could see what had happened to them.

My trip home initially left me even more puzzled by the heat wave and the processes through which we have come to know it. There was an urgent need to conduct what I imagined as a social autopsy, yet the concept of such an undertaking—let alone a technique for performing it—did not exist. I began to ask how the tools of sociological inquiry—ethnographic fieldwork, in-depth interviewing, archival research, mapmaking, and statistical analysis—could help to build an account of how the nature, culture, and politics of the city crystallized in Chicago in the summer of 1995. Soon thereafter I became convinced that social scientific methods and theories could advance or answer questions about the heat wave that other investigations had not addressed. I initiated the research for what became a five-year examination, and the report before you recounts what I found.

INTRODUCTION
The City of Extremes

Thursday, 13 July 1995, was the hottest day in Chicago's recorded history, but the weather is only one of the reasons that Joseph Laczko died alone in his home soon afterward. Laczko, a sixty-eight-year-old man of Hungarian descent, lived by himself in an apartment on the city's Northwest Side. Although he had few visitors, Laczko apparently staved off loneliness by collecting his neighbors' unwanted mail and filling his home with phone books, old newspapers, and shoddy furniture.[1] Laczko preserved order amidst the chaos of broken radios and piled seat cushions by keeping a calendar, in which he recorded the daily temperature and noted the news stories that moved him. On 15 July he entered "94 degrees" in the book. On 16 July he was dead.

Aside from the calendar, investigators from the Office of the Cook County Public Administrator who searched Laczko's home for contact information about friends or family found only a few signs of a social life. Laczko kept a couple of letters sent to him from Hungary in the 1980s; a bank statement showing that his last withdrawal, on 1 July, brought his account down to less than a thousand dollars; a group of letters from legal cases in which he had been involved in the 1980s and early 1990s; and an Easter card he had written in 1991 but never sent. Most of Laczko's papers were taken to the Public Administrators Office, and the staff would later use them in their efforts to track down someone interested in claiming his possessions.

In their report, the investigators listed the results of their inquiry: "Unfurnished one bedroom apartment. Complete mess. . . . Living room: 4 chairs, 2 stereos, 2 stools, boxes, misc papers, junk, garbage. Bedroom: wardrobe, 1 single bed, 3 dressers, misc clothing, papers, garbage. Dining room: 1 dresser, 1 film projector, 1 table, garbage. Family: 0." They took two instant photographs, consulted with Laczko's landlord, and left for their next job. "There was so much to do that we lost all idea of time," an investigator on Laczko's case remembered. "We'd hit the streets and we just kept going until nightfall. We were so crushed that we had to write our reports from the field." It was the busiest week ever experienced by the Public Administrators Office, which is in charge of managing the estates of unclaimed decedents. Dozens of cases that would be similar to Laczko's remained.

Cook County officials brought Laczko's corpse to the morgue, where the intake staff of pathologists assembled by Chief Medical Examiner Edmund Donoghue was racing to keep up with the demand. After examining the body, pathologists determined that Laczko had died of artherosclerotic cardiovascular disease and heat stress. They penned these findings on his death certificate, entered his records into a computer database, and moved his cadaver into storage. The office waited for Laczko's next of kin to take care of his remains, but no one ever came. When it was clear that the body would never be claimed, the Public Administrators Office used funds from Laczko's bank account to have a private funeral home arrange for his interment in a cemetery nearby.

Solitary at the end of life, Laczko was joined by hundreds of other Chicago residents who died alone during the heat wave and were assisted by two potentially life-saving interventions—attention from state-sponsored service providers and artificial cooling—only after their bodies were delivered to the Cook County Morgue. Just a minority of the victims, including a mother and child who succumbed together and two sisters who lived in the same building, perished with company nearby. Hundreds died alone behind locked doors and sealed windows that entombed them in suffocating private spaces where visitors came infrequently and the air was heavy and still. Among these victims, the bodies and belongings of roughly 170 people went unclaimed until the Public Administrators Office initiated an aggressive campaign to seek out relatives who had not noticed that a member of their family was missing. Even then, roughly one-third of the cases never moved beyond the public agency. The personal possessions of dozens of the heat wave victims, including Laczko, remain filed in cardboard boxes at the County Building to this day.

THE SOCIAL AUTOPSY

In the years following the heat wave, several political commissions and city leaders have dismissed the solitary deaths of Laczko and the hundreds of other Chicagoans as anomalous and abnormal. The catastrophic week in July, they argue, was a freakish disaster that shows little more than our human frailty to the whims of nature. Immediately after the heat wave, for example, Mayor Richard M. Daley appointed a large commission to study, in its words, "the epidemiological, meteorological, and sociological aspects of the heat wave." The commission's major findings are summarized in the beginning of its report: "The heat wave was a unique *meteorological event* caused by a rare convergence of critical factors" (italics added), which it specifies as (1) a heat index above 100 degrees daily, including two consecutive days over 115 degrees; (2) cloudless skies with little night cooling; and (3) an *urban heat island effect**—whereby the concentration of buildings and pavement attracts and traps the heat—that heightened the temperature within the city. The subsection entitled *Why Heat Can Be Fatal* explains simply that "the link between human physiology and environment is delicate and pivotal. When body temperature rises enough above the normal range, heat injury occurs. Severe heat injury is fatal."[2] Social factors receive no attention in this crucial part of the report.

What the commission also buried in its publication is the connection between its work and the heat wave, since the title, *Final Report: Mayor's Commission on Extreme Weather Conditions,* makes no reference to the trauma it assesses. Disguised as a general statement about the weather, the report helped the city government hide its own public statement about the disaster by publishing it under another name. This strategic move was typical of the public and the political response to the crisis. Although the death toll from the one-week heat wave is unprecedented in U.S. history, the collective response to the trauma

---

* The climates of cities are generally different from the weather systems in the areas surrounding them, and the urban heat island effect refers to the elevated temperatures typical in urban spaces. According to a classic article by William Lowry (1967), "the city itself is the cause of these differences." Lowry identifies five principal causes for the city's exceptional climate: (1) "The predominantly rocklike materials of the city's buildings and streets can conduct heat about three times as fast as it is conducted by wet, sandy soil"; (2) "the city's structures have a far greater variety of shapes and orientations than the features of the natural landscape. The walls, roofs, and streets of a city function like a maze of reflectors, absorbing some of the energy they receive and directing much of the rest to other absorbing surfaces"; (3) "the city has many sources of heat that the countryside either lacks or has in far smaller numbers. Among them are factories, vehicles, and even air conditioners, which of course must pump out hot air in order to produce their cooling effect"; (4) "the city has distinctive ways of disposing of precipitation [with] drainpipes, gutters, and sewers. . . . Because there is less opportunity for evaporation in the city, the heat energy that would have gone into the process is available for heating the air"; and (5) "the air in the city is different in that it carries a heavy load of solid, liquid, and gaseous contaminants. . . . Although these particles collectively tend to reflect sunlight, thereby reducing the amount of heat reaching the surfaces, they also retard the outflow of heat" (Lowry 1967, 15–17).

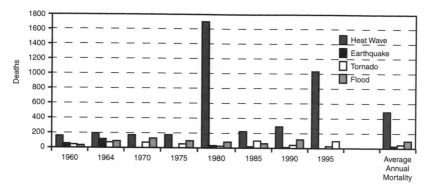

Figure 10. United States disaster mortality, 1960–95. Sources: heat wave, Vital Statistics of the United States; earthquake, USGS National Earthquake Information Center; tornado and flood, the National Oceanic and Atmospheric Administration.

has been marked by a will not to know the reasons that so many people died.[3]

Such treatment is not unusual. Given the attention that we pay to spectacular and camera-ready disasters such as hurricanes, earthquakes, tornadoes, and floods, Americans are often surprised to learn that in the United States more people die in heat waves than in all other extreme meteorological events *combined* (fig. 10). Heat waves receive little public attention not only because they fail to generate the massive property damage and fantastic images produced by other weather-related disasters, but also because their victims are primarily social outcasts—the elderly, the poor, and the isolated—from whom we customarily turn away.[4] Silent and invisible killers of silenced and invisible people, the social conditions that make heat waves so deadly do not so much disappear from view as fail to register with newsmakers and their audiences—including social scientific experts on disasters.[5] The introduction to a recent anthology of essays on urban disasters, for example, lists the most deadly urban events of the 1980s and 1990s, but inexplicably excludes the Chicago heat wave—and indeed all other American heat waves—even though the 1995 catastrophe killed more than ten times the number of people as the deadliest disaster in the table, the 1989 San Francisco Bay earthquake.[6]

In contrast with the public reluctance to look closely at the causes of Chicago's summer trauma, scientists from a range of fields have been drawn to study the heat wave because the prevalence and patterns of mortality defy easy explanation. As public health researchers have shown, the morbidity and mortality rates from the urban inferno surpass the levels predicted by standard scientific models. In analyzing the heat wave, medical and meteorological scientists discovered a series of puzzles that they have been working to solve for years. Why, for example, did so many Chicagoans die alone? Why was the overall death toll higher than meteorological models would predict? Why did some neighborhoods and groups experience greater devastation than others? And why did the support systems designed to protect vulnerable city residents fail to work? Unfortunately, the methods and theories used in conventional health and climate studies deprive scientists of the instruments they need to conduct a thorough investigation. There is little in their professional tool kit to help explain the social sources of the disaster. Although every major study and report has found that medical and meteorological approaches are inadequate to explain why so many Chicago residents died, no one has analyzed how the city's social environment contributed to the devastation.

This book is driven by two overarching concerns. First, it examines the *social conditions* that made it possible for hundreds of Chicago residents—most of them old, alone, and impoverished—to die during the one-week heat spell. As in Kai Erikson's *Everything in Its Path,* the social autopsy draws upon a wide range of social scientific studies, sifting "through the store of available sociological knowledge to see what light it might shed on a single human event."[7] Despite the insistence of several political commissions and journalistic stories that the heat wave fatalities were dispersed throughout the city—that the "casualties of heat," as a *Chicago Tribune* headline put it, were "just like most of us," or, as the *Sun-Times* proclaimed, "they were as varied as victims of a plane crash"—the patterns of mortality reflect the inequalities that divide Chicago.[8]

The victims were primarily elderly: 73 percent of the heat-related casualties were older than sixty-five years of age (table 1). African Americans had the highest proportional death rates of any *ethnoracial* group.[9] They were significantly more vulnerable to the catastrophe than whites, with a death ratio of 1.5:1 in the total, age-adjusted population* (table 2), 1.8:1 for middle-aged victims (aged fifty-five to

* Age-adjustment is the statistical technique in which the age distributions of specific populations are standardized so that the experience of those populations—in this case, heat-related mortality—can be compared in light of their age differences. For further information about age-adjustment in the analysis of mortality rates, see the National Center for Health Statistics Web site: <www.cdc.gov/nchs/datawh/nchsdefs/ageadjustment.htm#Mortality>.

Table 1. Total Heat-Related Deaths by Age and Race/Ethnicity: Chicago
Residents

Age	White	Black	Latino	Other	Total
<55	27	39	1	0	67
55–64	25	45	4	1	75
65–74	62	64	1	0	127
75–84	90	66	1	2	159
85+	48	42	2	1	93
Total	252	256	9	4	521

Source: City of Chicago, Department of Public Health.

Table 2. Age-Specific and Age-Adjusted Heat-Related Death Rates per
100,000 Population, by Race/Ethnicity: Chicago Residents, July 1995

Age	Non-Hispanic White	Non-Hispanic Black	Ratio: Black/White
<55	4	5	1.3
55–64	31	57	1.8
65–74	75	83	1.1
75–84	119	176	1.5
85+	222	429	1.9
Total*	11	17	1.5

Source: Whitman, et al. (1997, 1516).
* Standardized to the 1940 U.S. population.

sixty-four years), and 1.9:1 for very old victims (aged eighty-five years
or older). Indeed, although several officials and journalists emphasized
the virtual parity in numbers of heat-related deaths between African
Americans and whites, there was no age group in which African Americans did not have the highest proportional death rates in the city.
These stratified mortality figures reflect typical patterns in Chicago,
where African Americans daily face higher risks of death than whites,
as well as typical patterns of heat wave death. In contrast, Latino Chicagoans, whose overall level of poverty placed them at a heightened risk
of mortality, experienced a surprisingly low death rate. Although they
constituted at least 23 percent of the city's population in 1995, they
represented only 2 percent of the heat wave deaths. Accounting for
this "Latino health paradox," whereby Latinos experience better outcomes or conditions than their collective deprivation leads public
health scholars to predict, is one of the challenges for the social autopsy.[10]

There was also a significant and surprising difference in the mortality levels for men and women. Fifty-five percent of the heat-related

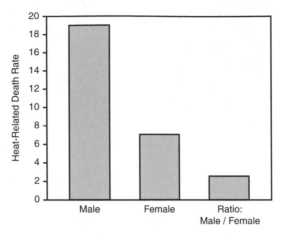

Figure 11. Age-adjusted heat-related death rates per one hundred thousand residents, by sex. Source: City of Chicago, Department of Public Health.

deaths were men and 45 percent were women; the age-adjusted death rates show that when the age factor is controlled, men were more than twice as likely as women to die (fig. 11). These patterns vexed some experts on aging, because elderly women are so much more likely than their male counterparts to live by themselves that many gerontologists consider aging alone to be a women's issue. Men's relatively high death rates are even more confusing when viewed in the context of gerontologist Hamilton Gibson's finding that women are more likely than men to report feeling lonely and isolated.[11] The pattern begs for explanation.

In addition to these group-level differences, there were also sharp contrasts in the prevalence of death among Chicago community areas.[12] In the city famous for the extent to which its spatial order reflects the social division of its residents, the geography of vulnerability during the heat wave was hauntingly similar to the everyday ecology of inequality. Heat wave deaths were concentrated in the low-income, elderly, African-American, and violent regions of the metropolis. The individual-level and population-based studies so common in epidemiology and demography explain only part of these geographical patterns. Social ecology, and its influence over the ways in which people interact and use public space, played a role that bears further investigation.

TOWARD A SOCIAL EPIDEMIOLOGY OF THE CITY

The group- and community-level death rates are simple portraits that begin to illustrate the impact of the heat; they suggest that the heat wave was an environmentally stimulated but socially organized catastrophe that sociological investigation can help decipher. The social autopsy dissects the underlying relations of the event by drawing upon but also extending the legacy of social epidemiology.[13] The analysis here departs from conventional demographic and sociological studies of mortality by placing the individual-level factors that affect death rates within a broader context of neighborhoods, social service systems, and government programs. Treating the city itself as the focal point of the study, it advances a multilayered analysis that integrates political, economic, and cultural factors with the individual- and community-level conditions that are prevalent in epidemiological reports.[14]

It is impossible to understand the deprivation that led to so many deaths during the crisis without situating the event in the social geography and political economy of Chicago in the 1990s.[15] The account here focuses on the social and political production of deprivation and suffering, but offers a broad perspective on individual, community, state, and symbolic levels of the city in order to illustrate the ways in which diverse actors and institutions are collectively implicated in making a major urban event that they experience individually. Drawing upon extensive fieldwork and in-depth interviews with Chicago residents, city officials and employees, social service workers, journalists, and research scientists, the book offers a vantage point on different positions and divergent experiences that rarely come together in social life.

Occasionally the accounts of social worker and scientist, state agent and single room occupancy resident, journalist and public official will appear incompatible or even contradictory. But together they will represent the range of positions and the diversity of viewpoints that constitute the heterogeneity of the modern city and account for the variations in the ways that the heat wave was managed and interpreted.[16] The counterposition of divergent views and different stories will help to illustrate the relationships between action in one sphere of the city—the journalistic field, for example—and activity in others, such as the emergency response agencies of the local government or the informal support networks in neighborhoods.[17] City dwellers and their institutions live and die in relation with each other—even when the relationship is based on exclusion. The heat wave puts into focus the ways that connections made or missed, visible or unrecognized, can determine the fate of the city and its residents.

The location of the heat wave makes the event an especially rich empirical resource for assessing the methodological and theoretical tools of urban sociology, and particularly the legacy established by the

Chicago school of urban research. For Chicago, with its famously divided segments, its infamous segregation, and its stark inequality, is not only the quintessential American city of extremes. It is also the city in and through which scholars founded and developed the American approach to urban studies, creating an agenda for investigation in the urban environment that shaped much of twentieth-century urban social science. Although in recent decades scholars associated with the new urban sociology have levied compelling criticisms of the Chicago school's "urban ideology"—most notably its failure to call attention to the political and economic production of inequality and domination in the city—the Chicago techniques for exploring the social fabric of the city offer rich possibilities for discovery.

The marks of both the first and second waves of the Chicago school are evident throughout this analysis of the heat wave: the case study; the emphasis on physical and social space; the focus on community and public life; the investigation of ethnoracial differentiation; and the assessment of the city as a total social system—all at the heart of the Chicago school problematic—are central to this project. Ironically, though, this analysis of the solitary deaths in the living laboratory of Chicago breaks from the school's traditional approach to the issue of *social isolation in the city,* one of the key concerns of the American sociology. For while the early Chicago school urbanists emphasized the isolation of different regions in the metropolis, here I treat the city as a complex social system of integrated institutions that touch *and* interpenetrate in a variety of ways. The distinctiveness of urban life lies in the spatial forms and the networks of actors and institutions that collectively organize a specific set of pressures, such as concentrated crime, crowding, and pollution, and possibilities, such as relationships with similarly disposed people and opportunities for political action. There has never been much evidence that urban regions are isolated as separate social worlds in the ways that the early Chicago sociologists described, and in retrospect, it appears that their method of focusing attention on one community or neighborhood oriented urban theory toward problems of segmentation rather than sources of contact and connection. But the heat wave helped to show that under contemporary conditions certain urban residents suffer from forms of *literal isolation,* the consequences of which can be dire. Assessing the social processes and spatial patterns that foster such isolation requires exchanging the Chicago school's biotic vocabulary for describing urban social processes with concepts and categories that recognize the significance of socially engineered inequality and difference. Moreover, it demands a method of investigation capable of comprehending the city as a complex system, where nature, culture, and politics conspire to determine the fate of its inhabitants.

The second major concern of this book is to analyze the symbolic construction of the heat wave as a public event and experience. My account pays particular attention to the processes through which political officials, journalists, and research scientists established the dominant analyses of the heat wave as well as the basic categories that organized public discourse about the trauma. Journalistic, scientific, and political institutions benefit from their symbolic power to create and to impose as universal and universally applicable a common set of standards and categories, such as *natural disaster* or *heat-related death,* that become the legitimate frames (or organizing concepts) for making sense of an unexpected situation.[18] For although everyone in Chicago experienced the severe climate, news reporters, politicians, and scientists were primarily responsible for explaining and interpreting it for different audiences. The heat wave was a cultural event as well as a public health crisis, yet for much of the nation it never registered as a major happening, and its legacy is difficult to trace. Examining the ways in which features of the catastrophe were brought to light or concealed helps to make visible the systems of symbolic production that structured the public understandings of the disaster. This part of the study helps to answer the question of why, despite the magnitude of the catastrophe and the spectacular journalistic coverage it received, the social life of the heat wave and its victims have been so easy to disregard or forget.

THE TYPICAL AND THE EXTREME

Although this book focuses primarily on the 1995 heat wave, the account offered here is not a conventional social history of the disaster. Instead, the analysis is motivated by two theoretical principles that hold that the case of the Chicago disaster can be used to open a broader inquiry into the life of the city. The first principle, which derives from the work of Marcel Mauss and Emile Durkheim, is that extreme events such as the Chicago catastrophe are marked by "an excessiveness which allows us better to perceive the facts than in those places where, although no less essential, they still remain small-scale and involuted."[19] The second principle is that institutions have a tendency to reveal themselves when they are stressed and in crisis.[20] There is no question that the weather that catalyzed the disaster was anomalous, but this book will show that many elements of city life that the disaster expressed are typical features of the local urban environment. Among the most important of these are a series of emerging conditions that have introduced new forms of vulnerability in U.S. cities, but that have been largely overlooked in the burgeoning literature on urban inequality.[21] The conditions that proved most consequential in the heat wave include the literal social isolation of poor senior citizens, particularly in the city's most violent areas; the degradation of and rising conflict in urban hotel residences, which constitute a large but often ignored sector of the low-income housing market; the changes in social service delivery and the threats to public health and welfare stemming from privatization and other radical shifts in local government administration; and the new social ecological conditions of neighborhoods abandoned by businesses as well as local governments and depopulated by residents. The conditions that the heat wave revealed did not disappear when the temperatures moderated, and their invisibility makes them all the more dangerous in the daily life of the city.

Take, for example, dying alone. The number of people whose lives ended in isolation during the one-week heat wave was unusually high, but the circumstances in which they were found are not uncommon in Chicago and other large U.S. cities. In a typical month the Cook County Public Administrators Office investigates roughly one hundred cases in which someone dies and no family members come forward to manage the estate or bury the body. These figures are not surprising when we consider the rapid increase in the number of Chicago residents, and of Americans in general, who live alone, especially in their old age. There is little public discussion of these trends, yet in recent years several cities have reported an increase in the number of their residents who die alone, often going undiscovered for days or weeks. In one major U.S. city, *The New York Times* reports, unclaimed bodies "are piling up faster than the city can handle them"; boxes containing the personal papers of the deceased are "piled floor to ceiling" in the county office.[22] "We had never been so busy before," one Cook County investigator explained, "but nothing about the heat wave was really unusual except the amounts" (see fig. 12).

For much of Chicago, however, the scale of isolation that the heat wave made visible defied the conventional narratives of community strength and solidarity through which this "city of neighborhoods" understands itself.[23] Few people outside of the Public Administrators Office were aware that so many Chicagoans were living and dying alone; and had it not been for the work of Chief Medical Examiner Edmund Donoghue (fig. 13), the city might never have been forced

Figure 12. An exhausted worker takes a break after transporting bodies at the Cook County Morgue. Source: *Chicago Sun-Times;* photographer: Rich Hein. Reprinted with special permission from the Chicago Sun-Times, Inc. © 2002.

Figure 13. Chief Medical Examiner Edmund Donoghue. Source: *Chicago Sun-Times;* photographer: Andre Chung. Reprinted with special permission from the Chicago Sun-Times, Inc. © 2002.

to acknowledge the devastation in its midst. For it was Donoghue's early reports that the outbreak of death was attributable to the heat that turned the public health crisis into a major public event.

Donoghue, a physician who grew up in a politically active Chicago family and began working at the Medical Examiners Office in 1977, had followed recent heat epidemics closely enough to know that reports about their severity often sparked political controversies. Heat waves are slow, silent, and invisible killers whose direct impact on health is difficult to determine. Extreme heat breaks down the body's resistance but leaves much of the environment around it untouched. The evidence that a person has suffered a "heat-related death" lies in the setting in which the death took place as well as within the body, and investigators do not always know to, let alone *how* to, examine a possible heat wave victim.

Donoghue's knowledge of previous heat disasters made him aware of two procedures that would be essential for properly diagnosing heat-related mortality. First was the importance of establishing clear criteria for determining a heat-related death and instructing investigators and medical examiners to look for these benchmarks. Setting the criteria would not be an easy process, in part because in 1995 neither the federal government nor the National Association of Medical Examiners had developed a uniform definition for a heat-related death, resulting in inconsistent diagnoses in cities across the United States. Drawing on the most current scientific standards, though, Donoghue established three criteria, and classified a death as being heat-related if it met any one of them: "(a) a measured body temperature of 105°F at the time of the death or immediately after the death, (b) substantial environmental or circumstantial evidence of heat as a contributor to death (e.g., decedent found in a room without air conditioning, all windows closed, and a high ambient temperature), or (c) a decedent found in a decomposed condition without evidence of other cause of death who was last seen alive during the heat wave period."[24]

Second, Donoghue recognized the necessity of documenting information about the heat wave victims as soon as possible, and of being prepared to mobilize the evidence in support of the autopsies. He knew from experience that someone would challenge the death attributions; the case records, he believed, would support his scientific work. What Donoghue had not expected was that the challenge to the credibility of his medical examinations would come from the most powerful political leader in Chicago's recent history, Mayor Richard M. Daley. At a news conference held on Tuesday, 18 July, Daley flatly denied the validity of Donoghue's death reports. His skepticism about the relationship Donoghue established between the weather and the surge in mortality resonated with other Chicago leaders, and journalists were quick to turn the mayor's remarks into the source of a controversy over whether the deaths were, to use the phrase that recurred at the time, "really real"—were they simply coincidental, or were they actually related to the heat? The day after the news conference *The Chicago Tribune* reported that the heat wave death toll had reached 199. But the paper also ran an article on coroners' disputes over heat wave death attributions as well as a column by the legendary Mike Royko headlined "Killer Heat Wave or Media Event?"

In the summer of 1995, Chicago's leaders and powerful boosters had ample incentive to question or deny reports that the city had become a cauldron of death and decay. After some thirty years of economic and social decline triggered by the flight of its manufacturing industries and the degradation of its neighborhoods and streets, by the 1990s Chicago had embarked on a political, socioeconomic, and symbolic recovery that promised to transform the metropolis.[25] Like most other major U.S. cities at the time, many residents and neighborhoods were enjoying the benefits of a durable and robust period of economic expansion, and even longtime critics had taken up the rhetoric of urban revitalization. Mayor Daley was winning praise from the local and national media for his campaign to reinvent the city government; new industries, including tourism, were replenishing the local employment base; suburbanites were moving back to the city after decades of retreat; and, to cap it all, the city was investing in a massive effort to beautify its streets and gloss its image in preparation for the Democratic National Convention of 1996. Well aware that its reputation had been tarnished by the violent 1968 convention, local leaders hoped that the 1996 event would be the showcase through which Chicago regained its reputation and lived up to its motto as "The City That Works."

The heat wave of 1995, though, threatened to cast a new stigma on Chicago's image and to undermine the city's resurgence at the very moment it was poised to ascend. The hundreds of deaths represented a massive social catastrophe, but in addition the ugly spectacle of death in the city was a potential public relations disaster, signaling to the world that Chicago could not shed the extreme poverty and insecurity with which its name had become associated. At home, Mayor Daley could not have helped but worry about the impact of the disaster on his political future. In a famous election just sixteen years before, Chicago mayor Michael Bilandic had lost his seat to Jane Byrne in part because of his inability to clear the city streets during a catastrophic but far less deadly blizzard. The consequences of failing to protect the city from an attack of the elements could be severe, and although the Medical Examiners Office was part of the county government and not the city, Donoghue faced great pressure to tone down his reports.

The Chief Medical Examiner, however, refused to bow to external pressure and change his death reports, effectively preventing city leaders and opinion makers from dismissing the severity of the disaster without a public battle. "Another more politically sensitive guy might not have told the full story," explained Lawrence Harris, a former president of the National Association of Medical Examiners. "He [Donoghue] has got to be admired for telling it like it is."[26]

The criteria for determining heat-related deaths require that police officers or medical workers who discover a dead body record information such as the room temperature, environmental conditions, and the state of the corpse, and that medical examiners use this information when conducting their autopsies. Most deaths, however, do not require extensive police reports or medical autopsies. During heat waves many of these casualties go uninvestigated because private funerary agencies take care of the bodies independently. Many other cases, Donoghue knew, would fall outside the city's initial counts because Chicago residents who died in suburban hospitals outside Cook County would not be included in the citywide mortality figures until their death certificates were filed by a state office in Springfield, the state capital. For these reasons, deaths that might be heat related are often left unclassified, so public health scholars argue that heat-related death measures generally understate the impact of extreme weather.[27] Donoghue believed that the scientific evidence would support his findings, and in the face of widespread skepticism he boldly announced, "We would be delighted to have the figures checked. But if anything, we're underestimating the amount of death."[28] By the time the county had finished counting the bodies, the official heat-related death toll was 465 for the week of 14 to 20 July and 521 for the month.

Within days Donoghue's death attributions would receive support from another leading Chicago public health worker, Steven Whitman. Whitman, a former researcher at Northwestern University who had left academia to create and direct an epidemiology program for Chicago's Public Health Department, decided to compare the figures coming in from the Medical Examiners Office with the death rates from earlier Chicago heat waves. He recalled, "I was stunned to discover that no one knew anything about the history of heat-related deaths. I found newspaper articles that listed a few deaths here and there during hot summers, but few major reports about heat-related mortality." Whitman and his staff initiated a study of the major urban heat epidemics in U.S. history. They found the meteorological reports for extremely hot periods in major cities, then tracked down the relevant mortality rates. "It was amazing," Whitman explained. "We found events in which there were hundreds of deaths above the normal rates, but there was no public health literature to explain them."

After carefully examining the records of previous heat waves, Whitman and his colleagues realized that the most accurate way to count heat wave deaths was to use the concept of "excess deaths."[29] Unlike heat-related death measures, excess death figures do not require special examinations of every case of mortality. Instead, epidemiologists can generate an excess death number by measuring the difference between the reported death rates for a given time period and the typical death rates for a comparable time. For their analysis of major U.S. heat waves, the Chicago epidemiologists compared the average mortality rates for cities in comparable periods before the heat epidemics with those during the extreme events. Their measures did not specify causes of death, so the researchers had to confirm that no other unusual event—such as a massacre or another epidemic—was responsible for inflating the mortality rates. But ultimately they were able to eliminate other potential causes of death from serious consideration, and they arrived at excess death figures for major heat waves in Chicago, Los Angeles, and New York that were more reliable than any statistics previously produced.[30]

The excess death study provided compelling evidence that Donoghue had been accurate on two counts. Not only were the Chief Medical Examiner's heat-related death attributions reliable, so too was his public statement that the early numbers had understated the severity of the disaster. According to Chicago's own excess death figures, 739 city residents above the norm had died during the week of 14 to 20 July—over 200 more than the county Medical Examiners Office had initially claimed. Equally important was the information that the epidemiologists obtained from Milwaukee, a city roughly ninety miles north that, though considerably smaller than Chicago, shares several social and demographic features with it. Using the excess death measure, Milwaukee had suffered a proportionally comparable catastrophe; yet the smaller number of total deaths and the media focus on Chicago kept reports from Wisconsin in the shadows.[31]

Finally, federal officials stepped in to support Donoghue's death attributions. Cynthia Whitney, an epidemiologist from the U.S. Centers for Disease Control and Prevention, told the media that "the medical examiner has given very, very good information. . . . Doctor Donoghue's criteria are very good."[32] City leaders who were skeptical of the death attributions found it difficult to challenge the wealth of scientific evidence and the legitimacy of the institutions that supported Donoghue's figures. "We're not going to talk numbers," one high-ranking official in the Health Department stated, signaling that the city's leadership would stop challenging the mortality figures and that one part of the political controversy had ended.[33] But the debate over the true impact of the heat wave continued.

After it became untenable to contest the validity of the coroner's mortality figures, city officials posed another question about the heat wave deaths: wasn't it likely that the heat wave simply affected a group of Chicagoans who were already on the verge of death, and whose demise was not so much caused as it was hastened by the heat? Everyone, of course, will die eventually, so it might seem disingenuous to ask whether the heat proved most consequential for the people who were, as some speculated, "about to die anyway." Unnecessary loss of life is significant, even if the loss is better measured in months than years. But the epidemiological question was at least somewhat more nuanced. If after the heat wave, for example, there was a decrease in the mortality rate substantial enough to counterbalance the 739 excess deaths during the crisis, some health scholars would consider the epidemic to be a case of "death displacement," because there was no net increase in the total mortality level.

The medical examiner's data show that disproportionate numbers of the heat wave victims were, in fact, members of the city's most vulnerable groups: the elderly, African-Americans, and the poor. But there is little reason to believe that the people who perished in the heat wave were already about to die. Two years after the catastrophe, the Illinois Department of Health analyzed the mortality patterns following the heat wave and found that, contrary to some officials' conjectures, there was no compelling evidence that the mortality levels during the crisis represented a displacement of deaths that would have occurred soon thereafter even without the extreme weather.[34] The heat wave, in other words, did not kill people whose deaths were imminent, but hastened the demise of vulnerable residents who were likely to have survived if the crisis had not occurred. Nonetheless, the skepticism voiced by Chicago officials and journalists made a major impact on the public inter-

Figure 14. A Chicago television news anchor asks, "Who's to Blame?"
Source: WBBM-TV (CBS affiliate).

pretations of the catastrophe; in the absence of more public verifica-
tion of the heat wave mortality rates, the debate over whether the heat
wave deaths were really real has continued to this day.

Once it became untenable for Chicago political officials to deny the
scientific reports about the heat wave death rates, the city's most vocal
residents and organizations embarked on another, equally distracting
inquiry: who was to blame for the disaster (see fig. 14). There was no
shortage of suspects. Some local activists and community leaders argued that responsibility lay in the hands of the mayor and his cabinet
members. According to their argument, the leaders of various city
agencies collectively neglected to recognize the danger posed by the
social and meteorological climates and failed to organize an effective
public response. One group of opposition African-American politicians on the city's South Side, for example, called for the resignation
of several top city officials after the disaster and demanded a formal
investigation of the event. For their part, city officials denied accountability and claimed that responsibility actually resided in groups and
institutions outside their control. Commonwealth Edison, the primary
utilities provider, became the target of the mayor and the city council

and was subjected to a public hearing. Official reports and public commissions criticized journalistic organizations that did not issue adequate warnings. Some, such as the daily newspaper the *Chicago Sun-Times,* countered by criticizing the city government for ignoring its own emergency plans. Top city officials faulted the families of victims for failing to attend to their kin. And the commissioner of the Department of Human Services simply blamed the victims, publicly declaring that "people . . . died because they neglected themselves."

But ultimately it is pointless to organize an inquiry into the heat wave as a search for a guilty party, as only the crudest forms of analysis could reduce such a complex event to a single actor, causal agent, or social force. There is no simple explanation for why so many Chicagoans died in the trauma, and there is certainly no individual or group responsible for the crisis. What makes the heat wave such a meaningful event is that it represents an exemplary case of what Marcel Mauss called a *total social fact,* one that integrates and activates a broad set of social institutions and generates a series of social processes that expose the inner workings of the city.[35] For when hundreds of people die slowly, alone and at home, unprotected by friends and family and unassisted by the state, it is a sign of social breakdown in which communities, neighborhoods, networks, governmental agencies, and the media charged with signaling warnings are all implicated. Showing how is the principal challenge of this book.

AN OVERVIEW OF THE BOOK

The inquiry presented here proceeds in layers, beginning with an account of individuals dying alone and extending to an examination of how communities and political agencies contributed to the vulnerability or security of Chicago residents. Chapter 1, "Dying Alone," explores the emergence of literal social isolation, the lack of contact with friends, family, and formal support networks that left so many Chicagoans uncared for and unprotected in the crisis. Two questions drive this chapter. First, what are the social conditions that explain why so many Chicagoans died *alone* during the heat wave? And second, to extend the first question, what conditions explain why, in the wake of this tragedy, so many Chicagoans continue to live alone, with limited social ties or contacts?

My answers to these questions are primarily based on sixteen months of fieldwork I conducted in Chicago. I spent much of that time alongside seniors who live alone, are poor, and report having few social ties. There is, unfortunately, little contemporary research on either the extent of isolation among city residents, particularly among the old and poor, or on the nature of this condition. Finding these seniors, let alone getting to know them, was not an easy task. Among the many paths I explored in search of the isolated elderly, the most fruitful went through social service agencies that worked with homebound seniors, city agencies that identify and assist the vulnerable elderly, single room occupancy dwellings that housed several older men, and one social organization whose mission is to provide companionship and support for older people who are on their own. Over the course of my fieldwork I interviewed or became acquainted with more than forty seniors, and the experiences I shared with them are central to my understanding of the varied nature of isolation and reclusion among the aged. Like most ethnographers, I developed particularly close relationships with a few of my informants, some of whose stories I tell in greater detail because they represent central features of being old, alone, and poor in the city.

It is, by definition, impossible to collect firsthand information about the experience of dying alone in an acute event.[36] The circumstances of the heat wave deaths, many of which went undiscovered for days, suggest some of the qualities of isolation in the city. Journalistic reporting immediately after the victims were discovered provides additional information about the decedents, some of whom had neighbors or relatives who spoke to the media during the crisis. But most of the accounts of individuals who died during the heat wave that I present here were garnered from research I conducted with seldom used sources, such as the Public Administrators Office files of personal belongings from people who died alone and were unclaimed by next of kin; a database compiled by the Medical Examiners Office; and police reports describing the conditions in which the heat wave victims were discovered. Finally, I conducted my own investigations into the life histories of several of the heat wave victims. I visited the places they lived and died, and spoke with neighbors, landlords, building managers, and, where possible, their friends and relatives.[37]

In chapter 2, "Race, Place, and Vulnerability," I consider whether there were place-specific conditions that heightened or reduced the risks of heat-related mortality for Chicago residents. Because several epidemiological studies have shown that social contact is a key factor in determining heat wave vulnerability, I examine the question of which community area social conditions facilitate strong and effective support networks and which conditions render frail residents even more susceptible to deprivation and isolation. Examining North Lawndale and

Little Village, two neighboring communities on the West Side of the city that had similar risk factors but radically different heat wave mortality rates, I consider how their specific social and ecological conditions influence the health and welfare of local residents.[38]

The research for this chapter is rooted in six months of near-daily observations made in the two neighborhoods between June and December of 1998, as well as in more than forty formal and informal interviews with local residents, merchants, political officials, religious leaders, community organizers, police officers, and neighborhood groups. The spatial contiguity between the two community areas, one almost entirely Latino, the other almost entirely African American, made it easy to move from one to the other. I split many days between the two areas, spending time among residents whose physical separation by a single street belied their experience of the border as a dividing point between what many referred to as "two totally different worlds." Religious institutions and community organizations were my primary sources of entry into the parts of North Lawndale and the Little Village that I got to know, with one of each becoming the base for my work in the neighborhoods. In North Lawndale two block clubs also took me in as an occasional guest, and I met several local residents through these groups.

The neighborhood comparison in chapter 2 is also the basis for my engagement with a major public debate concerning the nature of the heat wave mortality: why, despite similarly heightened levels of vulnerability, did Chicago's African-American community experience the highest proportional death rates of all ethnoracial groups, while Chicago's Latinos experienced the lowest? The comparative case study of North Lawndale and Little Village helps to show how variations in the social ecology of Chicago's neighborhoods affected the viability of collective life and neighborhood social support, and in turn determined the capacity of communities to buffer the dangers imposed by the heat.

The questions that motivated chapters 3, 4, and 5 grew out of my reviews of the political, scientific, and journalistic reports on the disaster. The commissions, hearings, and official studies produced by different political agencies suggest that several layers of government were involved in disaster management, playing roles in both the public efforts to assist city residents during the heat wave and in establishing the levels of vulnerability that made the event so deadly. In chapter 3, "The State of Disaster," I depart from the social scientific convention of limiting the study of government action during a disaster to the question of how its agencies *react* to the crisis. In addition to looking at the way that different city agencies responded to the heat and health emergencies, I ask whether and how governmental programs and policies contributed to the social conditions that placed so many Chicagoans at risk of breaking down in the heat. More specifically, I draw on fieldwork conducted alongside city employees of the Police Department and the Department on Aging, as well as interviews with members of the Fire Department and its paramedics division, to assess how the structure and spirit of the newly "reinvented" local government affects the capacity of various local state agencies to provide services to poor, old, and precarious city residents. The question at issue is not whether the new forms of urban governance are more or less effective at providing support to city residents than previous systems, but whether there is a *good fit* between the human capabilities and social resources held by the vulnerable—particularly the poor elderly—and the set of emergent programs, principles, and social service strategies in contemporary city governments.

Chapter 4, "Governing by Public Relations," considers the city's public relations campaign to manage the crisis as a fundamental part of the emergency political response to the disaster. Drawing upon Stanley Cohen's typology of the methods governmental regimes use to deny their implication in cases of violence, I show how city officials deployed rhetoric designed to defuse criticisms about their role in the crisis and shift the direction of public outrage toward other organizations.

In chapter 5, "The Spectacular City," I draw upon observations made in a local newsroom and more than twenty interviews with journalists, editors, and managers who contributed to the coverage of the heat wave for one of Chicago's major news companies, to examine the symbolic production of the disaster in the major media. This investigation also breaks with the conventions of researching disasters and other social problems. Although it begins with a comprehensive content analysis of the journalistic coverage of the event, the chapter does not simply show which dimensions of the disaster journalists explored or explained and then speculate on the reasons for these reportorial patterns. Instead, it analyzes the cultural production of news and information about the heat wave and illustrates the organizational structure and vocational practices through which media organizations transformed the public health crisis into a public news event. As gatekeepers of the so-called public sphere, the media does the crucial cultural work of reframing, and not simply reporting, major issues for their audiences. Social scientists have a long history of studying newsrooms, but in recent decades they have produced few major accounts of the social, technological, and organizational conditions that have changed the work of news gathering in the age of digital production. Looking closely at the story behind the story of the heat wave, then, will also afford us a perspective on the conditions of journalistic production in a major city news organization that is otherwise difficult to obtain.

The book concludes with an overview of recent Chicago heat waves and an explanation of why even well-executed heat emergency policies are insufficient to remove the risk of future catastrophes. The results of the social autopsy suggest that extreme exogenous forces such as the heat will prove deadly again so long as extreme forms of vulnerability, isolation, and deprivation remain typical features of the urban environment. The epilogue, "Together in the End," provides a cautionary tale about the consequences of our collective denial.

CHAPTER ONE

Dying Alone
The Social Production of Isolation

t the end of summer in the year 2000 I had my most personal encounter with the heat wave victims. They had been dead for five years by then, so it was hardly a typical meeting. But a generous invitation from a group of county employees who make their living working in what they call the "secret city of people who live and die alone" made the unlikely introduction possible.

A few weeks before, I had read an article that reported an increase in the prevalence of dying alone in San Francisco, a city that has a far smaller population of poor and elderly residents than Chicago. In the first six months of the new year, San Francisco officials discovered almost as many cases of solitary decedents as they had during the previous decade. "More people are dying alone, with no one to arrange their funerals, settle their estates or mourn their passing," the story explains. "Sometimes the bodies lie for months in the city morgue as officials search for heirs."[1] In San Francisco, the article continues, the public administrators office is in charge of these investigations, and stores the personal papers of solitary decedents for five years in case someone comes to collect them. This article was published close to the fifth anniversary of the 1995 heat wave in Chicago, and I wondered if the Office of the Cook County Public Administrator might have records of the cases it investigated during the disaster. One phone call later, I learned that the county had, in fact, maintained its files from the catastrophe and catalogued its work through the 1990s. Officials there had conducted roughly 1,000 to 1,200 investigations—about 3 per day—for almost every year during the 1990s. In the 1997–98 budgetary year, though, the total jumped to 1,370; and in 1998–99, the most recent year for which there were data, it was 1,562. That day I wrote to the office requesting permission to examine the files.

Soon after, I was sitting in a conference room on the twenty-sixth

floor of the County Building, surrounded by roughly 160 official reports and boxes full of the mundane belongings—watches, wallets, letters, tax returns, photographs, and record books—that had been in
the homes or on the persons of the heat wave victims. During the previous five years of my investigation I had spoken to neighbors, friends,
and family members of some of the decedents; immersed myself in
neighborhoods that had exceptional heat wave mortality rates; visited
the apartment buildings and transient hotels where people had died;
spent hours in the morgue looking over death certificates and speaking
with the Chief Medical Examiner; scoured police reports, public health
documents, and epidemiological studies; read hundreds of news articles; viewed dozens of television stories; and interviewed paramedics,
police officers, and hospital workers who handled the dead and the
dying the week of the heat wave. Yet nothing apart from the decedents'
files had given me such an intimate and human view of the people
whose isolation knew no limits, of the nature of life and death inside
the sealed room.

The public administrators' descriptions of the rooms are incisive
but curt, with simple, abbreviated terms summing up the destitution
surrounding most victims: "Furnished room," many reports began,
revealing the large concentrations of death in the city's single room
occupancy (SRO) dwellings; "roach infested," and "complete mess"
were common too. Most files contained instant photographs of the
apartments taken by the investigators; some showed barren spaces and
few signs of life, while others were so cluttered with objects as to suggest
that the material goods had replaced human company in the worlds of
the isolates.[2] The victims' mementos and photographs capturing better
times provided some relief from the terrible images everywhere else in
the files. One man, for example, died alongside a certificate awarding
him the Bronze Star for exemplary conduct in ground combat during World War Two, and two photographs of himself as a handsome
young soldier in full uniform. There is, however, a disturbing side to
such signs of vitality and success: they show how fleeting can be one's
security, how deep are the crevices in the city, and how invisible are
those who fall through the gaps.

The personal letters express the longings born of solitude, hinting
at the extent to which the victims suffered from their social deprivation.
Several weeks before the heat wave, one resident of an SRO dwelling
in the North Side's Uptown neighborhood penned a plea for companionship to an estranged friend in a nearby suburb, but ultimately kept
the note himself. "When you have time please come visit me soon at

my place," he wrote. "I would like to see you if that's possible, when you come to the city. Write when you can. I will be glad to hear from you." Another resident who died in the same hotel had received a letter from a distant relative shortly before July. The writer anticipated his family's demise, though his relative in the Chicago SRO was only fifty-three years old. "I don't have words to tell you how bad I feel about the troubles and sickness you are having," he began. "It seems to me that our family should have gotten along and been friends. As we near our end it seems it should be different."

While researching the heat wave I had become familiar with a series of popular books and scholarly publications that downplayed the difficulties of living alone, especially in old age, and enthusiastically celebrated the successes of people who managed to enrich their lives and build communities while living by themselves. Renowned writers such as Robert Coles, Arlie Hochschild, and Barbara Meyerhoff had published beautiful and influential books about the capacity of older people to flourish despite their separation from family and old friends; and even Robert Putnam, whose lament over the increase in Americans bowling alone captivated the public during the 1990s, emphasized that, relative to other groups, retired senior citizens were the nation's most active joiners. Yet none of the authors who celebrated the flourishing elderly living on their own established whether the subjects of their studies were typical or exceptional. Hochschild, in fact, had argued that her subjects were interesting precisely because they were not representative of most seniors, while the others had simply avoided the question.[3] The books had done the important work of illustrating the conditions under which it is possible to age well, but they said little about the fate of the people deprived of such opportunities. Older people who live as shut-ins and isolates are no more typical than the seniors who appear in these popular texts—but their absence in the literature leaves a knowledge gap that the Public Administrator's files help to fill.

Coles, whose book *Old and On Their Own* is the most recent of these works and the only one to focus on senior citizens living alone, produced a heartwarming collection of photographic and written portrayals of older Americans. Their success, as he describes it, is that they manage to "hold on—to maintain considerably more than a semblance of their privacy, their independence, their personal sovereignty, their 'home rule' " while living alone.[4] Coles presents the faces and stories of the seniors who are struggling to get through the daily challenges of aging alone but who, in the end, are making it. They manage, as one eloquently puts it, to "duck . . . bullets" such as bodily decline, boredom, depression, loneliness, illness, immobility, loss, and the constant proximity of death that come at the end of life. Neither Coles nor his informants hide the difficulties of aging alone, yet the portraits in *Old and On Their Own* offer few glimpses into the social universe apparent everywhere in the biographies at the Public Administrators Office. It was as if the stories of the most isolated and vulnerable seniors had been excised because they disrupted the triumphant tone of the book; they were, perhaps, too difficult to absorb.

Perhaps Coles and the photographers excluded the most difficult cases from their presentation, invoking them only as absences, ghosts we dare not see. Longevity means forging new opportunities for creating things, for making or developing meaningful relationships, for contributing to society, to family, and to friends, and it would be misleading to emphasize only the dangerous consequences of aging alone or the unusual problems of being isolated. Yet it is equally misleading to celebrate a long duration of life without thinking seriously about the quality of that life, or to let the successes of the fortunate seniors who age alone and well blind us to the difficulties of those who suffer the more severe consequences of spending most of their time by themselves.

The incongruity between the accounts featured in *Old and On Their Own* and the Chicago stories I was learning about became even more noticeable when I discovered the police reports of the heat wave deaths. Filed in the recesses of the Cook County Morgue, the hastily scribbled notes authored by Chicago police officers show that the circumstances under which many heat victims died only emphasized the isolation and indignity of their lives.

MALE, AGE 65, BLACK, JULY 16, 1995

R/Os [responding officers] discovered the door to apt. locked from the inside by means of door chain. No response to any knocks or calls. R/Os . . . gained entry by cutting chain. R/Os discovered victim lying on his back in rear bedroom on the floor. [Neighbor] last spoke with victim on 13 July 95. Residents had not seen victim recently. Victim was in full rigor mortis. R/Os unable to locate the whereabouts of victim's relatives.

FEMALE, AGE 73, WHITE, JULY 17, 1995

A recluse for 10 yrs, never left apartment, found today by son, apparently DOA. Conditions in apartment when R/O's arrived thermostat was registering over 90 degrees f. with no air circulation except for windows opened by son (after death). Possible heat-related death. Had a known heart problem 10 yrs ago but never completed medication or treatment.

MALE, AGE 54, WHITE, JULY 16, 1995

R/O learned . . . that victim had been dead for quite awhile. . . .Unable to contact any next of kin. Victim's room was uncomfortable warm. Victim was diabetic, doctor unk. Victim has daughter . . . last name unk. Victim hadn't seen her in years. . . . Body removed to C.C.M. [Cook County Morgue]

MALE, AGE 79, BLACK, JULY 19, 1995

Victim did not respond to phone calls or knocks on victim's door since Sunday, 16 July 95. Victim was known as quiet, to himself and at times, not to answer the door. Landlord . . . does not have any information to any relatives to victim. . . . Chain was on door. R/O was able to see victim on sofa with flies on victim and a very strong odor decay (decompose). R/O cut chain, per permission of [landlord], called M.E. [medical examiner] who authorized removal. . . . No known relatives at this time.

These accounts rarely say enough about a victim's death to fill a page, yet the words used to describe the deceased—"recluse," "to himself," "no known relatives"—and the conditions in which they were found— "chain was on door," "no air circulation," "flies on victim," "decompose"—are brutally succinct testaments to the forms of abandonment, withdrawal, and isolation that proved so dangerous and extensive in Chicago during the heat wave (compare with fig. 15). Yet, like the Public Administrators Office reports, they introduce more questions about the lives inside the rooms than they resolve.

This chapter addresses the first layer of the heat wave puzzle by assembling an account of the collective production of individual-level isolation. Two questions guide this inquiry. First, why did so many hundreds of Chicagoans *die alone* during the heat wave? Second, to extend the question outward from the heat wave to the present, why do so many Chicagoans, particularly older residents, *live alone*, with limited social contacts and weak support networks during normal times?

These questions carry significant social and symbolic meaning. Most contemporary versions of the "good death" in the United States emphasize that the dying process should take place at home, a familiar setting in which the person is more likely to be comfortable. But it is even more crucial that the process is collective, shared with a community of

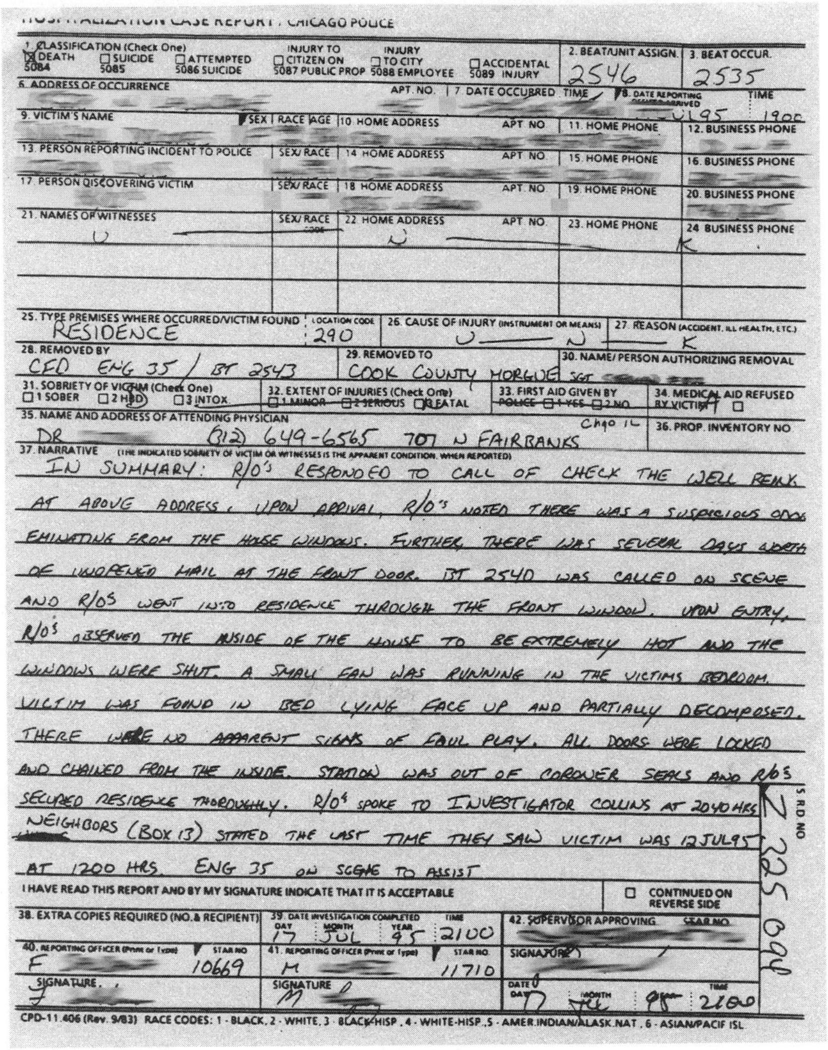

Figure 15. A police report notes the conditions of a decedent's apartment: "suspicious odor," "unopened mail," "extremely hot," "windows were shut."

attendant family and friends. When someone dies alone and at home, such a death can be a powerful sign of social abandonment and failure. The community to which the deceased belonged is likely to suffer from stigma or shame as a consequence, and often it will respond by producing redemptive accounts or enacting special rituals that reaffirm the bonds among the living.[5]

   In the United States, the social issues of living alone or lacking close
and durable communal ties are equally loaded. Despite considerable
evidence that Americans are relatively active participants in social organizations and community groups, the specter of the lonely and atomized individual in the great metropolis has long haunted the national
imagination. U.S. sociology is internationally distinct in that only here
do studies focusing on the isolation of individuals and the crisis of community account for five of the six best-selling books in the history of
the field, including texts entitled *The Lonely Crowd* and *The Pursuit of
Loneliness*.[6] Moreover, two of the most influential books in the last
twenty years of American social science, William Julius Wilson's *The
Truly Disadvantaged* and Robert Putnam's *Bowling Alone,* are based on
theories that "social isolation," broadly construed, is the fundamental
cause of numerous and varied social problems. To talk about social
isolation, it seems, is to touch a central nerve of U.S. intellectual culture.[7]

BEING ALONE

The issues of aging and dying alone are hardly limited to Chicago. The
number of people living alone is rising almost everywhere in the world,
making it one of the major demographic trends of the contemporary
era.[8] In the United States, the proportion of all households inhabited
by one person (the U.S. Census Bureau's best measure of people living
alone) climbed steadily in the twentieth century, moving from roughly
7 percent in 1930 to 25 percent in 1995; and the percentage of all
people who lived alone rose from 2 percent to about 10 percent in the
same period. According to the Census Bureau, the total number of
Americans living alone rose from 10.9 million in 1970 to 24.9 million
in 1996; about 10 million of these, more than 40 percent of the total,
are aged 65 years or older.[9] As figures 16 and 17 show, the proportion
of American households inhabited by only one person and the proportion of elderly people living alone has soared since 1950. These numbers are certain to rise even more in the coming decades, yet few studies
document the daily routines and practices of people who live alone in
their final years, and we know little about the experiential makeup of
their conditions.[10] We know even less about the fastest emerging group
of seniors: "very old" people aged 85 years or above who live alone,
often surviving the departure of their children, the death of their
spouse, and the demise of their social networks.

   It is important to make distinctions among living alone, being isolated, being reclusive, and being lonely. I define *living alone* as residing

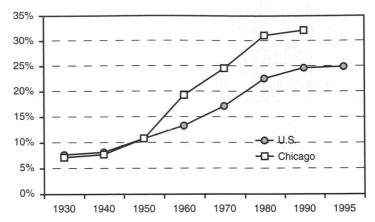

Figure 16. Proportion of U.S. and Chicago households with one inhabitant. Source: *The Statistical Abstract of the United States* (1980, 1989, 1999), U.S. Bureau of the Census.

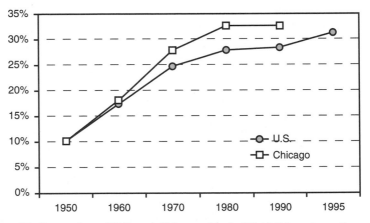

Figure 17. Proportion of U.S. and Chicago elderly (65+) living alone. Source: *The Statistical Abstract of the United States* (1980, 1989, 1999), U.S. Bureau of the Census.

without other people in a household; *being isolated* as having limited social ties; *being reclusive* as largely confining oneself to the household; and *being lonely* as the subjective state of feeling alone.[11] Most people who live alone, seniors included, are neither lonely nor deprived of social contacts. This is significant, because seniors who are embedded in active social networks tend to have better health and greater longevity than those who are relatively isolated. Being isolated or reclusive, then, has more negative consequences than simply living alone. But older people who live alone are more likely than seniors who live with others to be depressed, isolated, impoverished, fearful of crime, and removed from proximate sources of support than the elderly who live with others. Moreover, seniors who live alone are especially vulnerable to traumatic outcomes during episodes of acute crisis because there is no one to help recognize emerging problems, provide immediate care, or activate support networks.[12]

It is difficult to measure the number of people who are relatively isolated and reclusive. First, isolates and recluses are by definition difficult to locate and contact because they have few ties to informal or formal support networks or to researchers; second, isolated or reclusive people who are contacted by researchers often become more connected through the research process. In surveys and censuses isolates and recluses are among the social types most likely to be uncounted or undercounted because those with permanent housing often refuse to open their doors to strangers and are unlikely to participate in city or community programs in which they can be tracked. In academic research it is common to underestimate the extent of isolation or reclusion among seniors because most scholars gain access to samples of elderly people who are already relatively connected. One recent book about loneliness in later life, for example, makes generalizations about the prevalence of isolation and loneliness on the basis of a survey of seniors who participate in a university for the aged;[13] and even medical studies of isolation and health are likely to exclude people whom physicians and research teams never see or cannot locate.

Such methodological problems account for part of the reason that there are no systematic data on the extent of isolation and reclusion in the general population or even among the elderly.[14] But another reason is that despite the longstanding national conversation about being alone, few people or institutions have shown interest in learning about the truly isolated. U.S. city governments, though, are becoming increasingly aware that the emergence of isolated and reclusive residents has introduced a new set of challenges for social service providers and public health programs—in part because of the death reports they receive from public administrators and police departments. According to the director of one of Chicago's largest senior-citizen advocacy groups, "there are thousands of isolated seniors out there who we don't know."[15]

Though unnoticed in the everyday life of the city, the prevalence and danger of living alone without social contacts were apparent in the heat wave mortality patterns. According to the authors of the most thorough epidemiological study of the disaster, "During the summer

Figure 18. An elderly Chicagoan walks near Lake Michigan during the heat wave. Source: *Chicago Sun-Times;* photographer: Andre Chung. Reprinted with special permission from the Chicago Sun-Times, Inc. © 2002.

heat wave of 1995 in Chicago, anything that facilitated social contact, even membership in a social club or owning a pet, was associated with a decreased risk of death"; living alone "was associated with a doubling of the risk of death"; and "those who did not leave home each day" were even more likely to die.[16] Along with city residents suffering from frail health and/or confined to bed, those who were isolated faced the greatest risk of heat-related mortality (figs. 18, 19).

Figure 19. An elderly Chicago man tries to keep cool in his apartment after his power went out. Source: ABC7. Courtesy of WLS-TV.

THE SOCIAL PRODUCTION OF ISOLATION

Although the epidemiological reports on the heat wave established the relationship between isolation and mortality in the disaster, they offer little explanation for the deeper question of why so many Chicagoans lived and died alone. The political commissions that studied the heat wave, however, provided two major conclusions. The first was that relative to earlier times, more frail people are aging alone and living with everyday vulnerabilities that render them susceptible to the heat. The second was that most people who live alone take great pride in their independence and tend to refrain from asking for or accepting assistance, because doing so would spoil their identity as self-sufficient individuals. The result, as the Mayor's Commission on Extreme Weather Conditions states, is that "those most at risk may be least likely to want or accept help from government."[17]

There is some degree of truth in both of these explanations, and I will consider them seriously in this chapter. Yet even together they fail to provide a satisfying account of the reasons that so many Chicago residents died in solitude during the heat wave and that so many others continue to live in isolation. According to urban critic Jane Jacobs, "It took a lot of effort to make people this isolated." But the ways in which Americans have engineered such extreme forms of individuation and social segmentation remain mysterious.[18] Looking more closely at the conditions that made Chicagoans vulnerable to the heat helps to make visible a series of social transformations that contribute to the emerging phenomenon of being alone in the city.

This chapter focuses on four trends, all of which contribute to the vulnerability of the growing number of Americans who are old and poor:

• a *demographic shift,* the increasing number of people living alone and, in particular, of seniors who are aging alone, often with disabilities and barriers to mobility and sociability;

• a *cultural condition* related to crime, the coupling of a "culture of fear" stemming from the violence and perceived violence of everyday life with the longstanding American valuation of privacy, individualism, and self-sufficiency, particularly among the elderly and men;[19]

• a *spatial transformation,* the degradation, fortification, or elimination of public spaces and supported housing arrangements such as public housing clusters or SRO dwellings, especially in areas with concentrated poverty, violence, and illness;

• a *gendered condition,* the tendency for older men, particularly single men without children and men with substance abuse problems, to lose crucial parts of their social networks and valuable sources of social support as they age.

Together, these conditions create a new set of risks for a rising segment of the urban population, an everyday state of danger and deprivation whose impact on the life of the city is as severe as it is unspoken. This chapter examines each of these conditions in turn, then illustrates the potential for disaster when all come together in concentrated zones of isolation. The account begins with a discussion of aging alone and an extended portrait of one Chicago woman who barely survived the heat wave. Next, it addresses the isolating influences of crime and violence on urban seniors, whose daily routines and social practices are often constrained by insecurity and fear. Finally, it assesses how changes in two particular social environments, public housing for seniors and SRO dwellings, compromised the viability of public space and collective life for many of their residents during the 1990s.

AGING ALONE

If the heat wave was the most dramatic expression of the dangers of isolation, it was hardly a revelatory moment for the small number of foundations and social service agencies familiar with the condition. In 1988 the Commonwealth Fund published *Aging Alone: Profiles and Projections,* a widely distributed report highlighting the general aging of U.S. society and the rapid increase in the population of "very old" seniors, aged 85 years or older, who are more likely to be alone, frail, and unable or unwilling to stray far from home.[20] Roughly one out of every three Americans aged 65 years or older, and almost one out of every two aged 80 years or older, lived alone in the mid-1980s; and in the 1990s the proportions increased.

Aging Alone captured the attention of government and service agencies with its finding that most seniors who live alone are women, about two-thirds of whom are widows. Class status is a key determinant of isolation and living alone. The study showed that two out of every three seniors who are poor live by themselves, a situation that is dangerous because impoverished seniors are twice as likely as financially stable ones to report poor health (44 percent versus 22 percent), have health-related limitations in bathing, dressing, and other daily tasks (34 percent versus 17 percent), and experience depression at least once a week (47 percent versus 24 percent). The combination of isolation and depression often spins into a vicious circle that is difficult to break, since being alone leads to depression, which in turn reduces one's capacity to make contact with others, which then heightens the depression, and so on.[21]

Childless seniors are more likely than those who have living children to be socially isolated. Ties with children are crucial for sustaining a support network, and when a child dies or moves far from her parents there is generally no compensatory attention from other relatives and families. These patterns suggest that older African Americans and men are most likely to be alone at the end of their lives, since surveys consistently show that a higher proportion of black elderly than white elderly have dead or incarcerated children, and that a higher proportion of men than women are estranged from their children.[22] People who have mental illnesses and substance abuse problems, especially those who fail to get proper care, are also more likely to be alone late in life, since their instability often strains relationships with family and friends and complicates their integration into communities.

Strained or severed family ties are common themes in the histories of the isolated elderly. *Aging Alone* reports that 18 percent of all seniors living alone have no relative on whom they could depend for support for only a few days, and 28 percent had no one available for needs lasting a few weeks. Although the majority of seniors alone speak with family members often, 27 percent have no children and 6 percent have no phone. Among those who do have children, 60 percent see them less than once a week and 20 percent see them once a year or less. Very old seniors aged 85 years or older, who are more likely to be confined and to have special needs, see their children only slightly more often than other seniors: 32 percent get monthly visits, compared with 24 percent of seniors aged 75 to 84 years and 22 percent of those aged 65 to 74 years. More than two out of every three seniors have no monthly visit with their children.

Perhaps the most striking findings in the studies of seniors and isolation concern the extent to which some of the elderly have lost contact with their friends and families. Of all seniors living alone and below the poverty line, one out of three sees neither friends nor neighbors for as much as two weeks at a time, and one out of five has no phone conversations with friends. Seniors who never had children or who grew estranged from their families are especially susceptible to being alone and bereft of social support; but in the United States, where mobility rates are high and families are often spatially dispersed, it is common for seniors to be out of touch with relatives. National studies show that for seniors, geographical distance from friends and family is the strongest determinant of contact and social support. Decades of migration out of Chicago, where the total population decreased by more than a million between 1950 and 1990 and several neighborhoods lost more than half of their residents, increased the likelihood that the city's seniors would be isolated and alone. These patterns of migration and family dispersal are among the reasons that 48 percent of Chicago residents and 35 percent of suburbanites older than 65 years of age report having no family members available to assist them.[23]

Although some of these seniors live in specialized housing environments, the majority reside in apartments or single family houses, the kinds of places where most Americans spend their lives. And though some isolated seniors have endured decades of marginalization or estrangement, most moved through life in ways that Americans would regard as normal. As the story of Pauline Jankowitz shows, isolation in cities such as Chicago grows out of typical social processes and personal experiences. One need not fall victim to a trauma to find oneself alone and at home as death approaches.

"THE CLOSEST I'VE COME TO DEATH"

Pauline Jankowitz survived the heat wave, but her story helps to illustrate some of the fundamental features of aging alone and being afraid in the city. I first met Pauline on her eighty-fifth birthday, when I was assigned to be her companion for a day by Little Brothers Friends of the Elderly, a secular, nonprofit, international organization that supports seniors living alone by linking them up with volunteer companions and inviting them to the organization's center for a birthday party and a Thanksgiving and Christmas dinner every year. Although a stranger before the day began, I became her closest companion for the milestone occasion when I picked her up at the Northeast Side apartment where she had lived for thirty years.

Pauline and I had spoken on the phone the previous day, so she was expecting me when I arrived late in the morning. She lives on a quiet residential street dominated by the small three- and four-flat apartment buildings common in Chicago. Her neighborhood, a key site of departure and arrival for urban migrants, has changed dramatically in the time she has lived there. Her block has shifted from a predominantly white ethnic area in which Pauline was a typical resident to a mixed street with a sizable Asian and increasingly Mexican population. The small urban enclave remains home to her, but she is less comfortable in it because the neighbors are no longer familiar to her. "They are good people," she explained, "but I just don't know them." Her situation is similar to that of thousands of Chicago residents and millions of seniors across the country who have *aged in place* while the environment around them changes and their local friends leave.

Other major sources of discomfort for Pauline are her physical infirmities, which worsen as she ages: a bladder problem that left her incontinent, and a weak leg that requires her to walk with a crutch and drastically reduces her mobility. Pauline's fear of crime, which she hears about daily on the radio and television, contributes to her confinement. "Chicago is just a shooting gallery," she told me, "and I am a moving target because I walk so slowly." Acutely aware of her vulnerability, Pauline reorganized her life to limit her exposure to the threats outside, bunkering herself in a third-floor apartment in a building that has no elevator. The stairs give her trouble when she enters and leaves her home, but she prefers the high floor because "it is much safer than the first floor. . . . If I were on the first floor I'd be even more vulnerable to a break-in." With a home-care support worker, delivered meals, and a publicly subsidized helper visiting weekly to do her grocery shopping and help with errands, Pauline has few reasons to leave home. "I go out of my apartment about six times a year," she told me, "and three of them are for Little Brothers celebrations."

Little Brothers Friends of the Elderly is one of the few organizations in the United States whose mission is to address the problems related to aging alone and to assist isolated seniors in their efforts to make or remake connections to a world that has left them behind. In 1997 the Little Brothers Friends of the Elderly Chicago operation coordinated more than 8,000 personal visits and 11,000 calls to isolated and reclusive seniors; brought more than 2,000 isolated elderly to their various holiday activities; and welcomed about 1,800 to birthday celebrations. "The problem," the organization states clearly in its reports, "is isolation and loneliness. . . . Our old friends don't have a social network of family and friends. They identify themselves as lonely and they seek companionship and friendship. . . . Our role is to become the family and friends the elderly have outlived, never had, or from whom they are estranged."[24]

It is, I would learn, a challenge for Little Brothers to help even the seniors with whom they have contact. Pauline and I made it to the birthday celebration after a difficult and painful trip down her stairway, during which we had to turn around and return to the apartment so that she could address "a problem" that she experienced on the stairs— one apparently too embarrassing to discuss with me. Pauline's grimaces and sighs betrayed the depth of the pain that the walk had inflicted, but she was so excited to be going out, and going to her party, that she urged me to get us to the center quickly. I was supposed to have brought two other seniors to the celebration who had confirmed their intention to me the day before, but when I arrived at their apartments they both told me that they had decided to stay home.

Pauline had an extra incentive to get to the party. Edna, one of her two "phone buddies" who lived a few blocks away but saw her only at Little Brothers events, would also be there for the day. The two were thrilled to see each other, and at the end of the excellent meal and sing-along that highlighted the joyous event, Edna arranged to get a ride back with me so that she could extend the visit.

Edna got out more than Pauline, but both explained that the telephone has become their primary link to the world outside. Pauline has two phone buddies with whom she speaks regularly; one is a romantic albeit physically distant attachment. A few other friends and family members also call occasionally. Pauline has two children, who both live out of the state and visit infrequently but call about once a week. Although they phoned to wish their mother a happy birthday, neither could make it to Chicago to celebrate the occasion.

Pauline's other main sources of companionship are the major media, mostly television and radio, and the odd things she receives in the mail, which a neighbor brings up to her apartment and leaves on a pile of boxes outside the door so she doesn't have to bend over to pick it up. Recently, Pauline has started to phone in to talk shows, where she likes to discuss political scandals and local issues. These contacts helped keep her alive during the 1995 heat wave, as she and her friends checked up on one another often to make sure they were taking care of themselves.

Pauline knew that I was studying the disaster and during one visit she announced that she wanted to tell me her story. "It was," she said softly, "the closest I've come to death." Pauline has one air conditioner in her apartment, which gets especially hot during the summer because it is on the third floor. But the machine "is old and it doesn't work too well," which left her place uncomfortably, if not dangerously, warm during the heat wave. A friend had told her that it was important for her to go outside if she was too hot indoors, so she arose very early ("it's safer then") on what would become the hottest day of the heat wave, to visit the local grocer to buy cherries ("my favorite fruit, but I rarely get fresh food so they're a real treat for me") and cool down in the air-conditioned store. "I was so exhausted by the time I got down the stairs that I wanted to go straight back up again," she recounted, "but instead I walked to the corner and took the bus a few blocks to the store. When I got there I could barely move. I had to lean on the shopping cart to keep myself up." But the cool air revived her enough to buy a bag of cherries and return home on the bus.

"Climbing the stairs was almost impossible," she remembered. "I was hot and sweaty and so tired." Pauline called a friend as soon as she made it into her place. As they spoke she began to feel her hands going numb and swelling, a sensation that quickly extended into other parts of her body, alerting her that something was wrong. "I asked my friend to stay on the line but I put the phone down and lied down." Several minutes later, her friend still on the line but the receiver on the floor, Pauline got up, soaked her head in water, directed a fan toward her bed, lay down again, and placed a number of wet towels on her body and face. Remembering that she had left her friend waiting, Pauline got up, picked up the receiver to report that she was feeling better and to thank her buddy for waiting, and then hung up. Finally, she lay down once more to cool off and rest in earnest. Before long she had fully recovered.

"Now," she concluded, "I have a special way to beat the heat. You're going to laugh, but I like to go on a Caribbean cruise"—alone and, as she does nearly everything else, without leaving her home. "I get several washcloths and dip them in cold water. I then place them over my eyes so that I can't see. I lie down and set the fan directly on me. The wet towels and the wind from the fan give a cool breeze, and I imagine myself on a cruise around the islands. I do this whenever it's hot, and you'd be surprised at how nice it is. My friends know about my cruises too. So when they call me on hot days they all say, 'Hi Pauline, how was your trip?' We laugh about it, but it keeps me alive."

Pauline's case is hardly unique. Sharon Keigher, a professor at the University of Wisconsin who conducted a multiyear study of housing risks for the Chicago elderly, reports the following case study of a woman identified through Chicago's Emergency Services program. Her account of Viola Cooper suggests how much more difficult isolation can be when it is compounded by extreme poverty:

> At similar risk . . . is Viola Cooper, a thin 70-year-old black woman who continues to live alone in isolation in her basement apartment. She greeted us in the hallway with a toothless, pleasant smile. Her three-room apartment, furnished with odd items of run-down furniture, was cluttered, dirty, and in poor condition. . . . This apartment, for which she pays $250 of her $490 monthly income, was not much of an improvement over the last apartment where ES [Emergency Services] workers found her.
>
> She had just come home from the hospital after 8 days in intensive care for treatment of an infected bite on her face received from a rabid rat. She had been bitten while sleeping in her apartment. After the fire (2 years before), ES determined that repairs on her apartment were 'in process' and 'relocation (was) not needed,' although follow-up (*sic*) services record the deplorable conditions she was living in.
>
> Fortunately, she was referred by the City to a private agency which helped her move and gave her some furniture. . . . She now lives too far from her church to attend, for the first few months she had no running water or working toilet, her only friend in the building died a few months ago. . . . Alone, sick, and depressed, her condition is aggravated by the unhealthy conditions under which she lives.[25]

VIOLENCE AND ISOLATION

Pauline Jankowitz and Viola Cooper are merely two of the 110,000 seniors who lived alone in Chicago during the 1990s; and despite her many barriers to social integration, Pauline's location in the northeast part of the city makes her relatively safer than seniors living in other regions. Nonetheless, urban areas with high levels of violent crime impose real barriers to mobility for their residents, and during this period Chicago was among the most dangerous cities in the country. In 1995, for example, Chicago ranked sixth in robberies and fifth in aggravated assaults among all U.S. cities with populations exceeding 350,000; and in 1998 it was the national leader in homicides at 698—exceeding New York City's figure for that year by about 100, although it is roughly one-third as populous.

Most important for the story of the heat wave, though, is that during the week before the event Chicago experienced a spurt of homicides that put people living near the crossfire on alert. From Friday 7 July to Thursday 13 July 1995, there were twenty-four homicides in the city. Under the headline "City Murders on Rise with the Thermometer," the *Chicago Tribune* reported that the annual summer upsurge in violence had begun, with most killings "concentrated in South Side neighborhoods that carry a disproportionate share of the city's deadly violence."[26] The same areas produced an inordinate number of heat-wave-related deaths the next week. Though they were unlikely targets for the shootings, older residents of violent areas who refused to leave their homes during the heat wave had reason to be concerned about the risks they faced in the city streets.

In recent years a number of studies have shown that older people living in violent and deteriorated urban areas tend to be more isolated and afraid of crime than those in more robust regions.[27] Among the mechanisms producing this concentrated fear and isolation in ecologically depleted and politically underserved places are the lack of local commercial venues and service providers to draw people into the streets; barriers to physical mobility, such as broken stairs, crumbling sidewalks, and poor lighting; the psychological impact of living amidst signs of disorder; indifferent government agencies who neglect the local infrastructure; and the decrease of trusting and reciprocal relationships in areas with high levels of crime.[28] In extreme cases, social gerontologists Estina Thompson and Neal Krause report, "avoidance behavior" encouraged by degraded public areas "is so great among older people that many live in a virtual state of 'self-imposed house arrest.'" But "even if people only partially restrict their outdoor activities in response to their fear of crime, they still have fewer opportunities than those with lower levels of fear to establish the face-to-face contact that appears to be so important to receiving support."[29]

THE CULTURE OF FEAR

The urban elderly are hardly the only Americans to reduce their vulnerability to the dangers of the street by limiting their time in public as well as their social contacts. In recent decades, as sociologists including Elijah Anderson show, social avoidance and reclusion have become essential protective strategies for city residents whose concentration in high-crime neighborhoods places them directly in harm's way.[30] Moreover, Americans who live in objectively safer areas have been influenced by a sweeping culture of fear that is borne of both direct experience and sensationalistic representations of crime and danger in the media. In cities like Chicago a pervasive concern with crime is now a fundamental part of the cultural substratum of everyday life, playing a key role in organizing the temporal and spatial boundaries of mundane activities—many people refuse to go out at night or to visit "no-go" areas—as well as in shaping major decisions about where to live, work, and send children to school.[31]

According to several commentators who wrote about the heat wave, one barometer of the extent to which Chicagoans have adapted to the threats of contemporary urban life is that during the heat wave most of the city's public parks and beaches were empty at night. Throughout the city, but especially in the areas with high rates of violent crimes, people chose to suffer through the intense heat rather than cool themselves in the same areas in which their predecessors had congregated in severe heat waves of previous decades. "You'd have to be crazy, suicidal, or homeless these days to spend a sultry night sleeping in a park or on a porch," opined Bob Secter in a *Sun-Times* article placed beneath a photograph of two men resting by a harbor during a balmy night in 1964 (fig. 20). "But Chicagoans once did it by the tens of thousands to survive blistering heat waves."[32]

In an especially intense heat wave during 1955, for example, thousands of families packed up their bedding and beverages and camped outdoors in parks, on beaches, or simply on their front porches. Fewer than 10 percent of Chicago homes at the time had air conditioners, but the simple strategy of sleeping outside helped to keep the mortality rate during the 1955 crisis down to roughly half the level of the 1995 disaster. Alan Ehrenhalt argues that in the 1950s the streets and public areas in Chicago's ghettos supported vigorous social activity and provided safe spaces for residents to come together. Ehrenhalt depicts Bronzeville, Chicago's black metropolis, as typical of a 1950s city environment that was "an unrelentingly public world" in which "summer

Figure 20. Sleeping outdoors during the heat wave, 1964. Source: *Chicago Sun-Times* file photo. Reprinted with special permission from the Chicago Sun-Times, Inc. © 2002.

evenings were one long community festival, involving just about everybody on the block" and ending with people "sleeping on fire escapes to avoid the heat."[33]

There is good reason to be cautious about an overly romantic, even nostalgic view in this kind of account. But if the image of sleeping outdoors in summer is a central element of conventional portraits of urban decline, it is such a powerful and pervasive memory among older Chicago residents—including those who lived in the city's ghettos during the 1940s and 1950s—that it is difficult to discount.[34] Eugene Richards, a seventy-year-old African-American man who has lived in North Lawndale since the late 1950s, recalled that in the early days "when it got hot, the whole block would go to Garfield Park and sleep outside. We'd take out blankets and pillows, people would sleep on benches and in the grass. And we just left the dogs in the yard. And that was it." I asked Eugene whether people went to the parks during the 1995 heat wave. He looked at me incredulously and chuckled to himself. "Over here? Now? Are you kidding me? No, no, no. No one would sleep. I won't even walk at night around here. It's too dangerous. You can't trust your luck too much. People out at 2 or 3 in the morning will do anything. You have to be cautious."

Another indication of the extent to which this cautiousness has spread in Chicago is that during the heat wave many Chicago seniors refused to open their doors or respond to volunteers and city workers who had tracked them down and tried to check on them. Although the Mayor's Commission on Extreme Weather Conditions complained that such behavior was a sign of seniors' refusal to compromise their independence and face up to their own vulnerability, there is more to the story than this. According to seniors throughout the city, turning strangers away at the door has become part of a survival strategy for living alone in the city. "If someone comes to the door I won't open it," a woman in her seventies told me during a discussion in a local church. "I'll talk through the door because you never know."

In an environment where preying on the elderly is a standard and recurrent practice of neighborhood deviants as well as legitimate corporations, mail-order businesses, and salespersons, seniors report feeling besieged on an everyday basis. Whether the aggressors are local hoodlums who pay them special attention around the beginning of the month when Social Security checks are delivered, or outsiders who try to visit or phone and convince them to spend scarce dollars, the cumulative impact for the elderly of exposure to such threats is increased suspicion, especially when it comes to greeting unannounced and unknown visitors at the door.

Criminologists have long puzzled over the question of why the elderly, who are statistically less likely to be victimized by crime than almost all other demographic groups, are generally the most afraid of crime.[35] But seniors in Chicago can explain the basis of their concerns. Many of the elderly people I interviewed acknowledged that they were unlikely to be robbed or burgled, yet argued that they had special concerns about the consequences of being victimized that younger and more adaptable people did not share. Economic insecurity is one source of their fear. Seniors living on fixed and limited incomes worry about making ends meet most of the time, and for them a robbery or burglary could result in a loss of food, medication, rent, or resources to pay for utilities. In Chicago, where roughly 16 percent of the elderly live below the official poverty line and housing is in short supply, these are well-founded concerns.[36] Physical insecurity is another source of disquiet. The seniors I got to know expressed great concerns about their health, and awareness of their own frailty made them especially fearful of an act of aggression. Not only were they worried that they would be unable to defend themselves or flee from an attack, they also feared the possibility that an assault would leave them disabled or even dead.

Sensationalized media representations of crime, particularly local television news stories about violence and danger in the city, fuel these concerns. George Gebner, former dean of the Annenberg School of Communication at the University of Pennsylvania, has shown that "people who watch a lot of TV are more likely than others to believe their neighborhoods are unsafe, to assume that crime rates are rising, and overestimate their own odds of becoming a victim."[37] Chicago television stations contributed to anxiety about crime during the early days of the heat wave. The one local network affiliate, for example, opened its 5:00 P.M. news broadcast on 14 July with a warning that "the heat is also giving opportunities to thieves," accompanied by video footage of a home with open windows and an interview with police officers cautioning residents to look out for trouble.

In fact, another reason that seniors are especially fearful of crime is that older Americans are among the greatest consumers of the media, including broadcast news on radio and television, which are the greatest sources of urban crime stories. Barry Glassner sums up the research on the elderly, media consumption, and fear in language that resonates strikingly with the story of Chicago's heat wave. "Ample real-world evidence can be found among the nation's elderly, many of whom are so upset by all the murder and mayhem they see on their television screens that they are terrified to leave their homes. Some become so isolated, studies found, that they do not get enough exercise and their physical and mental health deteriorates. In the worst cases they actually suffer malnutrition as a consequence. . . . Afraid to go out and buy groceries, they literally waste away in their homes."[38]

These pressures to withdraw from public life in U.S. cities are especially dangerous because they join forces with another fundamental feature of American culture that fosters isolation: the idealization and valuation of independence and self-sufficiency.[39] The myth of the independent individual who determines his own fate and needs no help from others has evolved from frontier legend to become one of foundations of U.S. popular thought. Americans not only deny the extent to which their fate is shaped by their support networks and their ties with others, but also stigmatize people—historically women and the elderly—who are thought to be especially dependent. The elderly in general, but old men in particular, face the challenge of maintaining their sense of self-worth and dignity in a society that denigrates people having visible needs. For older men, most of whom built their identities around the role of the breadwinner, perhaps the primary struggle of aging is warding off the role of the dependent old-timer who is unable to provide for others or even himself. Many seniors find that retreating into isolation and refusing support is the best means of saving face. Better to be alone, they conclude, than to be disgraced.

Although fear and isolation are more prevalent in areas where violence is most prevalent, the conditions of insecurity and concern about crime penetrate every part of a city. As a consequence, a pervasive bunker mentality has emerged on a smaller scale throughout Chicago, affecting a broad set of buildings, blocks, and housing facilities. It is now common for city residents to protect their neighborhoods, streets, and homes with walls, cul-de-sacs, bright lighting, and alarms, and to patrol their territory with neighborhood watches and crime-control groups. The fortress architecture of gated communities is the most public symbol of this trend, but it is also marked by the make-shift home-security devices common in poor neighborhoods where residents face a greater risk of burglary or violent attack, and by the rise of private alarm systems and security workers in all realms of American life.[40]

Spatial degradation combined with concentrated criminal activity helped produce isolation and reclusion in some of the settings where heat wave deaths were concentrated, such as senior public housing units and SROs. The recent crises in these specialized housing complexes deserve attention because senior public housing and single room occupancy dwellings have historically served as crucial sources of security and social support for older people having little income or wealth.[41] The problems induced by the extreme heat were hardly anomalous: in fact, residents and activists concerned about the emerging hazards in these units had warned city officials about the potential for disaster long before the summer of 1995.

THE WORST COMBINATION

The Chicago Housing Authority's Flannery Senior Housing building is just a few blocks away from Cabrini-Green, the family housing complex long considered to be one of the most volatile projects in the city. Few of the residents in the 126-unit building had home air-conditioning during the heat wave, and although Arthur Chambers, the president of the resident organization, had lobbied the CHA to install air-conditioning in the first-floor social room there was no artificial cooling available in 1995. Worse, on Friday 14 July the building's

Figure 21. Police remove the body of a heat-related victim from an apartment on the South Side of the city. Source: *Chicago Sun-Times;* photographer: Brian Jackson. Reprinted with special permission from the Chicago Sun-Times, Inc. © 2002.

water service failed because so many of the local fire hydrants had been illegally opened, and most of the residents were trapped in the heat. "It's very bad these people had to suffer," Chambers told a reporter from the *Chicago Sun-Times.* "A real shame. It was pitiful. We lost a couple of elderly people in this hot heat." Mary Dingle, another Flannery resident, was equally moved. "I hope I go to the Good Place when I go," the seventy-one-year-old quipped. "I don't see how I can last down there. I can hardly take this."[42] Such responses were typical in CHA senior housing during the heat spell, when many buildings experienced heat-related fatalities despite the public awareness that residents there were endangered (fig. 21).

The loss of water and lack of air-conditioning were only part of the reason that seniors in CHA buildings such as Flannery were so vulnerable to the heat. They also suffered from the pressures of living amidst a systemwide crime wave created by the housing authority's new policies. In the early 1990s the CHA opened its fifty-eight senior buildings, which house about one hundred thousand residents and are dispersed throughout the city, to people with disabilities as well as to the elderly. The 1990 Americans with Disabilities Act had made people with substance abuse problems eligible for social insurance, so the CHA welcomed them into its senior housing units. Unfortunately, this act of

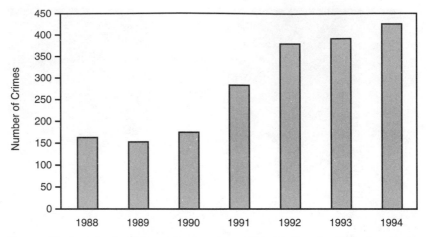

Figure 22. Part I crimes in senior housing, 1988–94. Part I crimes (as classified by the U.S. Department of Justice) include homicide, criminal sexual
assault, serious assault, robbery, burglary, theft, and vehicle theft. Source:
Building Organization and Leadership Development (1995).

accommodation has proven disastrous for senior residents and the
communities they had once established within their buildings. The mix
of low-income substance abusers, many of whom continue to engage
in crime to finance their habits, and low-income seniors, many of
whom keep everything they own, savings included, in their tiny apartments, discourages collective life in the housing complex.

In the four years leading up to the heat wave, conditions in the city's
senior public housing facilities bucked all of Chicago's crime trends
(fig. 22). Residents of these special units experienced a soaring violent
crime rate even as the overall crime levels in the CHA family projects
and the rest of the city declined, forcing many residents to give up not
only the public parks and streets that once supported their neighborhoods but also the public areas within their own apartment buildings.

In March of 1995, just a few months before the heat wave, the CHA
reported that from 1991 to 1994 the number of Part I crimes (the category under which the U.S. Justice Department includes homicide,
criminal sexual assault, serious assault, robbery, burglary, theft, and
violent theft) committed and reported within its housing increased by
more than 50 percent.[43] "The elderly in public housing are more
vulnerable than seniors in assisted or private housing in that they are
being victimized in many cases by their neighbors," reports Building
Organization and Leadership Development, a group of CHA tenants
and advisers. Moreover, BOLD shows that thefts, forcible entry, armed

robbery, "and other crimes of violence are substantially higher in those developments housing a large percentage of non-elderly disabled. . . . The reality appears to be that disabled youth are victimizing seniors."[44]

In their current arrangement, elderly residents of senior buildings voice the same complaint: they feel trapped in their rooms, worried that if they leave they might be attacked or have their apartments robbed. The most afraid refuse to use the ground-floor common rooms unless security workers are present; the degradation of public space that contributes to isolation all over Chicago is exacerbated here. Most residents, to be sure, do manage to get out of their units, but they have to organize their neighbors to secure public areas, elevators, and halls. Unable to improve the structural conditions of insecurity in the buildings, workers at the Chicago Department on Aging recently initiated a program to help residents develop watch groups in the senior complexes. True to its mission to enable as well as provide, the city government has increased the security services in the buildings but also encouraged the elderly and impoverished CHA residents to arm themselves with flashlights, cellular phones, and badges so that they can patrol their home turf.

Yet while one branch of the city government prepares the elderly for a feeble battle against the conditions that another one of its branches has created, the most worried and disaffected residents of the senior buildings respond by sealing off their homes with homemade security systems designed to ward off invaders. One woman I visited has wedged a piece of metal into her door so that it screeches noisily enough to awaken the neighbors when it closed. "It's my alarm system," she boasted. "And it works." According to a social worker I contacted, another resident of a senior building has wired his doorknob to an electrical current so that it shocks anyone who touches it before he disconnects the wiring.

Concern about the proximity of younger residents and their associates who are using or peddling drugs is ubiquitous in Chicago's senior housing complexes. During an interview in her home, a resident of a CHA building on the Near West Side expressed remorse that a formerly pleasant and popular patio on the top floor had been vandalized and looted by younger residents and their friends. The group had first commandeered the space and made it their hangout spot, then decided to steal some of the furniture and even the fire extinguishers. Some older residents, she explained, did not want to make a big deal out of the problem because they worried that their young neighbors would retaliate against the informant. The fear of young people and demonization of drug users common in contemporary American society rendered the situation more difficult, as many building residents presumed that the younger residents would cause trouble and were scared to approach them. Despite their frustration, the building's seniors have been unable to fix up the area or win it back. "Now," the elderly woman sighed, "no one uses that space. It's just empty, dead."

Trouble stemming from the forced cohabitation of some of the city's most precarious and most apparently threatening groups only compounds the typical problems within the CHA's notoriously underserviced buildings. "For the most part," a former commissioner of the Chicago Department on Aging explained, "the senior buildings are maintained poorly." Elevator breakdowns and malfunctions are common, making it difficult or impossible for seniors and disabled residents to get outside. In one building I visited an impressive health-care clinic that was inaccessible to some residents because the elevator wouldn't stop on the floor where it was located. In another complex, the elevator stopped before it reached the higher levels, forcing residents to use the stairs for the remaining distance to their homes.

The heat wave, however, did inspire some important changes in CHA policy. After the disaster the housing authority promised to install and maintain air-conditioning units in the common rooms of every senior building in Chicago; residents citywide benefited immediately. In the year 2000, the new housing commissioner pledged to spend millions of dollars to renovate and repair senior housing facilities, but whether the expenditure will improve the residents' security remains uncertain. By 1996, after the Department on Aging held a hearing in which residents had a chance to share their experiences and concerns regarding the dangerous cohabitation arrangement, the CHA acknowledged the problem its housing policy had created and pledged to close the senior buildings to new applicants having substance abuse problems. For now, however, the current residents of the buildings will be allowed to remain, as will the fears of the older residents.

CRISIS IN THE SROs
The senior CHA buildings were not the most dangerous places in Chicago during the heat wave. But there is some evidence that the city's remaining single room occupancy dwellings (SROs), particularly the for-profit hotel residences clustered around Uptown and the South and West Loop regions, experienced the highest rates of heat-related mortality. In one region on the Northeast Side of the city, for example, medical records show that approximately 16 of the area's 26 heat-

related deaths took place in SROs, and several others occurred in one-room efficiencies nearby. Although there is no official record of the number of deaths that occurred in transient hotels and one-room apartments with shared bathroom facilities, 62 of the 160 death reports at the Public Administrators Office listed "Room"—the code word for hotel residence—as the place where the decedent was discovered.

The concentration of deaths in the SROs is partly due to the prevalence of vulnerable people in this kind of housing: men with low incomes and weak social networks, high levels of illness (both mental and physical) and substance abuse, and little contact with doctors and social service providers are especially prominent in Chicago's SRO population. According to a census of the city's hotel residences conducted in the mid-1980s, 77 percent of the occupants were male, 33 percent were aged 55 years or older, 60 percent were unemployed, 38 percent had serious illnesses (about two times the general national level), and 93 percent were single.[45] SRO occupants live on the verge of homelessness, and they generally move into hotel residences only when they have exhausted their other housing options and sources of support. A population with this profile is overdetermined to suffer high death tolls during almost any health crisis. But the conditions of the hotel residences have changed along with the composition of their residents, and together they create a dangerous social environment for at least some of the people who make them home.

For most of the twentieth century, SROs constituted an important alternative for single people and poor families looking for inexpensive housing in city centers; and at a time when homelessness is rampant in American cities, SROs remain a crucial source of protection from life on the streets. When managed and maintained well, these dwellings can be an effective source of housing for urban residents otherwise unable to enter the housing market, as well as a meeting ground for people in need of new contacts and support. According to Charles Hoch and Robert Slayton, who directed a thorough census of Chicago SRO residents in the mid-1980s, most of these residents feel safe in their units and manage to maintain autonomy by participating in reciprocal relationships with other hotel occupants. Yet for many, particularly those who are old and ill, hotel living has become less viable at the same time that it has become more necessary because there are so few housing alternatives. Political pressures to eliminate the few hotel residences and housing alternatives for the poor that have survived the sweeping assault on low-cost housing in recent years have constrained public discussions of the emerging crisis in SROs. Fearing that closer inspection of extant buildings would only embolden the political officials and real estate developers who would prefer to convert the units into market-rate family housing, advocates for hotel residents who might otherwise call attention to the problems in the buildings have largely chosen to hold their tongues. According to one political activist on the Northeast Side, these fears explain why no one analyzed or publicized the traumatic impact of the heat wave on hotel dwellers.

The concerns of housing advocates are well founded. In the last fifty years, two changes in government policy have eliminated or degraded the stock of hotel buildings and reduced the quality of life for their residents; moreover, additional pressures from realtors and neighborhood groups have led several hotel proprietors to sell their buildings. First, the urban renewal programs of the 1950s and 1960s and urban development programs of the 1970s led to the destruction or conversion of most of the old SROs, but neither the city nor the federal government has funded or assisted much new hotel-style public housing since then. From 1960 to 1980 Chicago lost 85 percent of its one-room units in the West Madison region, 48 percent of its units in the South State Street area, and 84 percent of its units on the Near North Side, for a total loss of more than seven thousand units in these three areas alone. Nationally, historian Paul Groth reports, "estimates usually refer to 'millions' of rooms closed, converted, or torn down in major U.S. cities" since the 1960s. Using a more conservative measure from the Census Bureau's American Housing Survey, Christopher Jencks claims that the number of one-room rental units dropped nationwide by 325,000 from 1973 to 1989, but nonetheless agrees that "most of the old SROs were torn down during the 1960s and early 1970s."[46] The destruction of these dwellings continued into the mid-1970s and 1980s, with Chicago losing roughly eighteen thousand units from 1973 to 1984. Building code restrictions and unrest among hotel proprietors inhibited the development of new transient hotels, and by the mid-1980s Chicago was left with a mere 11,822 hotel units.

Second, changes in mental health policy during the 1970s and 1980s sparked a massive influx of mentally ill people into the low end of the housing market, notably the SROs. At the same time, Groth explains, "welfare departments were referring more unemployed downtown people—especially the elderly—to hotels for temporary housing that tended to become permanent."[47] By the 1970s the population base of the hotel residences had changed dramatically. Gone were most of the families, and many of the day laborers and migrant workers who had counted on empty hotel rooms when they arrived in town found that the SROs were either full of unstable people or simply full.

In the 1990s the increase of residents circulating between hotels and criminal justice facilities added new burdens to SRO residents and staffs. The dwellings became repositories of people shunned by other protective institutions: the mentally and physically ill, substance users and abusers, drug dealers looking for places to work temporarily, parolees and probationers who cannot find other housing—and the impoverished seniors who once constituted the core population of hotel residents. Together, these predominantly male tenants make up an "impossible community" that can isolate and endanger some residents even as it integrates and protects others.[48]

In their census, Hoch and Slayton, who argue that most hotels in the 1980s provided decent support for collective life and resident support, also found SROs in which the "inability of the former patients to collaborate in the maintenance of the fragile social order of the hotel . . . threatened to overwhelm the balance of reciprocal exchanges that kept the hotel secure" for generations. In their interviews they discovered that fully "half the residents in the hotel . . . complained that the crazy newcomers were replacing the old tenants," creating a public impression that the residence had been taken over by "crazy folk" who were often getting in trouble with police or loitering around the building and making other occupants insecure.[49]

Sitting in his room on the third floor of the Uptown SRO where he has lived for almost thirty years, Bob Greblow lamented that the environment has "changed for the worse." Although he used to fraternize with other hotel residents, a series of bad experiences ultimately made him distrustful of the people nearby:

> I don't bother other people and I don't want to be bothered by other people. That's just my way. Once a month I might go have a couple of beers just to get away from the boredom of lying around and doing nothing. I have nowhere that I want to go.
>
> I never go out at night because the streets are rotten. Young people are on the streets when I go to the currency exchange to get my check. There's robberies every day. It's too dangerous out there. Even during the day, that's when they get you—you know, when you go get your money. It's scary, but you got to do it. What else are you going to do?

The degradation of the hotel environments made the buildings vulnerable to another pressure that SROs faced in the late twentieth cen-

tury: gentrification and the rising demand for housing in neighborhoods such as Uptown and the South and West Loop, where hotels
could be easily converted into expensive property or sold to a developer
for a handsome profit. By the 1990s many of the city's hotel owners,
including the most civic minded and socially responsible, had grown
exhausted from the challenge of managing and maintaining decent
buildings for such an assortment of society's discarded people. Hotel
proprietors recognized that they were being asked to provide the safety
net that governments, health-care providers, and families had cast
aside, and they had ample incentive to follow suit. As a well-educated
hotel manager known for his fairness, tolerance, and support of hotel
residents told me,

> This is a family business that I've been working in since I was a kid. And
> trust me, I'm devoted to it. My father still works here with me. And we've
> put a lot into it. But do you have any idea what it's like to run this place?
> I have to be a security guard, a policeman, a counselor, a drug therapist,
> *and* a hotel manager. Can you imagine what's that like, what a hassle it
> is? And believe me, there are *a lot* of people who want to buy this build-
> ing, and there are *a lot* of other things that I could do. I have to say that
> these last few years have been almost impossible, and I think I'm finally
> getting ready to give up.

Hotel residences continue to vary greatly in quality and form. In
Chicago federal housing grants fund roughly one thousand units, and
most of the publicly subsidized buildings are well kept, staffed by
trained social workers, and busy with programs for job training, substance abuse treatment, and habilitation for working life. Most for-
profit buildings lack these services entirely. SROs are realistic housing
sources for poor Chicagoans, yet the pressure exerted by developers
who want to tear them down and build more profitable properties,
coupled with the weak political support for SROs within the city, imperil the few thousand units that remain.[50] Although recent evidence
shows that the most successful SROs are those that receive direct subsidies and supports from the federal government, in current Chicago and
national politics most housing advocates and policy experts agree that
it is unrealistic to expect much government assistance with housing for
the poor, so they are scrambling to create alternatives in the private
sector.

Although there are many decent hotel residences in the city, some
SROs are bleak enough to resemble the "cattle sheds for human beings" common in industrial Britain 150 years ago.[51] In one large hotel

on the Northeast Side where at least two residents died during the heat wave, managers have used plywood to subdivide the building into hundreds of units large enough to fit only a bed, a dresser, and a chair. The wooden partitions stop several feet below the high concrete ceilings, but residents and their property are protected by key-lock room doors and chicken wire pleated atop the walls to serve as ceilings where none other exist. There are a few windows on the exterior walls and fire escapes on every floor, but these offer little ventilation to the residents lodged in the belly of the building, and there is no air-conditioning in the dim public space on the ground floor.[52]

Unlike the nonprofit SROs, the hotel offers no services connecting residents to medical or vocational support structures in the area; management's policy of nonintervention in the lives of building residents is guided by a principle of tolerance and respect that would be admirable were so many of the building's residents not so dangerously ill.[53] Health crises are not uncommon there, nor in the other nearby SROs that were also home to multiple heat wave deaths. "I was surprised that [the SRO death rate] wasn't higher," the alderman of one Northeast Side ward told me. "I'm sure those people were unhealthy and didn't have access to health care. I would guess that 90 percent of the people living in efficiency apartments and single room occupancy apartments have no health insurance. And they [always] have health problems." Local political leaders and neighborhood residents, who have tried for years to have the SROs improved, know from the frequent arrival of ambulances on the block that it does not take the heat to put SRO occupants at risk.

As we rested by the front stairs of an efficiency building on a small Uptown street where Lorraine Ranger, a woman in her fifties, died during the heat wave, the manager told me about the times when he had found residents dead in their apartments after noticing a strange smell. Lorraine's case, he explained, was fairly typical—except even his efforts to help her stay healthy failed.

> She lived by herself, maybe for half a year. She kept to herself, and her people would help her pay the rent but other than that I didn't see them. She stayed in her apartment, didn't even go to the back porch. Too burrowed up. She would go shopping for herself, but other than that her world was just she and the walls.
>
> The problem was mental, she didn't want any help. I wanted to give her a fan, window fan, but she refused and said she didn't have the money for it. I said, "I'll give it to you free," but she still wouldn't take

it. Some time later I did not see her at all, and I knocked on the door. There was no response. The next day I tried again. No response. So I went in with the keys and she was laying in the bed. I called the medical examiner and the police and they took her. Then the relations came and they blamed it all on me.

Although the manager was convinced that Lorraine's mental illness had made it impossible to help her, he also explained that the substance abusers and unstable young residents in the building created a difficult social environment for female residents.

I got to watch constantly for the drugs. Young people are lawless. Once the drugs are in the building people are afraid. The butts are in the hallways, and that is more difficult. Women [here] are afraid to go out to the bathroom at night. They're groped in the building.

The alcoholism, substance abuse, and mental illness that are rampant in hotel residences create additional barriers to supportive social relations among residents. Drinking alcohol is particularly dangerous during hot summer weather because it contributes to dehydration as well as liver disease and, insofar as it exacerbates problems with depression, can engender isolation. Heavy liquor and drug consumption is a known risk factor for heatstroke; and although alcoholism appears as a contributing cause of death in fewer than ten of the five-hundred-plus medical autopsies for the heat-related decedents, there is good reason to suspect that the health of many heat wave victims had been affected by long-term drinking. People taking medications for mental illnesses also face heightened risks of heat-related mortality, since neuroleptic drugs and other antidepressants sometimes impair the body's capacity to regulate its own temperature and induce hyperthermic disorders.[54]

WARNING SIGNS

Several studies of private SROs in Chicago have shown that hotels foster reclusion, fear, and isolation among senior residents. Paul Rollinson, who conducted ethnographic research in thirteen Chicago hotels and interviewed fifty-three elderly residents during 1986, found that "the hotel environment imposed geographical isolation upon the elderly tenants."[55] Rollinson describes the public areas in the hotels as "noisy and even dangerous," especially at night, when "people often drifted in off the streets" and "drug activity was common." The rooms, he found, "were small (averaging only 225 square feet), sparsely furnished, dark, dirty, and infested with vermin. . . . The carpeting throughout the hotels was torn and damaged. . . . The elevators . . . were old, in a state of neglect and disrepair, and often were not working."[56]

For senior residents, many of whom are ill and suffering from physical problems that limit their mobility, these conditions make socializing difficult and turn even a simple trip to the lobby into a struggle. A report to the city government published in 1991 states clearly that in SROs "physical barriers like long or treacherous stairways, heavy doors, and poor lighting are simply taken for granted"; yet "these structural problems present real deterrents to the elderly and disabled."[57] The internal state of the buildings helps to explain why Rollinson found that 81 percent of the tenants in his study spent their typical days inside their rooms and 83 percent received no regular assistance from friends or neighbors.[58] Hoch and Slayton, who found that 36 percent of hotel residents had no personal support network, also note that the elderly had the fewest contacts and smallest support systems.[59]

Together, Rollinson's ethnography and the survey of Chicago SROs provided warnings of the dangers for older SRO residents during hot summers several years before the heat wave disaster. Specifically, the authors of these studies showed that senior SRO occupants were concerned about problems stemming from the heat. In their census, Hoch and Slayton learned that 34 percent of hotel dwellers complained about the heat in the summer even without the prompting of a question about the weather.[60] Rollinson discovered that only about half of the hotel residents had fans and that many lived in rooms where the window shutters had been sealed shut and were impossible to open on even the hottest days. Sharon Keigher had reported on heat wave deaths in the SROs long before the 1995 crisis. During a 1988 heat wave, Keigher noted that "one older black woman who was reclusive was found dead during the summer heat wave. . . . Her window could not be opened due to the way the phone in her room was hooked up, though the staff believed that, even if she could, she wouldn't have opened it anyway."[61] Rollinson's informants told him that "a number of elderly tenants had died and it was not until a neighbor had called the police about the stench that the bodies were removed."[62] Residents discovered several corpses in hotel rooms during the Chicago heat wave as well, and the addresses of SRO buildings figured prominently in the files of unclaimed decedents at the Public Administrators Office.

In contrast, at Lakefront, the federally subsidized single room occupancy complex a few blocks away from the SROs where many deaths were concentrated, residents were well guarded from the dangerous weather. With the large staff, comfortable air-conditioned lounges, and well-maintained residential units made possible by public funding and Section 8 housing subsidies, Lakefront's managers can help occupants through emergencies such as the heat wave as well as the daily struggle to protect personal health and security in the city. Roughly one year after the disaster, longtime Lakefront resident Greg Porter remembered how the building's supportive social environment and strong ties with service providers helped him survive.

Well, we knew we were in trouble when it got up to 105 degrees with 90 percent humidity. And, ah, we don't have AC, just downstairs in the lounge. I have a fan, and the only thing that did was circulate warm air that didn't do much good of anything.

I was feeling it so I went downstairs and we were playing cards and it was about 5 or 6 in the evening. During the day we could come in the lounge and it was nice and cool, wonderful. I mean, it would be nice if we could have central air but we don't. Let's look at reality, you know? But we do have access to this place. That's one thing I like, that this is open 24 hours a day, 7 days a week.

The lights dimmed first. We, I didn't think anything of it because they usually do, we usually get a brownout when it gets overheated. And then it just went off completely for 24 hours—actually 26 hours. 26 hours without electricity of any kind. The thing that got me was that I just went shopping that day. And I put in food in the refrigerator, a lot of frozen stuff and it all spoiled, every single piece. The power went out on Friday and it came back on Sunday. But by the time it came back on . . . it was too late. There were too many people suffering from it. And I almost was sent to the hospital. And it came very close. It was a disaster, and I hope to God that I never have to go through it again.

We did one good thing. One thing that really impressed me was that we united together, people came together closer. Ah, it was very, very fascinating. We came, well, we came closer as a family type thing. Well, others were just getting more and more unapproachable. But for the most part people helped other people to survive this.

Desk clerks called the Salvation Army and they came out. And, ah, thank God for the Salvation Army because they brought the canteens out. And they treated it like the disaster that it was. And they sent out hamburgers, tons of hamburgers from McDonald's and, ah, lemonade and stuff like that and they treated us, really, really, like we were victims. And, and we were.

The fire department came. The paramedics came to see if everything was alright. And, I gotta admit . . . there's a janitor over at the Delmar, a good friend of mine. He, he was great 'cause he was here all the time helping out and trying to make sure everybody was OK, he did such a fantastic job. I mean, I gotta give credit where credit is due.

In marked contrast with the stories of SRO residents who endured the heat alone, Greg's account illustrates how the state-subsidized and professionally staffed hotel residence creates social as well as political conditions for group cohesion and support. The air-conditioned lobby gave occupants a safe place to socialize and relax; the building's janitor went door to door to check on residents; staff members called local support agencies and requested special services; and representatives of local government agencies were on the scene to help. Few of these resources were available to occupants of the for-profit buildings nearby.

The problem, though, is that facilities such as Lakefront achieve this social integration only at the expense of those whom it excludes. With just one thousand units of publicly supported hotel housing in the city, there are not enough secure rooms to go around. In the late 1990s there were so many applicants for the government-subsidized buildings that semipublic housing complexes often refused to accept more names to the waiting list. Those who do reach the top of the list must pass an elaborate screening and selection process—designed to weed out applicants who are using illegal drugs or give evidence of behavioral problems deemed unmanageable by the staff—to obtain a unit. This process helps to protect the residents who make it into the complex, but it leaves those whom it rejects all the more likely to be concentrated in the less supportive and more dangerous hotels. The residual housing seekers, Keigher found, express a preference for subsidized or CHA housing but recognize that they have few chances of getting in.[63] In the early 1990s Lakefront expanded the number of buildings it operates; by 2000, however, there were no plans for reproducing the Lakefront model on a scale large enough to improve the housing opportunities for the thousands of Chicago SRO occupants on the verge of homelessness.

In a series of interviews, residents of the Lakefront buildings explained that not only did their administrative and social-worker staffs personally check on occupants and encourage them to come down to the air-conditioned lounges, but police and fire department officers as well as local social service agencies such as the Red Cross also visited, bringing food and cold drinks. Residents of for-profit SROs received far less assistance. "We asked about the situation when we got to the hotels," an investigator from the Public Administrators Office remembered. "But the managers would tell us that they don't check on people: 'It's not our business.' I know those buildings pretty well by now anyway. We could park the car on Broadway and Lawrence and spend the day walking to investigate cases. A lot of people live these nondescript lives in those hotel rooms. And"—he nodded toward the piles of death reports in the room—"that happens."

THE GENDER OF ISOLATION

Although it is miles away from the SRO dwellings on the Northeast Side and the other places in Chicago where people live and die alone, the Public Administrators Office affords a bird's-eye view of both the products and the production of urban isolation. The investigators who spend their days searching throughout all regions of Chicago for discarded people and the social lives they lost carry a practical knowledge about the causes and consequences of being alone that extends far beyond official explanations. They recognize, for example, the truth contained in the mayoral commission's finding that heat wave victims who died alone were discovered in nearly every part of the city. But they also know the truths that such a statement conceals. For, as an investigator and a staff attorney told me, the public administrator's work tends to be concentrated in the parts of the city where conditions foster isolation and reclusion. Staff members visit some hotel residences so frequently that building managers sometimes gather the papers and belongings that they know the investigators will want, even though their assistance often interferes with the administrators' work.

The mortality records maintained by county and state offices also provide useful information concerning the patterns of isolation. The paradox that older women are far more likely than elderly men to live alone but significantly less likely to be cut off from social ties, appears with even greater clarity in the heat wave death files. I found records of fifty-six heat wave decedents whose unclaimed bodies had been buried by the county or state government. Forty-four of the fifty-six unclaimed people, roughly 80 percent, were men—the most powerful indicator I know of the extent to which males suffered disproportionately from the consequences of social privation during the crisis.[64]

Ample sociological and historical research would predict the gendered character of dying alone in the city. In *The Politics of Pensions,* Ann Shola Orloff reviews nineteenth-century demographic patterns in Europe and North America which show that once they could no longer work, single or widowed men had difficulty maintaining close ties with family members. Contemporary research in U.S. cities shows that these trends have continued. In his study of urban American social networks, for example, Claude Fischer found that "old men were the most isolated" (in terms of the number of social contacts) of all groups; and the survey of Chicago's SROs conducted by Hoch and Slayton shows that in 1980, 78 percent of all hotel dwellers and 82 percent of all hotel veterans were men.[65]

There are a number of reasons that men have relatively more difficulty than women in sustaining intimate relationships with relatives and friends. Conventional social practices among the generation of Chicago residents that was most devastated by the heat inhibited the cultivation of intimate ties among men. Historically, gendered patterns in education and child-rearing have encouraged girls to develop skills in supportive social action and domestic caring, while boys have been trained to invest their energies in less social endeavors. In addition, the gendered division of labor has relegated most family responsibilities and friendship-making efforts to women, while men developed core relationships in the workplace. When they are no longer capable of working, men often not only lose their habitual identity as breadwinners, but also tend to fall out of their work-based networks and become dependent on their partners' social connections and sources of support.[66] Widowers and divorced men often suffer from failing physical and mental health after they become single, while divorced women and widows are more likely to gain support from their social networks and suffer fewer health consequences from their status change. Men with children are more likely to reintegrate with a supportive family than those without. But compared with women, who are more likely to have provided direct care for their children and sustained close ties as they age, single men experience greater difficulty moving in with or becoming dependent upon their children. If they do become estranged from their informal social networks, men are often excluded from formal programs sponsored by local governments and social service providers.[67] They are more likely to be picked up by the dragnet of the criminal justice systems than by the safety net of the welfare state.

Men also face particular emotional constraints to intimacy and friendship, in part because conventional models of masculinity encourage forms of toughness and independence that undermine the cultivation of close ties. The literature on men who live alone consistently emphasizes the individuality and detachment that mark their experiences. It is no accident that Robert Rubinstein titles his trenchant book about older men who live alone *Singular Paths,* and opens his introduction with a note that "essentially, the men we interviewed were known to us as individuals: what emerged in our research were a number of memorable persons, each with a distinctive style, worldview, social world, and 'slant' on life."[68] If most single men experience such individuating pressures, men who fail in work or in their family responsibilities face a distinctive set of difficulties in relationships because they tend to feel great shame and humiliation about their inability to live up to social expectations and fulfill obligations. As Elliot Liebow shows in *Tally's Corner,* the street-corner society of poor African-American men he observed was "a sanctuary for those who can no longer endure the experience or prospect of failure"; and despite the "traditional characterization of the lower-class neighborhood as a tightly knit community," "transience is perhaps the most striking and pervasive characteristic of this streetcorner world" of men.[69] Like depression, such despondency and mobility can cause a vicious cycle that leads to isolation, particularly when men partake of the alcohol that is commonly available in their subcultural world. Shame, stigma, and alienation affect men's relationships with institutions as well with individuals, leading the most anguished to feel a sense of total rejection and marginalization from the mainstream.

Although during my fieldwork it was impossible to observe the processes through which men become emotionally detached from relations and develop outsider identities, the dispositions to keep to oneself and avoid social bonds were visible in many of the men I met. According to SRO resident Bob Greblow, a lifetime of rejections, deceptions, and failures have taught him that no one is trustworthy and that staying alone is the only way to protect himself.

> I've always been suspicious. I just, like, I know that I don't make it with people. Everybody I've ever met are freeloaders, alright. Everybody seems to want something for nothing. They want you to help them some way, and you do—you know, if you're easy that way—and then you never see them again. When you need the help you don't see them, alright. People who work here are that way [too], so I just stay away from them.
>
> Nobody brings nothing to me. I don't ask somebody to do nothing, nobody volunteers anything. It just seems to be trouble. The last one I did buddy up with, or help, he ripped me off! You know, ripped me off of jewelry. And watches. I had a watch, because my girlfriend, she got, I'll show you, stuff to make this watch, alright. But this woman, she ripped

me off. I let her cook in here. While I'm not paying attention or while I'm in the bathroom or something, she was helping herself to it. That's the way they are.

I can hardly make it myself on my Social Security. And when you get old the government wants you to fade away. They ain't worried about you.

I don't even have a doctor. I'm 76, 76 years old. I don't know if I got any problems or not. The last time I saw a doctor was 1985. I had an operation, prostate operation. And that, that cured me. I don't cure easy most of the time. I still have problems. My bladder and prostate. When you get older that happens. You swell up, there's no way you can heal yourself.

I just hope I end up all right where I don't, you know, get sick or something. That's probably the only thing that bothers me, my health. But I'm all right. And that's the main thing in life. You got your health, you got it made.

Bob's words, which resemble those of several men I met in the hotels, illustrate the reproduction of a cycle in which experiences of perceived abandonment or abuse by friends and institutions help motivate his own abandonment of them. Bob withdrew not only from other residents of his hotel, but also from the medical providers and government services that, he believed, wanted him to "fade away." It had been forty years since he had been in touch with his family, and no one other than the hotel managers kept an eye out for him once Bob retreated to his room.

Although men who live alone face the greatest risks of being isolated and lacking social support, it is important to emphasize that women such as Pauline Jankowitz and Viola Cooper constitute the great majority of seniors who live alone, and are by no means spared from social deprivation and its most horrifying consequences. The special *New England Journal of Medicine* article examining persons found in their homes helpless or dead, for example, reports that while very old men had the highest rate of incidence, women accounted for 51 percent of the cases in the city of San Francisco.[70] There was a similar pattern in the distribution of heat wave mortality. Men were more than twice as likely as women to die (once we control for age with a statistical age-adjustment procedure), but women represented 45 percent of the total victims. The social pressures and spatial constraints that push city dwellers to live and die alone exert their force across the gender lines.

There are more elements to the collective production of isolation than we have explored thus far. After examining the demographic trends, cultural changes, housing arrangements, and gender patterns that help explain why certain individuals died in the heat, we can assess whether there are any broader community- or neighborhood-level conditions that contribute to the vulnerability or security of city residents. It is to this matter, and specifically the question of how an urban area's ecology affects the health and welfare of its residents, that the social autopsy turns next.

CHAPTER TWO

Race, Place, and Vulnerability
Urban Neighborhoods and the Ecology of Support

O n 21 July, while Chicago still simmered from its week of treacherous heat, a team of researchers led by the U.S Centers for Disease Control and Prevention arrived in the city to conduct an urgent epidemiological investigation into the risk factors for heat-related mortality. The project was ambitious for a quickly planned inquiry; yet, as one city official who helped coordinate the research explained, "the CDC is an extraordinarily powerful and rich organization, and when they come they bring an army." The case-control study design called for researchers to compare matched pairs consisting of one heat wave decedent and one survivor of similar age who lived nearby, either on the same street or in the neighborhood. Holding constant the age and location of the subjects, the epidemiologists would be able to determine a set of individual-level factors—such as living alone, having a medical problem, or owning an air conditioner—that affected a person's capacity to survive the heat. The scientific challenge was to locate the personal characteristics that proved most consequential during the catastrophe. But the "main objective," lead researcher Jan Semenza and his collaborators would later write, "was to identify public health strategies for reaching people at risk and preventing deaths in future heat waves."[1]

With roughly seven hundred heat wave victims scattered around Chicago, the CDC team had to select a random sample of decedents large enough to generate reliable findings but not so great as to overwhelm their resources. The research staff—which included roughly eighty participants—decided to visit and inspect the residences of 420 pairs of victims and controls; interview a friend, relative, or neighbor who knew the decedent well enough to answer questions about their social networks, medical conditions, and daily routines; and complete a standard survey questionnaire for each case. "It was a gigantic operation," Semenza explains. "We had to do more than eight hundred interviews and we obviously couldn't do them ourselves. We drummed up support from all kinds of agencies. We got all different kinds of people who were willing to go out into the streets. And it's hard to get through this questionnaire, especially with the relative of a decedent. It was a painful job." The team acquired death certificates, police reports, and a list of the names and addresses of persons older than twenty-four years of age who had died between 14 and 17 July and whose death certificates listed heat or cardiovascular disease as a primary, contributing, or underlying cause of death.[2] The official records led the researchers to the doors of the decedents' former residences; once there, they searched for a matching person (or case) by tossing a coin to determine their direction and walking from unit to unit until the paired individual emerged.

Using this method, the CDC completed the research for 339 matched pairs, or 678 persons, as well as an additional 33 unmatched decedents between 21 July and 18 August. After conducting a statistical analysis of the survey responses, the CDC team honed in on a series of risk factors that heightened the probability of death during the crisis, and the findings were ultimately published in the most prestigious medical journal in the United States, the *New England Journal of Medicine*. Among the most significant conclusions were that city residents were more vulnerable if they did not leave home daily, had a medical problem, were confined to bed, lived alone, or lacked air-conditioning, access to transportation, and social contacts nearby.[3] These findings were disseminated to an international audience of public health agencies and medical practitioners, and they have been influential in shaping morbidity and mortality prevention strategies in U.S. cities where heat waves are common.

What the epidemiological study did not do, however, is move beyond the population risk factors to identify the social environmental conditions that elevate or reduce the probability that residents would survive the heat. By studying matched pairs culled from the same location, the CDC researchers ruled out the possibility that their study would capture neighborhood or regional differences in heat wave mortality or the broader social context of the catastrophe.[4] If there were risks of living in an impoverished, institutionally depleted, or politically neglected neighborhood or region, the CDC analysis would not help to identify them. The CDC study directs the attention of public health agencies to the particular set of individuals who are most vulnerable to heat-related problems, but not to the places where such problems are likely to be concentrated. In recent years, a number of scholars have called attention to the ways in which the social ecology and political economy of urban areas affect the health and welfare of residents during normal times,[5] but few have asked whether such conditions alter health risks in extreme events. There were clear spatial patterns in mortality during the heat wave. Yet (as we will see in chapters 4 and 5) much of the official and journalistic discourse about the event, such as the summary statements that "all community areas in the city were affected" by the disaster, render these trends invisible.

Sociological theories and qualitative research techniques make it possible to conduct a different kind of epidemiology. Rather than ending an investigation with individual-level information, we can add a layer of regional or social ecological analysis to the study of urban health—for both extreme events and everyday, typical situations. Demographers and geographers can use census tract or neighborhood-level data to assess the extent to which place-specific conditions—such as land-use and development patterns, segregation, violence, and microclimate—influence health risks in disasters. The geographer Karen Smoyer, for example, shows that in the 1980 St. Louis heat wave "low-mortality tracts were predominantly in the cooler, more affluent and more stable south and west sections of the city"; whereas the high-mortality tracts were concentrated around the relatively warm central business district and the declining neighborhoods with low housing density and depleted population bases. These findings are largely consistent with the few studies of the geography of heat wave vulnerability that preceded Smoyer's work, which show significant associations between disaster mortality and neighborhood poverty, low-quality housing, lack of vegetation, and concentrated urban heat island effects.[6]

The spatial distribution of mortality in the 1995 Chicago disaster shared some characteristics with heat waves in other cities, but with a distinctly local pattern.[7] The map of the Chicago community areas that experienced the highest heat-related death rates (fig. 23) shows that the community areas hit hardest are concentrated on the South and West Sides of the city, the historic Black Belt where the city's African Americans have been concentrated and segregated.[8] This map is particularly striking because it illustrates a block of high-death areas, beginning at Burnside in the south and banking west before it reaches the most affluent areas on the North Side where residents had less difficulty protecting themselves from the heat. Although several predominantly

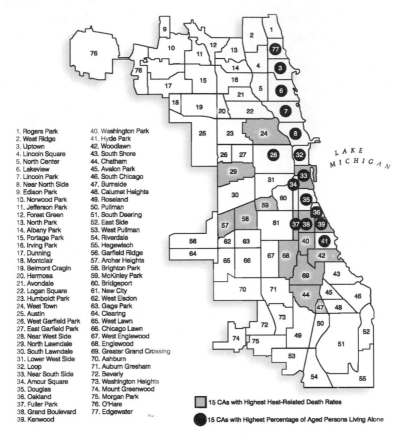

1. Rogers Park
2. West Ridge
3. Uptown
4. Lincoln Square
5. North Center
6. Lakeview
7. Lincoln Park
8. Near North Side
9. Edison Park
10. Norwood Park
11. Jefferson Park
12. Forest Green
13. North Park
14. Albany Park
15. Portage Park
16. Irving Park
17. Dunning
18. Montclair
19. Belmont Cragin
20. Hermosa
21. Avondale
22. Logan Square
23. Humboldt Park
24. West Town
25. Austin
26. West Garfield Park
27. East Garfield Park
28. Near West Side
29. North Lawndale
30. South Lawndale
31. Lower West Side
32. Loop
33. Near South Side
34. Amour Square
35. Douglas
36. Oakland
37. Fuller Park
38. Grand Boulevard
39. Kenwood
40. Washington Park
41. Hyde Park
42. Woodlawn
43. South Shore
44. Chatham
45. Avalon Park
46. South Chicago
47. Burnside
48. Calumet Heights
49. Roseland
50. Pullman
51. South Deering
52. East Side
53. West Pullman
54. Riverdale
55. Hegewisch
56. Garfield Ridge
57. Archer Heights
58. Brighton Park
59. McKinley Park
60. Bridgeport
61. New City
62. West Elsdon
63. Gage Park
64. Clearing
65. West Lawn
66. Chicago Lawn
67. West Englewood
68. Englewood
69. Greater Grand Crossing
70. Ashburn
71. Auburn Gresham
72. Beverly
73. Washington Heights
74. Mount Greenwood
75. Morgan Park
76. O'Hare
77. Edgewater

■ 15 CAs with Highest Heat-Related Death Rates

● 15 CAs with Highest Percentage of Aged Persons Living Alone

Figure 23. Chicago community areas with the highest heat-related mortality rates and highest proportion of elderly persons living alone. The top quintile is represented on the map.

African-American community areas had exceptionally low heat wave mortality rates, there was a clear clustering of deaths in Chicago's segregated black regions.

The heaviest concentration of high-death areas is in the region immediately south of the Loop, beginning at the Near South Side, progressing south into the old Black Belt and beyond to the newer African-American communities, such as Woodlawn and Chatham, east and farther south; another pocket with high mortality rates starts west of the Loop in the Near West Side area, extending through the western portion of the city. As figures 24 and 25 show, both of these large regions are notable for their high levels of poverty and violent crime.[9] Another cluster of heat-related mortality is on the Near Southeast Side, which,

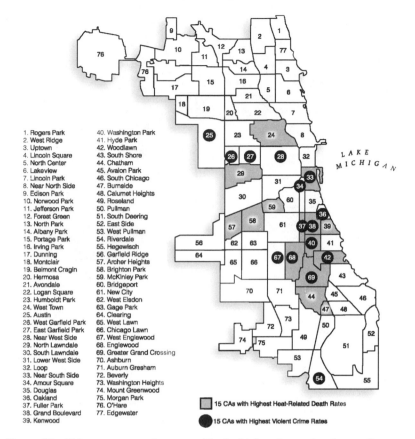

1. Rogers Park
2. West Ridge
3. Uptown
4. Lincoln Square
5. North Center
6. Lakeview
7. Lincoln Park
8. Near North Side
9. Edison Park
10. Norwood Park
11. Jefferson Park
12. Forest Green
13. North Park
14. Albany Park
15. Portage Park
16. Irving Park
17. Dunning
18. Montclair
19. Belmont Cragin
20. Hermosa
21. Avondale
22. Logan Square
23. Humboldt Park
24. West Town
25. Austin
26. West Garfield Park
27. East Garfield Park
28. Near West Side
29. North Lawndale
30. South Lawndale
31. Lower West Side
32. Loop
33. Near South Side
34. Amour Square
35. Douglas
36. Oakland
37. Fuller Park
38. Grand Boulevard
39. Kenwood

40. Washington Park
41. Hyde Park
42. Woodlawn
43. South Shore
44. Chatham
45. Avalon Park
46. South Chicago
47. Burnside
48. Calumet Heights
49. Roseland
50. Pullman
51. South Deering
52. East Side
53. West Pullman
54. Riverdale
55. Hegewisch
56. Garfield Ridge
57. Archer Heights
58. Brighton Park
59. McKinley Park
60. Bridgeport
61. New City
62. West Elsdon
63. Gage Park
64. Clearing
65. West Lawn
66. Chicago Lawn
67. West Englewood
68. Englewood
69. Greater Grand Crossing
70. Ashburn
71. Auburn Gresham
72. Beverly
73. Washington Heights
74. Mount Greenwood
75. Morgan Park
76. O'Hare
77. Edgewater

□ 15 CAs with Highest Heat-Related Death Rates

● 15 CAs with Highest Violent Crime Rates

Figure 24. Chicago community areas with the highest heat-related mortality rates and highest violent crime rates. The top quintile is represented on the map.

as figure 23 shows, is distinctive for its concentration of seniors and elderly people living alone. Table 3, which shows the community areas with the highest heat wave death rates, is equally striking. Of the fifteen community areas with the highest death rates during the heat wave, ten contain populations that are between 94 and 99 percent African American, and another is 77 percent black.[10] The four remaining community areas are distinctive for other reasons. West Town, which is a largely Latino and Puerto Rican region, faced elevated heat mortality risks because it has more Chicago Housing Authority senior public housing units than any other community area in the city. Archer Heights, McKinley Park, and Brighton Park, the three contiguous community areas on the Southwest Side, were especially vulnerable both

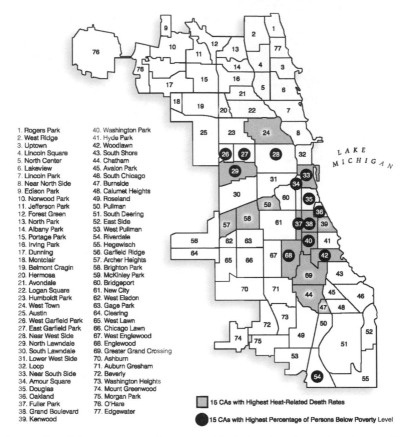

1. Rogers Park
2. West Ridge
3. Uptown
4. Lincoln Square
5. North Center
6. Lakeview
7. Lincoln Park
8. Near North Side
9. Edison Park
10. Norwood Park
11. Jefferson Park
12. Forest Green
13. North Park
14. Albany Park
15. Portage Park
16. Irving Park
17. Dunning
18. Montclair
19. Belmont Cragin
20. Hermosa
21. Avondale
22. Logan Square
23. Humboldt Park
24. West Town
25. Austin
26. West Garfield Park
27. East Garfield Park
28. Near West Side
29. North Lawndale
30. South Lawndale
31. Lower West Side
32. Loop
33. Near South Side
34. Armour Square
35. Douglas
36. Oakland
37. Fuller Park
38. Grand Boulevard
39. Kenwood
40. Washington Park
41. Hyde Park
42. Woodlawn
43. South Shore
44. Chatham
45. Avalon Park
46. South Chicago
47. Burnside
48. Calumet Heights
49. Roseland
50. Pullman
51. South Deering
52. East Side
53. West Pullman
54. Riverdale
55. Hegewisch
56. Garfield Ridge
57. Archer Heights
58. Brighton Park
59. McKinley Park
60. Bridgeport
61. New City
62. West Elsdon
63. Gage Park
64. Clearing
65. West Lawn
66. Chicago Lawn
67. West Englewood
68. Englewood
69. Greater Grand Crossing
70. Ashburn
71. Auburn Gresham
72. Beverly
73. Washington Heights
74. Mount Greenwood
75. Morgan Park
76. O'Hare
77. Edgewater

LAKE MICHIGAN

▨ 15 CAs with Highest Heat-Related Death Rates

● 15 CAs with Highest Percentage of Persons Below Poverty Level

Figure 25. Chicago community areas with the highest heat-related mortality rates and highest proportion of persons below poverty level. The top quintile is represented on the map.

because the red-brick and blacktop buildings ubiquitous in the region intensify the indoor heat,[11] and because the historically Polish communities concentrated there (especially in McKinley Park and Brighton Park) have aged in place while new, mostly Latino residents move in, leaving the white elderly culturally and linguistically isolated from the emergent populations.

The maps illustrate a clear correlation between heat-related mortality and certain community area conditions, and Illinois researchers used statistical research similar to Smoyer's to further investigate the sources of these varying death rates. After the disaster Tiefu Shen and his colleagues at the Illinois Department of Public Health found that, relative to other regions, community areas with high levels of violent

Table 3. Chicago Community Areas with the Highest Heat-Related
Death Rates

Community Area	Heat-Related Deaths per 100,000 Population	Percent Population Black	Percent Population 65+	Percent Population Lost, 1960–90	Overall Violent Crime, Rank, 1994–95 (77 CAs)
Fuller Park	92	99	19	64	1
Woodlawn	73	96	18	66	8
Archer Heights	54	0	21	13	56
Gtr. Gr. Crossing	52	99	18	39	15
Washington Park	51	99	11	56	2
Grand Boulevard	47	99	14	55	3
McKinley Park	45	0	13	21	46
North Lawndale	40	96	9	62	18
Chatham	35	99	19	16	30
Kenwood	33	77	15	56	31
Englewood	33	99	11	50	13
West Town	32	10	9	37	38
Brighton Park	31	0	15	15	50
Burnside	30	98	6	0	21
Near South Side	29	94	13	34	5
Chicago	7	39	12	22	—

Data based on 521 heat-related deaths located by Illinois Department of Public Health (1997), Chicago Fact Book Consortium (1995), and City of Chicago, Department of Public Health (1996).

crime and high proportions of elderly residents were significantly more likely to experience heat wave deaths.[12] The group did not examine whether there was also an association with the proportion of community area residents living below the poverty line, so the study yielded no information about place-based deprivation and vulnerability. Public health colleagues were convinced that there were reliable and significant differences in the neighborhood-level mortality risks, but they left it to others to explore and explain them.

In the years following the heat wave, however, no official or scientific report did revisit the issue of place-based risks, and subsequent public discussions and policy debates about heat-related health risks have not moved beyond individual- or population-level conditions. A smattering of quantitative evidence about heat waves in Chicago and St. Louis has shown that certain community area characteristics, such as poverty, high senior populations, lack of vegetation, and high crime, are associated with high heat wave mortality rates. But although demographers have ample data to examine these conditions, no studies have explained how neighborhood environments imperiled or protected residents during the extreme summer climate, and no qualitative research has identified significant contextual conditions that lie outside the scope of standard statistical data sets on urban regions.[13] Part of the reason for this absence is that community studies designed to identify the mechanisms through which neighborhood conditions affect the health and security of residents require intensive fieldwork and deep engagements with local residents, institutions, and public places. Without such research it would be impossible to learn whether community-level practices that fall outside the scope of quantitative studies—such as the ways in which residents use sidewalks and public spaces, the role of commercial outlets in stimulating social contact, the strategies through which residents protect themselves from local dangers, and the role of community organizations and institutions in providing social protection—affected the mortality rates.

The enormous amount of personnel, resources, and time that would be necessary to replicate the scale of the CDC heat wave study at the community area level makes it impossible to conduct an identical analysis.[14] Yet smaller-scale projects that focus on particular areas can deepen our understanding of the relationships among place, health, and risk during extreme events as well as normal times. Blending the CDC's case-control method with techniques honed by generations of urban sociologists, I turned my attention to a matching pair of neighboring Chicago community areas that have strong demographic similarities but drastically different heat wave mortality rates. The comparative case study would lack the large scale and predetermined variables of the CDC epidemiological inquiry, and it would no doubt be difficult to establish all the connections between the neighborhood social environments and the specific contexts in which residents died alone. But deep and intensive scrutiny of the two community areas would introduce novel ways of understanding place-based vulnerability or protection and, in turn, generate insights into how the social and ecological conditions that are unmeasured in conventional surveys affect the capacity of residents to survive the heat.[15]

MATCHING PAIRS

Like the CDC epidemiologists, my first challenge was to find a matching pair of cases that experienced different outcomes during the disaster. Since previous studies of place-based conditions that influenced heat wave mortality highlighted the significance of poverty, crime, elderly inhabitants, and lack of vegetation, I searched for two residential areas with similar compositional makeup on each of these measures and population levels high enough to generate reliably contrasting death rates.[16] One set of neighboring community areas on the West

Table 4. Characteristics of North Lawndale and South Lawndale

Condition	North Lawndale	South Lawndale	Chicago
Senior poverty level	26%	22%	16%
2× below poverty level	71%	62%	41%
Poverty level	44%	22%	18%
Population aged 65 years or older	4,029	3,965	334,046
Seniors living alone	956	1,256	106,792
Percent aged 65 years or older	8.5%	4.0%	12%
Percent seniors living alone	24%	31%	32%
"Minority" population	99% (96% black)	94% (85% Latino)	58%
Heat-related deaths	19	3	521
Heat wave death rate	40/100,000	4/100,000	7/100,000

Source: Chicago Fact Book Consortium (1995) and Lawlor, Almgren, and Gomberg (1993).

Side appeared to provide such a contrast: North Lawndale, which experienced 19 heat-related deaths for a rate of 40 per 100,000 residents; and South Lawndale (colloquially known as Little Village), which had 3 deaths and a rate of less than 4 per 100,000 residents—ten times fewer than North Lawndale. The two areas share more than a name. In the 1990s North and South Lawndale had similar microclimates and almost identical numbers and proportions of seniors living alone and seniors living in poverty. The community areas, then, naturally controlled for the weather and the subpopulation of people thought to be most at risk of heat wave death.

According to most observers, the obvious difference in the populations of the community areas was the ethnoracial composition of the residents. In North Lawndale 96 percent of the population was African American, whereas in Little Village 85 percent of the official population was Latino. Public health researchers had found that Chicago's African Americans faced the greatest risk of mortality in the heat wave, while Latinos were most likely to survive; after the heat wave, government officials, journalists, and scholars alike puzzled over the question of why, despite high levels of poverty and risk, Latinos fared so much better than blacks and whites.[17]

Though the areas are easily distinguishable to those who know them, an outsider who sees North and South Lawndale on paper would have little reason to believe that they would experience such great mortality disparities during the heat wave. As table 4 shows, the two Lawndales had almost identical numbers and proportions of seniors living alone and seniors living in poverty. In Little Village 1,256 seniors, or 31 per-

Table 5. Reported Overall Violent Crimes: Districts 10 and 11, 1994–95

Violent Crimes	11th District	10th District	Chicago
Number	4,714	2,973	218,894
Victimization rate	10/100,000	4/100,000	8/100,000
City rank			
(out of 77 community areas)	18	59	—

Source: City of Chicago (1996). The Eleventh Police District contains much of North Lawndale, and the Tenth includes Little Village and a slice of North Lawndale.

cent of the elderly population, lived alone, compared with 956, or 24 percent of the elderly population, in North Lawndale. Each of the areas also had distinctive risk factors. Although both had high levels of poverty relative to the rest of Chicago, North Lawndale, where 71 percent of local families earned below twice the poverty level and 44 percent lived below the line, was worse off than South Lawndale, where the poverty rates were 62 percent and 22 percent.[18] As table 5 shows, North Lawndale also had higher levels of violent crime; but it is important to note that in 1994 and 1995 its crime rate was not in the top quintile of Chicago's high-crime areas. The risks specific to Little Village stem from its high population of the people whom policy makers and scholars call cultural or linguistic isolates, who fit the demographic profile of the Chicago residents most likely to die in the heat. Roughly 46 percent of the seniors in Little Village were white "old-timers" who aged in place when the younger generations left, whereas only 2 percent of the seniors in the mostly African-American North Lawndale were white.[19]

To date, the most prominent explanations of the variance in death rates between the two areas, and between African Americans and Latinos more generally, have focused on the ethnoracial composition of the groups.[20] The two most popular cultural arguments that attempt to explain the variance in death rates are, first, that Latinos are acculturated to the heat and have strategies for coping with it because many have recently lived in hot Latin American climates. One of my Latino informants summed up this position when he told me that "people south of the border are more used to the heat. You have to realize that in the south of Mexico or Cuba or Puerto Rico the average temperature is about eighty-five or ninety degrees." The second cultural explanation is that Latino seniors benefit from strong multigenerational and extended family ties that facilitate close contact during normal times as well as crises. As another informant opined, "Among the three big groups that we have in Chicago—the Caucasians, the African-Americans, and the Latino people—the Latino group tends to be the less isolated group. . . . Latinos are the ones that probably get a little bit closer to their own families."

The primary "racial" argument, which I heard from a large number of Chicagoans when I discussed the heat wave with them, is that there is something about the physiology of Latinos that protects them from the heat.[21] "I guess naturally we are more equipped to resist the heat," one of my Latino informants told me. "I would say that there is something in our skin or our genes that makes us a little bit more comfortable with the heat." Another informant, this one a white woman who works with seniors regularly, added that Latinos' "metabolism and body chemistry . . . lends itself more to coping with high temperatures." None of these arguments provide a persuasive account of the differences in heat wave mortality between North Lawndale and Little Village. The racial argument is rooted in mythology rather than science. Not only is there no credible scientific evidence that Latinos have genetic or physiological traits that allow them to withstand the heat, there is also no distinct Latino "racial" type that unifies the heterogeneous groups having Latin-American ancestry, including residents of Little Village.

Cultural arguments concerning adaptation to the heat and family ties are also unsatisfying. For although social scientists and service providers often distinguish among ethnically organized cultures of care, there is little evidence that these caring practices and routines are inherent features of a group's identity. The claim that older Latinos are strongly connected to friends and family through multigenerational networks and extended family ties might be persuasive at first glance, especially given the important traditional role of the grandparent in Latino communities. But there are at least two reasons to treat it with caution. First, recent surveys of Mexican-American seniors have found that the native-born Mexican-American elderly are significantly more likely to live away from and out of regular contact with their children than are foreign-born Mexican-American seniors.[22] Clearly, ethnicity alone cannot explain this difference, but variations in the social environment in which Mexican Americans live can account for much of the cultural change. Second, many scholars argue that African Americans also have, or have had, both strong multigenerational family networks, extended family ties, and highly-respected and well-integrated grandparent figures.[23] Again, ethnicity alone cannot explain differences in support networks for the elderly.

The other claim, that some groups are acculturated to the heat because their members once lived in a warm climate, would likely be as applicable to Chicago's older African Americans, the majority of whom were born in the southern region of the United States and have ancestral roots in Africa, as it would be for any other group in the city. Yet, as we have seen, older African Americans experienced the highest death rates of all ethnoracial groups. Finally, both the "racial" and ethnic arguments about the differences in community area mortality rates overlook a crucial part of the heat wave story: *the social environment of Little Village protected not only the area's Latino population, but the culturally or linguistically isolated white elderly, who were at high risk of death as well.*

Together, these findings show that if in Chicago social connections proved to be more tenuous in North Lawndale than in Little Village, or among African Americans more generally, we will have to explain why this is the case and not simply attribute the differences to ethnicity or "race." For if it is true that the social support practices vary within groups as well as between them, a strong cultural argument about networks of care and support requires taking a closer look at the social environments of the two community areas.[24]

VARIATIONS IN THE SOCIAL ENVIRONMENT OF POVERTY

It takes only a few minutes of observation in the two community areas, or even a casual drive on Cermak Road, the border between the neighborhoods with the railroad line to the west, to see that the two Lawndales are, as numerous residents on both sides of the tracks told me, "totally different worlds." Most residents and outside observers differentiate the areas by the ethnoracial characteristics of the two distinctive local groups, but the differences extend far beyond the identities of the populations. To begin, North Lawndale and Little Village differ in their *ecological characteristics*—what Robert McKenzie called the "spatial and temporal relations of human beings as affected by the selective, distributive, and accommodative forces of the environment," or the spatial distribution of people and institutions that organize a local area. The two areas also differ in their *social morphological conditions*—which Marcel Mauss defined as "the material substratum of societies, that is, the form they assume in settling across the land, the volume and density of their population, the manner in which it is distributed as well as the ensemble of things that serve as the basis for collective life."[25] The social ecology of a community area is the foundation for local social life, the soil out of which social networks grow and develop or, alternatively, wither and devolve.[26] Thus, urban regions such as North Lawndale and Little Village can be distinguished not only by the identities of their inhabitants, but also by the structure and texture of their social and physical environments.

The prevailing U.S. tradition of thinking about urban poverty, however, involves focusing on poor people and their individual characteristics rather than on places and their social ecological features. This logic is most apparent in the culture of poverty arguments about the ways in which the practices of poor people contribute to the production of their own deprivation, but it informs more liberal theories as well. Yet there is also a rich heritage of research on city neighborhoods that highlights the spatial context of social order in the city.[27] Although most contemporary urban scholars argue that high population density undermines social cohesion within neighborhoods, Jane Jacobs draws a distinction between *high density* and *overcrowding*, which suffocates residents and stifles community life. According to Jacobs, density and public activity are necessary preconditions for vigorous neighborhood social networks. Residents of city neighborhoods without comfortable and secure streets and sidewalks, without places that draw people out of their homes and into the public, are more likely to suffer from literal isolation and social distance.

This chapter argues that place-specific social ecology and its effects on cultural practices account for much of the disparity in the heat wave mortality rates for the two Lawndales. The local social environment has a strong impact on older residents, for whom health problems that limit mobility can make it difficult to access places out of the neighborhood. In North Lawndale, the dangerous ecology of abandoned buildings, open spaces, commercial depletion, violent crime, degraded infrastructure, low population density, and family dispersion undermines the viability of public life and the strength of local support systems, rendering older residents particularly vulnerable to isolation. In Little Village, though, the busy streets, heavy commercial activity, residential concentration, and relatively low crime promote social contact, collective life, and public engagement in general and provide particular benefits for the elderly, who are more likely to leave home when they are drawn out by nearby amenities.[28] During the heat wave, these local conditions directly affected residents of the two community areas by constraining (in North Lawndale) or creating (in Little Village) the possibilities for social contact that helped vulnerable Chicagoans to survive.

AN ABANDONED COMMUNITY

Despite a recent resurgence of economic development, the major streets and the majority of the residential areas in North Lawndale bear the marks of decades of abandonment by factories, businesses, and residents, and of the devastating fires sparked in riots after the death of Martin Luther King Jr. in 1968. The physical landscape of North Lawndale's largest thoroughfares and many of its residential streets is dominated by boarded or dilapidated buildings, rickety fast-food joints, closed stores with faded signs, and open lots where tall grass and weeds, broken glass, and illegally dumped refuse give testament to the area's decline. North Lawndale lost roughly 50 percent of its housing stock (which fell from 30,243 units to 15,686 units) and about 60 percent of its population between 1960 and 1990, and the social and ecological consequences of these changes have been devastating for the residents who remain.[29]

The decay of the local infrastructure has gone hand in hand with the decline of the community's manufacturing, commercial, and residential presence. In the early twentieth century North Lawndale was a magnet for Polish and Czechoslovakian immigrants, many of whom benefited from or were attracted by the major employers clustered around the local railways, such as the Western Electric Company; Sears, Roebuck and Co.; and the McCormick Reaper Company (International Harvester, which later became Navistar International Corp.) nearby. The population doubled from 46,226 to 93,750 between 1910 and 1920 when Russian Jews arrived en masse. By 1930 the community area was bursting with residents and retailers and had reached a population density two times above the general city rate. Roosevelt Road became a commercial and cultural core of Chicago's Jewish community, and sixty synagogues, many of which exist as churches today, sprouted up around it. Douglas Park to the south, Garfield Park to the north, and Franklin Park to the east offered refuge from the tightly packed streets. Grand houses and apartment buildings made of limestone and brick provided a touch of elegance to the residential blocks.

Jews remained the majority group in the area during the 1930s and 1940s, but most local residents rented their homes instead of buying them and the community never established deep roots in the area. In 1939, for example, 81 percent of the housing units in North Lawndale were tenant occupied.[30] In 1940 only 380 African Americans lived in North Lawndale, but when the second wave of black migration from the South brought thousands of African Americans to the West Side of Chicago during the 1940s, whites throughout the city grew anxious about an incipient "invasion" that would transform and stigmatize their neighborhoods. Once the stream of African-American migration reached North Lawndale, more than seventy-five thousand white resi-

Table 6. Population in North Lawndale, 1950–90

Year	Population	Population Change (%)	Population White (%)	Population Black (%)
1950	100,489	—	87	13
1960	124,937	+24	9	91
1970	94,772	−24	3	96
1980	61,523	−35	2	97
1990	47,296	−23	2	96

dents abandoned their neighborhood. Roughly one hundred thousand blacks replaced them during the 1950s alone.

By 1960 North Lawndale had completed one of the most rapid and complete ethnoracial transition processes in U.S. urban history, turning over from almost 90 percent Caucasian to more than 90 percent African American in a single decade (table 6).[31] Although the composition of the population had changed, local factories and tertiary businesses continued to provide tens of thousands of working-class jobs to area residents. "Most people here could walk to work," one long-time resident told me. "Sears, Harvester, Western Electric, those companies were on the main line." There was no shortage of poverty within North Lawndale's black community, but the predominantly industrial economy generated enough demand for labor to support Lawndale families, and it paid workers enough to animate the area's public and commercial life. "It was a regular neighborhood then," long-time resident Ernie Stewart recalled. "We had lots of stores, meat markets, laundries, everything."

TURNING OVER

The fate of the area began to change in the late 1950s and 1960s, when the first stages of Chicago's industrial decline undermined the foundations of North Lawndale's economy. International Harvester, which once employed fourteen thousand laborers, left the community at the end of the 1960s. Sears, Roebuck, and Co. closed down the original Sears Tower (fig. 26) on Homan Avenue and moved its world headquarters, along with roughly seven thousand jobs, from Lawndale to the Loop in 1974. The catalog distribution center, which it left behind, stayed in the area and provided work for some three thousand employees until 1988, when Sears took it out of the neighborhood. Western Electric gradually shifted its facilities out of Lawndale and trimmed its labor pool until the Hawthorne plant, which had employed forty-three

Figure 26. An open lot near the original Sears Tower in North Lawndale.
Photo by Caitlin Zaloom.

thousand people, shut its gates for good in 1984. By 1970, 75 percent
of the businesses that had been in the area in 1950 were gone, and in
the 1980s and early 1990s North Lawndale experienced little economic
growth. The impact of these losses extended into other sectors of the
labor market as well, undermining the economic foundations of local
banks, small businesses, food stores, restaurants, and entertainment
facilities. The loss of this second-tier commercial economy deflated
the area, removing not only jobs but goods, resources, and places for
socializing and congregating as well. Lawndale residents lacked *places
to go* in the neighborhood as well as *places to work.* "The stores closing
down affected everything," a long-time resident told me. "There's not
very much in the streets for people to do here anymore."

The collapse of North Lawndale's commercial institutions and local
economy was devastating for the public life of the area.[32] As Jane Jacobs
argues, a substantial quantity of stores and other public places sprin-
kled along the sidewalks of a district is the basic requisite for establishing public safety through informal social control. Commercial institutions draw residents and passersby out into the sidewalks and streets,
inviting foot traffic and promoting social interaction among consumers, merchants, and people who simply enjoy participating in or observing public life. Moreover, Jacobs explains, stores and restaurants bring
"storekeepers and other small businessmen [who] are typically strong

proponents of peace and order themselves; they hate broken windows and holdups; they hate having customers nervous about safety," and they therefore play a vital role in preserving the quality of the public areas surrounding them.[33] Streets and sidewalks are the city's "most vital organs," but if they lose their animating institutions they break down, becoming instead the sources of violence, insecurity, and fear. By 1970 the loss of factories and stores had undermined the basis of collective life in the area, and in the next three decades the situation would only grow worse.

With few jobs, stores, or other public amenities to attract them to the area and a depleted infrastructure after the 1968 riots, the more mobile North Lawndale residents fled the area—almost as quickly as the local Jewish population had a few decades before. Between 1970 and 1990, roughly one-half migrated outward, leaving behind empty homes as well as the neighbors who were either committed or condemned to stay. The area entered a cycle of withdrawal and decline that the political scientist Wesley Skogan has characterized as a typical pattern of decay: "When communities become unpleasant to live in, and encounters leave people feeling uneasy and unsafe, many residents will try to leave. . . . Families and members of the middle class tend to leave first, often to be replaced by unattached and transient individuals. Those who cannot leave physically, withdraw psychologically, finding friends elsewhere or simply isolating themselves."[34] As these residents left, North Lawndale's community experienced transformations similar to those that Chicago's white population had undergone in previous generations: families and extended kinship networks were spatially separated as children or parents went to other African-American neighborhoods in the segregated city, suburban areas, or out of the metropolitan region. By the 1990s, members of African-American families that had once lived in North Lawndale were dispersed throughout the region, and their distance from one another limited their capacity to support the elderly.

In 1995 most of Chicago's poor black neighborhoods looked nothing like the crowded Rust Belt ghettos prevalent in the postwar years, and neither family nor extended family networks were rooted in local ecologies that facilitated close contact as well as they did during the 1950s and 1960s.[35] Migration and dispersion have changed the nature of family ties, with relatives communicating by phone or making occasional visits to one another rather than living in the area. Proximity matters during crises because it is easier and more convenient for people to provide emergency or casual support to their relatives if they

Figure 27. "Bombed Out": an empty lot in the residential area in North Lawndale. Photo by Caitlin Zaloom.

Figure 28. Another empty lot in once-prosperous North Lawndale. Photo by Caitlin Zaloom.

Figure 29. Ogden Avenue, once a major commercial artery in North Lawndale. Photo by Caitlin Zaloom.

live nearby; moreover (as we saw in chapter 1), it is particularly important for seniors because family members are more likely to check up on the elderly when they reside in the same area. The spatial fragmentation of family networks heightened the vulnerability of older African-American residents throughout Chicago during the heat wave.[36] In North Lawndale, the dangerous social ecology produced by decades of continuous abandonment and neglect rendered local seniors even more at risk (figs. 27, 28, and 29).

THE VIOLENCE OF EVERYDAY LIFE

The depleted physical infrastructure of North Lawndale has affected every aspect of neighborhood life. When I asked residents to describe the major streets that anchor their neighborhood, "bombed out" was the phrase that recurred most. As the editor of one of the community newspapers explained, "North Lawndale looks like a war zone. It has been bombed out. There's not very much infrastructure." Sarah Jones, who has lived in North Lawndale for more than forty years, used similar language to characterize the streets. "Sixteenth Street is almost null and void. Ogden Avenue has nothing. This used to be a car-dealing community. Now we only have one left." A few blocks down from her, another long-time resident drew a similar picture: "You ain't got no houses. You got nothing but lots. . . . All this land you lookin' at and you don't see people. You ain't even got no store open. And Roosevelt [Road] used to be full of stores." Her perception is well founded. According to one local development organization, more than 40 percent of the land in North Lawndale was vacant in 1990. A woman in her thirties complained about the difficulties of living in an area that has so few resources and so little public life: "There's no grocery store, no Walgreens, no pharmacy, nothing for us here. . . . On this street, from here to Twenty-sixth Street [the major commercial artery of Little Village], Twenty-sixth Street is the only place you can see life. All of the places here are deserted."[37]

During the heat wave, as in their everyday lives, older North Lawndale residents had few incentives to leave their homes and seek relief or social contact in public places. The area lacked the social and commercial attractions that draw people—especially the elderly—outdoors.[38] Unable to pick up many desired products on foot, residents had to drive or be driven several miles to the closest suburb to get staples such as fresh vegetables and medications that are easily available in other parts of the city.[39] Darcy Baker is similar to many others in the neighborhood in that, as she explained, "I never shop in this area." Few older residents walk to do their shopping or to take in the local street life, and the sidewalks are often devoid of foot traffic during the day as well as at night. During an interview, a nurse who runs a geriatric clinic at a nearby hospital argued that local dangers and the lack of decent food stores represented a genuine public health crisis in the community. "There's a high incidence of obesity and all of the things associated with that—hypertension, diabetes, renal failure. Nutrition is a big issue in this community. And I think it's lack of exercise and also poor diet [that are responsible]. I spend a lot of time with counseling. People say it's not safe to walk. And so I don't know how I can tell them to walk when they don't feel safe. They don't want to go out of their house. And a lot of them say, well, the things that they like, like vegetables, are expensive and hard to find. . . . The food is a big issue."[40]

North Lawndale's older residents not only lack animated public spaces and basic resources that pull them into the streets, they also face a range of local social and spatial pressures that push them to remain at home. A booming informal economy in illicit drugs has replaced the formal commercial economy that once supported the neighborhood, and the violent conflicts among young dealers and gang-bangers who battle for territory and market share have made North Lawndale a dangerous region, day and night. In 1995, a group of residents in one of the neighborhood's many criminal hot spots told me, drug dealers occupied several corners in the area. "They were up and down this block, all day long," a neighbor emphasized. Although residents generally felt safe around the local youths whom they had known all their lives, they fear getting caught in gang cross fire when there is trouble.

And there is often trouble. According to statistics from the Chicago Police Department and processed by the Chicago Department of Public Health, in 1994 and 1995 there was roughly one violent crime for every ten residents of North Lawndale.[41] The local police district, whose central office is close to the northern border of the area and whose territory encompasses parts of East and West Garfield Park as well, was considered "one of the hottest [most dangerous] areas around" by all the officers I met. One day, as a group of officers derided the Los Angeles Police Department for botching the O. J. Simpson investigation and explained that their experience handling homicides would have assured a conviction, a local sergeant told me that "one year of work in the Eleventh [District] is a career of training." "After working here," another veteran officer continued, "you're ready for anything."

During one of my visits to the District 11 police station, Officer Fred Handler, a veteran who had earned several advanced degrees while working on the force, brought me over to a computer terminal and showed me the crime statistics for the surrounding area. Even he was surprised to see the extent of the action. We decided to check the district's arrest figures going back from that day to the year before. District 11, which contains a little less than one hundred thousand residents, had been the site of more than twelve thousand narcotics arrests, for an average of roughly thirty-three per day, during that year alone— and this is an area where residents accused the police of letting dealers do their work with impunity and local alderman Michael Chandler complained that "open market drug sales are allowed here by police and the mayor." Turning back to the computer, Fred clicked in to see the reported activity during the heat wave. The temperatures between 12 and July 1995 were hot enough to reduce the action, or at least the arrests, in the region,[42] but there were still 134 narcotics arrests, and reports of 178 batteries, 95 thefts, 51 robberies, 50 assaults, and 2 homicides in the Eleventh District (fig. 30).

Crime levels this high make it impossible for the overwhelming majority of the people who live in North Lawndale and want nothing to do with drugs and violence to feel secure. "Of the people who live here, 97 percent of them are not involved in any way in guns, drugs, or anything," Alderman Chandler told me. "It's just that the 3 percent

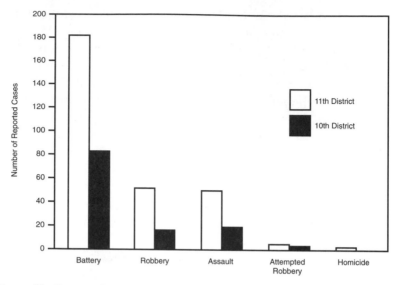

Figure 30. Reported crimes per one hundred thousand residents: Police Districts 10 and 11, July 12–19, 1995. Source: Chicago Police Department.

that are involved, they are going to walk all over us unless we organize and do something positive." Fighting against local drug dealers and other law breakers would be easier if they all lived in North Lawndale themselves. But, as one resident told me, "a lot of the guys who are selling rocks and blows [slang for crack and heroin] around here don't come from the neighborhood. There's nothing we can do to them."

Another reason that it is difficult for North Lawndale residents to fight the violence and the drug trade and establish more security in their neighborhoods is that the social ecology of the area attracts and fosters dangerous underground activity. Social scientists have long argued that young people who have no formal jobs or sources of respect in mainstream society will be lured into the drug trade, which offers income, community, and social recognition.[43] But street-level drug dealers also come to North Lawndale because the spatial conditions in the area facilitate their work. The open corners and fields, empty lots with tall grass and high cover, abandoned buildings with free spaces, and dark streets with poor lighting create relative security for dealers at the same time that they instill insecurity among residents. The economic, political, and physical abandonment of North Lawndale—processes that current residents were not responsible for or had no control over—has made the area a hub for an underground market organized around violent struggles over management decisions and territorial control. The spatial conditions in the area account for much of the danger that North Lawndale inhabitants experience in their daily lives, and exert strong pressures on the most precarious and insecure residents to seek protection by staying at home.[44] "Safety is the major issue here," a resident told me, and the neighbors' own understanding of the significance of space motivates and directs local organizing.

The proximity of North Lawndale residents to the unruly world of drug trafficking means that, as one woman explained a few weeks after two young people had been killed on the street next to her home, "Everybody's afraid of being caught in other people's problems. They might be driving around and doing drive-by shootings. And even if you're not in the gangs . . . you're afraid of a shooting like this."[45] Darcy Baker, who has lived in North Lawndale for more than forty years, told me that in her neighborhood the problems were particularly bad in the mid-1990s. "If you were standing here [in 1995] you'd see someone selling drugs on every corner . . . groups of people. . . . There were dealers standing in front of your home, hiding drugs in your yard. We spent all our money planting flowers and putting grass down, and they were hiding their drugs *in front of our house.* . . . There were bullets coming down our block. You couldn't sit out any longer. We used to sit outside all night and just talk and do whatever. But that's changed."

"EVERYBODY HERE IS VERY CAUTIOUS"

As much as the North Lawndale community tries to maintain a peaceful and stable neighborhood, action in the streets that residents cannot thwart on their own undermines the basis for the kinds of collective life that might have protected isolated residents from the heat. Elijah Anderson has observed that "the awareness of this constant danger fosters anxiety and skittishness even among decent people,"[46] the most vulnerable and fearful of whom protect themselves by staying at home. The cautiousness one finds among all local residents, and the fear apparent in others, restricts the public activity of the area for the elderly as well as for the younger and healthier people who are best positioned to support them.[47] "Fear prevents people from going out," Alderman Chandler explained. "That's real."

Living with fear, and even organizing one's routines around it, is a consequence of residing in high-crime areas with violent drug markets in the streets and a degraded public infrastructure. The impact of proximity to violence is particularly acute for the elderly, who are not only susceptible to street crime, but also vulnerable to serious physical injury as a consequence of an attack. Many of the middle-aged residents of

North Lawndale observed that, as Sarah Jones put it, "seniors here are always afraid to go outside." Yet Mrs. Winter, a North Lawndale resident in her seventies, took a more moderate view when she explained that although "most everybody you talk to [here] is scared, during the day most people don't mind [the danger] too much." A few blocks from her, Ernie Stewart tried to articulate the process of coping with the crime that has become an embedded feature of the local environment: "For me, it's caution, not fear. Everybody here is very cautious." Ernie's cautiousness filters into his daily habits and establishes the borders in which he lives. He feels safe within the few blocks that he considers his neighborhood, but he rarely walks outside of this area; moreover, like most of the local elderly, he rarely walks outside at night. Among his peers, though, Ernie is notably healthy and active, and his willingness to walk even a few blocks from his home makes him more of a risk taker than the other seniors.

Mrs. Freeman, an old-timer in her seventies, was typical of the seniors who felt comfortable in front of their homes and around young people they knew well but did not like to stray far from their own blocks and avoided encounters with strangers. She lived on a street that, like most others in the area, was frequented by drug dealers and users, including many whom she knew. Mrs. Freeman expressed comfort with the kids on her street but concern about their deeper intentions and the company they keep. "The kids around here all know me and they won't mess with me themselves," she declared. "They don't mess with me. They know me like the back of their hands. But they get their friends and they have them do it. They tell them who's got what." Fear of being burgled while she is out of the house further compounds Mrs. Freeman's insecurity. She believes that the local youths watch her and are waiting for an opportunity to break in, and her conviction was strengthened when a neighbor found a local man trying to force open her back door. "It's hard leaving your house," she told me, "especially in this neighborhood. People are looking to see who's out. They'll come and rob you."

Long-time residents of North Lawndale internalize and naturalize their strategies for coping with crime. Newcomers, though, have to be instructed on how to manage the dangers of living in the area, and the advice they receive from local residents carries with it the folk knowledge that grounds residents' protective strategies. Sister Mary, a black nun in her thirties who had come from Africa to work and live in a local church, summed up the tips that she had picked up from her neighbors: "Don't go out at night. Don't walk on my own. Don't stand somewhere by an empty building. It's risky to be there. It's risky to be here. It's risky. If you want to go to the store you have to come and take me out in the street to go to the store and buy something. . . . And, you know, I believe that whatever can happen at night can happen during the day too. Even the night doesn't make much difference once you are in a place where the people kill."

During an interview, Father Michael, an African priest in his thirties, told a similar story.

> I had no fear until they told me, oh no, it's not safe. These people steal on the corners and so on. They might cause trouble. . . . They would tell me that there would be drive-by shootings. They would fight among themselves, but I would be caught in the crossfire and I would be shot. And some feared even that if you walk they can come and snatch you. I've never experienced that but people have warned me. . . . And those whom I work with, they always tell me to be careful. Don't go through the alley. It can be dangerous. You never know. . . . I've never experienced it but I have had people who have experienced it. I have talked to some and I've seen the news on TV. So I took precaution. But at the beginning I had no idea.
>
> This building, it's been shot at several times. The windows in front, they've just been replaced. They shoot at it, not intending to shoot at the church but they are shooting among themselves and then the bullets come. If we were in the office then you would have had a bullet in your head.

The concentration of gang violence and drug dealing in the area has altered the social and physical landscape, making public life less attractive and viable for everyone who lives there. The degraded physical ecology of the area also imposes a specific set of dangers for the elderly. Old people in all parts of Chicago complain about the difficulties of navigating across broken sidewalks, rickety stairways, and forbidding open spaces left dark by burnt-out street lamps.[48] The fear of falling is a real concern of senior citizens, who know all too well that a stumble from which they once would have recovered could cripple or kill them when their bodies become frail. In North Lawndale, where the city government has done little to repair streets, sidewalks, alleys, and empty lots in the area and poverty prevented many residents from making major repairs on their homes, porches, and stairways, the condition of the physical environment contributes to the local seniors' sense of precariousness and increases the risks of leaving home. The social costs of fear in and of the streets made a brutal appearance during the heat wave, when the barriers North Lawndale residents established to keep themselves safe became the sources of their demise.

SOCIAL TIES IN THE UNRAVELING NEIGHBORHOOD

The pressures that restrict opportunities for social contact in North Lawndale do not make social cohesion altogether impossible nor render sociability within the neighborhood undesirable: local residents work hard to overcome the burdens of their environment and support one another. There is a considerable variation in residential transience and stability among the blocks within North Lawndale. Some have relatively high levels of home ownership and residential stability, and others have high levels of vacancy, tenancy, and turnover. One notable feature of the more stable (if not less violent) areas that I observed is that the residents, many of whom had lived on their street since the 1950s, were deeply rooted in and engaged with life on the block: they knew not only what the major issues, events, and problems on their street were, but also the people who were involved with them. They rarely had the resources that they needed to adequately address local problems and concerns, but residents of at least certain blocks in North Lawndale had the intimate familiarity with their neighbors and their neighborhood that is typical of those of the most cohesive communities.[49] North Lawndale residents suffered not from lack of knowledge about their neighbors or from disorganization, in the lay sense of the term, but from local pressures and challenges that overwhelmed their capacity to respond.

I made this observation during one of my initial visits to the community, when a long-time resident of a relatively stable block with three empty lots, two abandoned buildings, and a booming drug trade set against rows of solid limestone buildings led us up her street, then sat on her stoop and proceeded to tell stories about the families living in each house around her. "I know everybody on my block," she asserted, and she could account for several generations that she had seen on the street. In fact, keeping close tabs on neighbors and neighborhood activity was one of the strategies that North Lawndale residents used to reduce their vulnerability to violence and other local social problems and to gauge which other members of the community they could trust. The important distinction is that residents have less reason to be attuned to the older members of the community than they do to others, since shut-ins or recluses pose little threat to anyone other than themselves. For many residents, living in the violent area *required knowing* the scene, but they needed such practical knowledge so that they could *avoid* as well as participate in public life.

Throughout North Lawndale, though, there are two main sources of formal community participation: the church and the block club. Residents joke that the two institutions exist in such great numbers that one would think that their neighborhood would be the most holy and the most organized area on earth. For example, a local directory of services in North Lawndale produced by a community organization in 1998 lists 120 churches around the area and 73 block clubs within it.[50] Why, then, were these institutions unable to protect the most vulnerable residents of the area during the heat wave?

CHURCHES AND BLOCK CLUBS

African-American churches, from the large congregations that number in the thousands to the midsize corner chapels and the storefront varieties with a mere handful of congregants, have long been one of the main anchors of social life in black urban communities in general, and of black Chicagoans in particular.[51] Since the mid-1990s, when welfare reform legislation and other urban policies removed federal support for the urban poor and delegated more responsibilities to local organizations, the church has reemerged in numerous political and academic debates as a possible source of regeneration in low-income black urban communities.[52] There is good reason to look closely at the role that churches play in the social support systems in North Lawndale. For by examining the challenges that religious institutions face when they try to support residents of poor neighborhoods, we can identify potential strengths and shortcomings of faith-based solutions to the problems of urban danger and deprivation.

Not all residents of church-rich areas such as North Lawndale belong to local congregations, and although neighborhood churches often assist people outside of their congregations, it would be difficult for them to actively track down people who need help even if they had incentive to do it. Providing protective and supportive services to people with limited mobility and extreme needs is a difficult job, even for organizations that are explicitly designed to do this. It may be true that, as the Mayoral commission studying the heat wave concluded, service providers are most effective when they are "reaching out to those who are most isolated and fearful through networks they already know and trust."[53] But local organizations such as the neighborhood church cannot do this work effectively unless they, too, have financial and material support.

Other conditions further complicate the task of protecting vulnerable local residents through the churches. North Lawndale residents, like those in all urban neighborhoods, often attend churches in other areas of the city rather than those nearby. Similarly, churches in North Lawndale often had large memberships from other parts of the city. Residents who were most active in the neighborhood had generally gotten to know the leaders of the closest church that was involved in community work, thereby maintaining ties with both their congregations outside of North Lawndale and the local religious leadership. But these local activists, whose vocation or avocation involves supporting and protecting others, are usually not the people who need to be supported and protected by the church. Residents who attended churches outside their neighborhood but were less locally engaged were only loosely connected to church networks near their homes. If the religious community in which they were active was too far away to provide social support during normal times or crises such as the heat wave, it is unlikely that the local church group would know to look out for them.

Generally, though, it is the lack of time and resources rather than the lack of social commitment that undermines churches' contributions to the local community. The clergy in most of the churches are not paid to be full-time religious leaders, and the church leadership is made up of people with busy schedules of their own. Religious officials and active members have to work other jobs and take on "the Lord's work" in their spare time. Providing adequate support for people living in extreme poverty, and particularly for older people living alone who need help with shopping, cooking, and cleaning, demands more time and attention than most church networks have to offer.

Churches and church-based networks in North Lawndale did reach out to local seniors and sick people during the heat wave, and their efforts surely protected a number of vulnerable residents. But the conditions in which churches operate in North Lawndale—including the nonparticipation of many residents, the dispersion of different religious communities and leaders, the extreme poverty of the area, and the dangerous environment that undermines public life—make it impossible for these institutions to fill in all the gaps in the city social net.[54] Churches play a major role in supporting neighborhood social, political, and even economic activity, and when they work with other local organizations and state agencies they can be even more effective. But offering sufficient levels of these key support services requires human and financial resources that religious organizations with additional missions find difficult to provide.

The other major institutions that help support local social networks are block clubs, which have long been a core part of Chicago's neighborhood communities but have become even more popular in recent years, as the local government has actively promoted them.[55] Organized by residents as a means of asserting local control and establishing standards for public behavior and property maintenance, block clubs can be a key resource in building social cohesion in neighborhoods. These associations can provide a formal structure that facilitates residents' efforts to check up on one another during emergencies such as a heat wave or to work collectively to address various social problems. "We come together, we network, we make sure we bring the social services to the community and take care of our needs," explained a local leader who has organized many of the North Lawndale block clubs into a larger collective. But block clubs also require certain conditions and human resources to succeed, conditions that are difficult to achieve in neighborhoods with as much turnover, poverty, and violence as North Lawndale.

The most basic resource necessary to build a strong block club is a core group of active residents who are rooted in and committed to their block to the extent that they are willing to spend time and energy fighting threatening characters from the world of the street in order to control their neighborhood. Proponents of community organizing models that encourage residents to "take back the streets" like to tell stories about small groups of old women who have forced drug dealers off of their blocks by sitting outside on folding chairs and writing down the license plate numbers of all the cars that drive through the area. "You only need a few dedicated people, and you can beat back the dope dealers and rebuild your communities," one advocate of neighborhood reclamation programs proclaimed.

Although there are numerous examples of successful campaigns to reclaim neighborhoods,[56] taking back the streets can be difficult work in practice and residents have to be strongly motivated to fight. If they value the territory and they do not live there themselves, dealers will retaliate against the block club, intimidating residents with threats of various sorts and, in a tactic I saw several times during my fieldwork, taking down block club signs to symbolically deny the neighbors' claims to the street.[57] On her stable block, Dorothy Graham told me how she initiated a project to clean up one of the empty lots on the street and turn it into a neighborhood garden.

The grass and weeds had been, oh, somewhere between three and five feet high, and I went out there with a saw and a mower to cut them down. You know, I needed to go to the neighbors' and get some of their electrical equipment to get that grass down. It was that high.

Now, I'm working in there, cleaning things up, and then some dumb person walks over and tells me to stop because his gang needed the weeds for its business. He told me, "You shouldn't be cutting that grass."

And I said, "Why not?"

He said, "We need that grass."

They like open, grassy places that are unkempt so that they have a place to hide their drugs. And this way when the police come around and catch them they can't go down and find the drugs.

We had a lot of drugs, prostitutes, and drive-by-shootings then. Like everyone else, I had been complacent. But then we got fed up.

So I looked up at this young man, and I told him, "I don't care what turf you claim, you're in the wrong place when you're here. You got your thing that you need and we have our thing that we need. Right now we need a clean neighborhood and if cutting this down takes something away from you then I apologize but I will continue."

And he looked at me funny, but then he just walked away.

It took commitment to the area as well as courage to stand up to the young man in this way, and had Dorothy not been so invested in the area she might not have been willing to do it.

The trouble with some blocks in North Lawndale is that the high turnover of residents has both depleted the supply of old-timers who have strong emotional and financial ties to the area and unraveled or loosened local social networks, so that neighbors are not as personally attached to one another as they may be in other areas. Urban sociologists and city planners have long argued that residential stability is one of the keys to local social cohesion, and much of the reason for this is that it takes time and shared experience of various events and issues to develop bonds of affiliation, obligation, or reciprocity that are strong enough to motivate collective action or social support.[58] In North Lawndale, where decades of out-migration and economic dislocation have destabilized the community and 77 percent of the homes are occupied by tenants, the conditions that facilitate efforts to build strong block associations exist only on the most stable streets.

Strong block clubs can anchor efforts to establish cohesiveness and assert local control, but since they rarely get the participation of the very old and the young people in the neighborhood who most need support, they have to make a targeted effort to reach out to them. The block meetings I visited were attended and organized mostly by women between forty and seventy years of age, with a few middle-aged men and younger (twenties and thirties) women participating but no men younger than age thirty-five or very old residents around. Mrs. Winter told me that she had struggled to get her older neighbors to attend block meetings because "people never go out at night and you can't get enough people to neighborhood meetings because they're too afraid." Dorothy, who lives a few blocks from her, has helped to build one of the strongest block clubs in the area. But, she pointed out, "I don't have a regular block club meeting because the seniors can't always get out. . . . They shouldn't be out at night." Block clubs can become good resources for older residents, but only if participants know whom to help and how to do it effectively. In the 1990s even the most vigorous neighborhood associations in North Lawndale were overwhelmed by the pressures of everyday life in the West Side region, and the 1995 heat wave proved too dangerous to control.

SOUTH LAWNDALE: GROWING LITTLE VILLAGE

Cross just one street south of North Lawndale, though, and immediately the landscape changes. Although a statistical snapshot of South Lawndale (Little Village) shows that the community shares with North Lawndale comparable proportions of poor seniors, seniors living alone, and people living below twice the poverty line, the social ecology of the two areas could not be more distinct. The empty lots and abandoned buildings so prevalent in the African-American area give way to dense concentrations of busy sidewalks, active commerce, and residential buildings packed with more inhabitants than they can hold. The public discourse concerning the two areas focuses on the ethnoracial identities of their dominant populations, yet the contrast in the public spaces of Little Village and North Lawndale is equally extreme. Whereas the social morphology of North Lawndale undermines the collective life of the area, the material substratum of busy streets, dense residential concentration, proximate family habitation, and booming commerce in Little Village fosters public activity and informal social support among area residents. Although many residents are concerned about crime in the area and there is an active network of local gangs,[59] in 1994 and 1995 Little Village ranked fifty-ninth out of seventy-seven Chicago community areas in its overall violent crime rate—almost three times lower than the rate for North Lawndale and more than twice as low as the general level for Chicago—and violence had not significantly compromised the quality of public life in normal times.[60] Older residents reap special benefits from these ecological conditions because the amenities and the vital public spaces that surround them draw seniors out of their homes and into the sidewalks and streets. Once in these public places, the elderly can make social contacts with neighbors, proprietors of nearby stores, community institutions, and service providers that older shut-ins find difficult to establish.

During the heat wave the elderly in Little Village were doubly protected from the dangers of isolation. First, the action in and relative security of the local streets pulled older people into public places, where contacts could help them get assistance if they needed it. Second, the array of stores, banks, and other commercial centers in the area provided seniors with safe, air-conditioned places where they could get relief from the heat. Seniors felt more comfortable in and are more likely to go to these places, which they visit as part of their regular social routines, than the official cooling centers that the city established during the heat wave. Older whites who have stayed in Little Village as it has become predominantly Latino were the most vulnerable local residents during the heat wave, yet they, too, were protected by the local ecology. The robust public life of the region draws all but the most infirm residents out of their homes, promoting social interaction, network ties, and healthy behavior.

The differences in the ecological foundations of Little Village and North Lawndale have helped to establish a rigid physical border between the two communities that deepens the ethnoracial divide. Residents of Little Village explained that there is "a fixed line between us and North Lawndale," and political organizers, church leaders, and economic developers similarly noted that "if we plan events near or in Lawndale, people won't come" because "going over there is like going to a foreign land." There is also a symbolic separation of the two areas that maps onto the ethnoracial and ecological differences.[61] In the 1950s, as Albert Hunter has written, white residents of South Lawndale mobilized to change the community name to Little Village and "placed large painted signs on many railroad overpasses which read 'Welcome to Little Village' in "an attempt to distinguish the area from the neighboring community of North Lawndale,"[62] whose stigma they wanted to avoid. As the area turned over from white to primarily Latino after the 1950s, local residents became even more aggressive about marking the territory as distinct from Lawndale. There are numerous signs claiming the area as Little Village, with the largest of them being a giant arch at the east entry to Twenty-sixth Street (or *Calle Mexico*), the main commercial artery of the community, that greets visitors with the words "Bienvenidos a Little Village."

Figure 31. Commercial activity supports a booming street life on Twenty-sixth Street in Little Village. Photo by Rona Talcott.

A visitor need only go a few steps beyond the arch to see that the community, and especially its commercial strips, is bursting at the seams with shops, people, and activity. Twenty-sixth Street (fig. 31), as local boosters and economic developers were eager to tell me, is by some measures the second busiest commercial strip in Chicago, after Michigan Avenue. Just as residents of North Lawndale described their once-flourishing commercial roads such as Sixteenth Street as "bombed out," nearly all of my informants in Little Village used the word "booming" to convey the feel of Twenty-sixth Street—just ten blocks away—and the area around it. During my fieldwork I observed that, as resident Miguel Ramirez put it, "the streets here are always busy [fig. 32], from early morning to 9:30 P.M. there are people outside"— "more people than there is room," pointed out Daniel Nardini, the editor of a community paper. On weekends the traffic jams from shoppers and visitors to the area are so thick that it can take an hour to travel a few miles. During all but the coldest months, the sidewalks are lined with street vendors (fig. 33) peddling fruits, flowers, *aguas frescas, helados, churros,* and other goods; in fact, they are so prevalent that local business owners worry about losing revenues and have organized a campaign to keep them off the streets.

"Twenty-sixth Street is the heart of the area," explained Ricardo Munoz, the alderman of a ward covering much of Little Village. "It pumps economic vitality into the community and the residents are the blood." According to Frank Aguilar, president of Little Village Chamber of Commerce, stores and businesses on Twenty-sixth Street employ more than fifteen thousand workers, and much of their wages go back into the local economy. The vigorous circulation of people and goods has animated the surrounding streets as well: by the late 1990s stores, small businesses, and local organizations began opening up all over the area, even on largely residential streets. It is apparent that, as Nardini put it, "people are always coming and going and buying things."

South Lawndale has long been a little village of sorts. According to a local historian, the community area is "arguably Chicago's oldest working-class neighborhood, with roots stretching back into the 1830s" even though most parts of the area were not formally annexed by the city government until 1869 and 1889.[63] The ethnic solidarity of the local community facilitated the creation and cultivation of Chicago's famous Democratic political machine, which was founded by neighborhood hero and Chicago mayor Anton Cermak in Little Village's Twenty-second Ward. The community then consisted largely of people of Czechoslovakian, German, and, after 1910, Polish descent, migrants who came to South Lawndale for the same industrial jobs at the McCormick Reaper plant and the Western Electric Company that attracted people to North Lawndale a few blocks away. The community area experienced its first period of major growth in the late nineteenth and early twentieth centuries, but it boomed after the Douglas Park branch of the city's elevated train network arrived in the area in 1890 (and opened another station in the northwestern corner in 1902), providing better access to downtown and other city regions. By 1920 there were

Figure 32. "The streets here are always busy." Photo by Rona Talcott.

more than eighty-four thousand local residents, with "only a few vacant lots remaining in the southwestern part of the area."[64]

South Lawndale's white ethnic population was caught up in the wave of Chicago residents who took advantage of state-subsidized opportunities to move to the suburbs, and in the process distance themselves from the African Americans who were moving into North Lawndale

Figure 33. Street vendors attract shoppers outdoors. Photo by Rona Talcott.

Figure 34. A family relaxes in the yard on a hot day. Photo by Rona Talcott.

Table 7. Population in South Lawndale (Little Village), 1950–90

Year	Population	Population Change (%)	Population White (%)*	Population Hispanic (%)
1950	66,977	—	98%	NA
1960	60,940	−9	94	NA
1970	62,895	+3	86	NA
1980	75,204	+20	45	74
1990	81,155	+8	27	85

* The Hispanic category was first used in the census in 1980, and most Hispanic residents of South Lawndale were classified as white before this change. In the 1980 and 1990 censuses respondents could count themselves as both white and Hispanic.

and parts of Little Village as well, in the 1950s and 1960s (table 7). The out-migration in Little Village was more gradual than in North Lawndale, though, in part because in 1940 the home ownership rate of 36 percent in Little Village was more than twice the rate in North Lawndale, where only 16 percent of the homes were owner occupied.[65] The relatively slower pace of suburban out-migration from Little Village meant that the area did not open itself to African-Americans to the extent that North Lawndale did, and instead local realtors marketed housing in the area to the city's growing Mexican-American communities as well as to Mexican immigrants. Beginning the mid-1950s, Mexican Americans who had been displaced from their Near West and North Side homes by urban renewal programs and new highways took refuge in Little Village, and by the late 1960s the area had acquired a decidedly Latino identity. In one telling sign of the transformation, the Bohemian Settlement House, which had been founded in 1896 and was a major community institution, changed its name to Casa Aztlan in 1970.[66]

There are at least two reasons that Little Village was spared the fate of North Lawndale and other predominantly African-American communities in Chicago. The first has to do with processes of exclusion and oppression that we conventionally call racism, but which require more analytic specification because the loaded term connotes no identifiable and specific set of social or institutional practices. Douglas Massey and Nancy Denton capture part of the process in their argument that North Lawndale "became a wasteland" while Little Village evolved into "a beehive of commercial activity" because of "the degree of segregation" in North Lawndale.[67] Yet the differences between the two areas—both of which are dominated by so-called minority populations and had few whites—clearly extend beyond segregation. Unlike African Americans in North Lawndale and several other Chicago community areas, Latinos in Little Village did not experience the particular constraints of ghettoization, the rapid and continuous abandonment of institutions and residents, or the arson and violence that contribute to the destruction of the local social ecology.[68] The second crucial reason that Little Village developed into a commercial and residential hub is that since the 1960s the area has become a magnet for Mexican and Central American migrants and immigrants as well as for Mexican Americans already in Chicago, groups whose presence in the city has increased dramatically while the population of whites and blacks has declined.[69] The continuous migration of Mexican Americans to this community area has replenished its human resources and regenerated the commercial economy of retailers and small local businesses, such as food stores, travel agencies, health-care providers, and telecommunications companies. While North Lawndale lost more than half of its population between 1970 and 1990, Little Village grew by roughly 30 percent. There are only a handful of abandoned buildings and empty lots in the area, and those that exist are sure to be developed quickly in what *Chicago* magazine has dubbed one of Chicago's "hottest real estate markets."[70] "In Little Village," Frank Aguilar told me, "there is no such thing as an empty lot." In 1995, the year of the heat wave, the commercial vacancy rate was about 2.5 percent, compared with rates four times as high downtown and many times more than that in North Lawndale, where commercial vacancy is common.

"THE STREETS HERE ARE ALWAYS BUSY"

The active street life in Little Village attracts older and younger residents into the public areas where informal interactions and casual observations of others are typical forms of social cohesion. Many of the elderly I interviewed explained that during the heat wave they sought relief in the air-conditioned stores on Twenty-sixth Street, just as they do on ordinary summer days. Not only did elderly residents in Little Village have less to fear on the sidewalks and streets than did their neighbors in North Lawndale: living in a region with busy commercial traffic and active streets, they also had more incentive to go outdoors and walk to places where they could get relief. The rich commercial resources and a flourishing sidewalk culture animated public areas throughout the neighborhood; and there were always people, including seniors with their pushcarts full of groceries and small bags of goods, in the streets when I did my fieldwork. "Street life," as Gerald Suttles argues, "is a vital link in the communication network of the [neighborhood] and, as a result, governs much of what the residents know of one another."[71] This remains true in Little Village today, where the sidewalks are primary conduits for social contact and control. The relative security of these public areas makes it easier for residents of Little Village—even the older whites—to engage with their neighbors and participate in community events.

But in addition to this instrumental role in facilitating social integration, safe sidewalks, local retailers and grocers, and vigorous public activity provide intrinsic benefits for the health and welfare of local residents, particularly seniors. As Dr. John Herman, a neighborhood physician, explained, "People walk more here. That's healthy. People get more sunshine, so they get more vitamin D and less osteoporosis. They feel better." Health workers in North Lawndale found it difficult to get older residents to exercise because seniors felt vulnerable walking outdoors. In Little Village, though, walking was part of the daily routine for most of the older residents I interviewed, especially during the warmer months. Unlike their neighbors in North Lawndale, many of whom drive to the suburbs or Little Village to shop, Little Village seniors had ample reason to be outdoors. According to the glossy *Business Directory* published by Little Village Chamber of Commerce, there were seventy-one grocery stores of various sizes in the area in 1998, fifteen bakeries, ninety-six restaurants, thirty discount stores, and two department stores. There is also an active and cash-driven market in health and medical services as well as several not-for-profit providers, with dozens of clinics and alternative medical suppliers offering care to residents who have no health insurance. The commercial life is particularly important to local seniors, for it not only draws them out when they need goods or services but also gives them an excuse to leave home when they are feeling lonely or bored.

With one of the largest commercial strips in Chicago and a specialized market for Mexican products, Little Village is, in the words of several local residents, "a kind of self-contained community." As one long-time resident explained,

> We've got a lot of people in Little Village who don't leave Little Village if they don't have to. And that includes older white ethnic groups. For example, our neighbor. Until my wife took her downtown a month before she died, the last time she was downtown was in 1940. She hadn't been there in fifty-five years. She was ninety-two years old.
>
> People stay here because they like walking to the stores. They can get their food here. They can go to the bakery. Little Village has a lot of

banks [in 1998 there were seven major banks on Twenty-sixth Street alone, and six others in the area, with more on their way], so if they want to save their money they can do that here.

These resources pulled everyone into the streets. As Father Green noted, "Kids are out. Old people are out. People are shopping. The commercial attraction is just phenomenal. There's really no need to get in the car and go anywhere. You can certainly do things within walking distance and people do."

Although the high population density and active commercial sector imposes certain strains on local residents, including cramped living quarters and traffic congestion, they also foster tight social networks among families and neighbors and support a relatively secure public environment. In sharp contrast with North Lawndale, in Little Village the local ecology has strengthened family and friendship ties that might have been weakened by migration, because proximate conditions encourage and even force social interaction.[72] Latino residents do not necessarily perceive the residential crowding and busy street life as pleasant or desirable. "People here are living on top of each other," Javier Montes told me. "We're crammed into a little bit of space." Life-long resident Rosa Hernandez, a young woman in her twenties, complained, "I feel trapped in this neighborhood sometimes. I need to get out of here or I start to choke." Further, during one day of my field-work, a few minutes after a North Lawndale community leader had explained that open lots and empty space were causing much of his neighborhood's trouble, the director of Little Village Chamber of Commerce opined that "the biggest problem in Little Village is that, basically, there is no room."

Some of the more recent immigrants noted the irony that, as far as they have traveled from home, they see many of their old *compadres* in Little Village. "People come here because of family or friends from the old village or city," said Father Morales, a migrant himself. "They're rarely on their own." Yet these same conditions provide the ecological foundations that enable residents to attend closely to frail, unhealthy, or otherwise needy family members, *compadrazgo* (fictive kin) and friends. One local resident, a man in his thirties and the second of three generations of family members in the area, stated that most of his friends are moving out of their parents' homes, "but they're still very close to the family, as opposed to the kid who graduates from college and then just leaves and disappears and never comes back. I mean, I live two blocks from my mother. My dad lives [a few blocks away]—my parents are separated. So they're here."

Grandparents play a particularly important role in the many Little Village Latino families in which parents are working long hours and have little time for child care or other family activity.[73] Since working-age residents were likely to be toiling in one or more low-wage jobs, they relied on grandparents and other family members to look after children and help with other domestic work. The integration of older family members into the lives of their children, grandchildren, and great-grandchildren results not only from cultural values dictating that, as one Latino service provider for the local elderly put it, "it's important for these elders . . . that they are still kept around," but also because "they are important for the family because they have something to give." "Families around here can't afford to leave the older folks alone," one of the few Latino clergy members in the area told me. "They need them." Father Green, who works at the largest Catholic church in the area, reported that "it's phenomenal the number of elderly who are waiting outside to pick up the kids and take them home" after school. There is a downside to these conditions. Some of my informants complained that the low-wage economy in which they were embedded made it necessary to turn their mothers into "a kind of slave with no payment." But others had a more sanguine view. "We have to realize that they are more or less getting a kick out of it," Miguel Ramirez explained.

Although there was a gendered structure to the domestic work within Little Village, with grandmothers doing far more unpaid labor than grandfathers, few of the seniors I met in the community complained that they were overworked by their families. Their experiences illustrate how the cultural practice of caring is embedded in an ecology and economy—including the clustered households of multi-generational networks, the busy sidewalks, and the relative security of the neighborhoods—that promote social support even while creating other strains. During the heat wave the synergistic relationship between the cultural dispositions of the dominant local group and the neighborhood ecology allowed residents of Little Village to leave their homes, check up on vulnerable residents, and minimize the impact of the heat.

There are many parts of Chicago in which fear of crime and the degradation of public space has pressured older residents to shut themselves into their homes during the day as well as at night, but in Little Village even the old and frail residents felt comfortable going out except late at night. As Jacobs argues, "a well-used city street is apt to be a safe street. A deserted city street is apt to be unsafe. . . . There must be eyes on the street."[74] During the heat wave, older residents of Little Village who would have been vulnerable to the heat had they stayed at home were secure enough in their neighborhood to brave the outdoors, visit local stores or neighbors, and get the care that they needed. As a leader of a local Catholic church recalled, "During the peak hours of the heat you would not think twice about getting outside. You heard these stories of people who were locked into their houses for fear of coming out. That definitely wouldn't be true on a summer day here. The streets, especially in summer, are quite safe. There are isolated incidents. But the streets are vibrant until about ten o'clock at night."

We have already seen that in 1994 and 1995 the violent crime rate in Little Village was roughly three times lower than it was in North Lawndale and two times lower than in Chicago as a whole, setting a general social context in which Little Village residents had less to fear than did other city dwellers. These trends were visible during the week of the heat wave, when the Tenth Police District, which includes Little Village (and a slice of North Lawndale), and the Eleventh Police District, which contains much of North Lawndale, had great disparities in their reported rates of violent crime. Between 12 and 19 July 1995, District 10 reported 83 batteries, 17 robberies, 20 assaults, 1 attempted robbery, and 0 homicides for every 100,000 residents, whereas District 11 reported 181 batteries, 52 robberies, 51 assaults, 4 attempted robberies, and 2 homicides for every 100,000 residents[75] (see fig. 30). Though free from neither crime nor fear, residents of Little Village had good reason to feel safer in the streets than did the inhabitants of most other parts of Chicago.

According to the local residents I got to know, one of the reasons that they can easily manage walking or hanging out in the streets is that there is a clear spatial and temporal order to violence in the area, with most of the action taking place at night and in clusters of blocks that are off the major thoroughfares. In general, one resident explained to a police officer during a community meeting, "most of the violence we have happens at night;" and although several older residents I interviewed told me that they were growing more fearful of gang violence and avoided the streets after dark, many others found even this common self-protection strategy to be unnecessary. As Frank Kruk, a white old-timer who had spent his life in Little Village insisted, "I am not afraid of my neighborhood. We walk in the streets in the middle of the night when we come home." Frank's location within the community's safer and more middle-class southwestern corner accounted for some of this confidence. The real problems, he explained, are on the north side of the area, where Latino and black youths are closer together and the gangs are more active.

Residents believed that gang activity was on the rise while I was in Little Village, becoming a top priority for the community at precisely the moment when the neighborhood economy had begun to boom and property values to climb. At several community policing meetings I attended, residents complained that they were hearing gunshots after dark and growing concerned that, as one mother remarked, "gangs control the area at night."[76] Yet the ubiquity of "decent" public activities counteracted the threats of danger and disorder, preserving a safe environment during most hours of the day despite occasional instances of violence. "Even though we have gangs, people still feel comfortable in the streets," noted Father Morales, one of the few Latino Catholic religious leaders in the area. "You walk around and you see people sitting on the front steps everywhere." Casual street users provide the watchful eyes that, as Jacobs argues, facilitate neighborhood safety. "We look out for each other in our neighborhood," reported James Grabowicz, another of the white old-timers who had remained in the area. "If something is going on we'll see it and call each other or the police."

CENTRALIZED CHURCHES

In addition to the informal ties that connect Little Village neighbors, powerful church networks provide crucial forms of protection to local residents. Churches contributed to local efforts to protect seniors during the heat wave, but the nature of isolation and vulnerability in Little Village meant that the community's elderly were less at risk for heat-related problems even without religious organizations. With roughly twenty churches in the area, Little Village did not have as numerous a supply of religious organizations as did North Lawndale.[77] But the relative size, wealth, and centralization of these organizations in Little Village allowed the church networks to absorb and support large numbers of local residents. Just as the churches in North Lawndale had difficulty learning about and attending to reclusive seniors, churches in Little Village struggled to integrate older whites who lived alone, even those who were once active members.

The ethnoracial makeup of local religious institutions had turned over along with the neighborhood, and the same buildings that had long anchored the community life for the area's Poles, Czechs, and Slavs became predominantly Latino places where Spanish was the dom-

inant language, services took on a Latin-American style, and cultural
events were based on Latino traditions. Although few of the church
leaders were Latino, most pastors and administrators spoke fluent
Spanish. Many of the churches conducted special services and events
in English or Polish for the handful of white members who remained
participants in religious life, but church leaders throughout the area
expressed concerns that local changes had estranged the old-timers
and that the clergy possessed neither the human nor cultural resources
required to alleviate the difficulties of aging alone in the neighborhood. "We have plenty of old-timers living alone here," Father Morales
explained. "The old-timers more than the Hispanics. And it's a sad
story sometimes because we can't bring [the services] to them. Services
for that kind are important, but there are limitations and we can't do
much unless you have somebody on the staff. It's really hard to do it
with volunteers." Like the churches in North Lawndale, most religious
institutions in Little Village worked hard to assist local seniors but recognized that the job required time, money, organization, and labor
that they could not offer.

As in North Lawndale, churches in Little Village played roles in
many realms of neighborhood life, but in the latter community, religious institutions placed special emphasis on helping immigrants and
Spanish speakers cope with the pressures and demands of living and
working in Chicago. In addition to offering social, political, vocational,
and health services and programs similar to those provided by churches
in North Lawndale, religious organizations in Little Village offered
courses in English as a second language, helped recent immigrants
connect with social and economic networks, and counseled newcomers
from rural areas who had difficulty acculturating to the urban environment. In a city where the political and community organizations are
generally foreign and intimidating to migrants, many newcomers find
that the Catholic Church is the most familiar and trustworthy source
of stability and support.

The most significant difference between the religious institutions in
North Lawndale and Little Village was the relative centralization of the
Latino churches, which were predominantly Catholic and structurally
tied to and supported by the Archdiocese of Chicago. Although the
pastors were mostly white men who had moved to the neighborhood
within the last few decades, the church leadership, membership, and
support networks were more rooted in community life than were their
counterparts in many North Lawndale religious centers. Most church

participants, pastors, and administrators lived in the area, often within walking distance of the churches themselves, providing an ecological basis for place-based projects and facilitating the delivery of various support services. "The church is a center for socializing," Father Morales said. "People make *compadres* at church."

There were, however, costs as well as benefits stemming from the affiliation between neighborhood churches and the broader Catholic Church. Unlike many of the smaller churches in North Lawndale, the Catholic churches in Little Village received substantial resources and support from the centralized archdiocese. These resources proved invaluable during difficult times and helped local religious organizations maintain their services and programs despite the relative deprivation of many of their members. But the archdiocesan support came at a price. Representative of and responsible to a larger religious institution, the Catholic churches in Little Village struggled to be as responsive to the particular and changing demands of local residents as smaller, more grassroots churches were able to be. Some of the Little Village residents I met had left the Catholic Church in favor of evangelical denominations because, they felt, the new churches were more attentive to their needs. When I did my fieldwork, though, these converts were in the minority of the strongly Catholic Little Village religious community.

With large Catholic churches dispersed throughout the area, residents had little difficulty finding a place to anchor their religious or, in some cases, social activities. Most of the churches are busy throughout the week because they run parochial schools and host numerous events and programs. Father James, who presides over a church with several thousand members, explained as we sat outside the church school: "On different nights we can have eight different activities going on outside of the church in our meeting halls. And a lot of people connect to us. Sunday morning we have a Polish mass which is very small. It's in Polish. We also have an English mass that's a bit larger, maybe one hundred people. And two Spanish masses. They are the largest, four to five hundred people." On Sundays the major weekly masses draw more than ten thousand people, most of them Little Village residents, out of their homes and into the local churches. According to Father Green at Saint Michael's Church, "We are the largest Hispanic Catholic church in the archdiocese and we are the fourth-largest parish in the archdiocese. We have about five thousand people who come on Sunday. We have mass every hour and a half from 7:30

in the morning to 4:30 at night. Easter we probably have ten thousand. Ash Wednesday we have fifteen thousand. Everything here is on the same magnitude."

Ultimately, though, it is the severity of the local problems rather than the size of the local churches that most determined the capacity of vulnerable residents to survive emergencies such as the heat wave and withstand the daily pressures of urban marginality. Although there were some areas of commonality, the challenges that stemmed from poverty and transition in the Little Village community were distinct from those that troubled residents of North Lawndale. A greater number of seniors lived alone in Little Village than in North Lawndale, but they suffered from linguistic isolation and status transformation (from becoming ethnic minorities in the neighborhood) more than from the kinds of insecurity, fear of the streets, loss of local resources, and literal isolation that threatened seniors in North Lawndale.

Little Village community leaders have good reason to build formal social networks for local Latino seniors. In the 1990s Latino residents of the area have experienced firsthand what other ethnic groups in Chicago have already witnessed: the rise of interfamily dispersion, suburbanization, and increasing social and spatial distance between seniors and younger generations. Acculturating to social practices and migration strategies typical of most other communities in Chicago, working-age Latinos in Little Village have begun moving to the suburbs, leaving parents and other older relatives behind as they make their go at the American dream. In our interviews, Chicago-area social workers expressed concern that cultural myths about Latino intergenerational family ties had in fact rendered invisible or unstated the indisputable demographic trend toward Latino isolation that they had witnessed in their work.[78] "The older generation of Hispanics are beginning to be left alone by their families," the director of one service agency explained to me. "And because no one likes to talk about it their isolation is all the more dangerous." Protected by proximate family and friendship ties during the 1995 heat wave, Latino seniors in Little Village are unlikely to be so well positioned in the coming generations. Ethnically cultivated dispositions common among Latinos may have helped to keep recent generations of families together in places like Little Village, but the social trajectory and spatial dispersal of Latino families are already threatening such cultures of care.

Like the CDC epidemiologists who conducted the case-control study, when I ended my fieldwork on Chicago's West Side I searched for ways to determine whether the sources of risk and protection that I had observed in North Lawndale and Little Village were apparent in other parts of the city. In casual observations in other regions I found patterns of ecological decay in high heat mortality areas and relatively robust social morphology in places with better survival rates. Field notes taken in three community areas with high heat death rates, for example, describe the commercial strips and public spaces in terms that would fit the landscape of North Lawndale as well.

> Area 1: A small area with little commercial activity and virtually no retail stores. Most blocks are lined with dilapidated and boarded-up abandoned houses, vacant lots full of rubble or trash, and small storefront churches. [There is] only one commercial strip, but it only includes a check cashing service and a few empty storefronts.

> Area 2: The main commercial strips are rundown, but there are a few small retail stores and old industrial buildings. The streets are wide, and there is little or no street life. There are many empty storefronts, boarded-up buildings, and large lots of empty open space.

> Area 3: Many of the buildings were once used for commercial purposes, but the windows are boarded and the signs are old, faded, and falling apart. The only stores are little groceries and a check cashing service. Besides that there are virtually no shops—only empty lots. The area feels abandoned. One side of the street looked incredibly deserted and bombed out.

Such superficial descriptions should be treated with caution because they do not reflect deep knowledge about the ways that elderly or other residents use the spaces. It was impossible to replicate the intensive ethnographic study in every Chicago community area, but the research hints at a set of ecological contexts and social processes that helped explain how place-specific conditions affected heat wave mortality rates. In addition, it suggests that the widespread ecological impacts of urban abandonment and deprivation have altered the social environments of many Chicago communities in ways that population-level data do not reveal.

Once we identify these social ecological conditions we can integrate more standard demographic evidence to consider the significance of related conditions in the city.[79] Table 3, for example, shows that several of the areas, such as Fuller Park, Woodlawn, Washington Park, and Englewood, shared the high levels of abandonment—some lost as much as two-thirds of their residents between 1960 and 1990, and ten

Table 8. Chicago Community Areas with Lowest Heat Wave Death Rates

Community Area	Heat-Related Deaths per 100,000 Population	Percent Population Decline, 1960–90	Percent Population Black	Overall Violent Crime Rank, 1994–95 (77 CAs)
Beverly	0	10	24	70
Ashburn	0	4	10	62
Riverdale	0	5	98	11
East Side	0	11	0	54
Calumet Heights	0	10	93	39
Montclare	0	10	0	61
Auburn Gresham	3	0	99	19
Garfield Ridge	3	16	13	60
West Lawn	4	13	0	65
South Lawndale (Little Village)	4	−33	9	59
City of Chicago	7	22	39	—

Source: Data based on 521 heat-related deaths located by Illinois Department of Public Health (1997), Chicago Fact Book Consortium (1995), and the City of Chicago, Department of Public Health.

of the fifteen areas lost more than one-third—and violent crime that make public life intimidating for elderly residents; and table 8 shows the reverse: in a city that lost more than 21 percent of its residents between 1960 and 1990, all but two of the ten community areas with the lowest heat wave death rates lost less than 11 percent of their population base; the others, which lost 16 percent and 13 percent, were still below the city's rate. Moreover, the three predominantly African-American community areas with exceptionally low death rates, Riverdale, Auburn Gresham, and Calumet Heights, lost only between 0 percent and 10 percent of their residents in the decades preceding the heat wave—a rare pattern among Chicago's African-American regions.

Just as the CDC's epidemiological study identified individual-level risk factors for heat wave mortality, the ethnographic assessment of how community-level social environments affect the capacity of Chicago regions to survive the disaster located a series of place-based, social ecological conditions that heighten health risks during extreme events and normal times. Areas with low mortality rates were distinctive not because of their ethnic or racial compositions. As can be inferred from table 8, of the ten areas with the highest heat wave survival rates three were more than 90 percent African-American, two were officially more than 39 percent Latino, and five were predominantly white. But in most cases they did not suffer greatly from ecological depletion, the collapse of local infrastructure and commerce, population decline, and high levels of violent crime;[80] and in others, such as Little Village, they gained vitality while the rest of the city declined.

The areas with high mortality levels also had distinctive compositional and ecological features. Previous studies of heat wave mortality have shown that residents of places with high poverty, concentrated elderly populations, poor housing, and low vegetation are especially vulnerable to extreme summer weather; and the Illinois Department of Public Health found that residents of Chicago community areas with high levels of violent crime also faced elevated risks of death in the 1995 disaster.[81] This analysis adds several place-specific risk factors, some of which, such as the quality of public spaces, the vigor of street-level commercial activity, and the centralization of support networks and institutions, concern the social morphology of regions; others, such as the loss of residents and the prevalence of seniors living alone, concern population-level conditions.

The principal contribution of this approach is that it deepens our understanding of the reasons that different community areas and different groups had such disparate experiences during the heat wave. As is typical in contemporary health research and public policy discourse, much of the discussion about the group-specific health outcomes during the heat wave has been cast in ethnic or racial terms, with ethnic difference or cultural variation serving as explanations for ethnic mortality rates. The tale of the neighborhoods suggests that a key reason that African Americans had the highest death rates in the Chicago heat wave is that they are the only group in the city segregated and ghettoized in community areas with high levels of abandoned housing stock, empty lots, depleted commercial infrastructure, population decline, degraded sidewalks, parks, and streets, and impoverished institutions.[82] Violent crime and active street-level drug markets, which are facilitated by these ecological conditions, exacerbate the difficulties of using public space and organizing effective support networks in such areas. There is little evidence that during the heat wave the most isolated and vulnerable residents of places like North Lawndale suffered because members of their community did not care about them. Yet there is good reason to believe that residents of the most impoverished, abandoned, and dangerous places in Chicago died alone because they lived in social environments that discouraged departure from the safe houses where they had burrowed, and created obstacles to social protection that are absent from more tranquil and prosperous areas.

Chicago officials might not have been able to identify the social and ecological conditions that threatened the health of residents on the city's South and West Sides when the heat arrived in 1995, but they were familiar enough with the typical patterns of health and vulnerability in the region to predict at least some of the spots where the extreme environment would prove most devastating. While Chicago residents and communities improvised their survival strategies to withstand the unbearable climate, city agencies scrambled to mount a political response that would fill in the gaps. A coordinated program for providing emergency medical care and social service support would be essential for a successful public health intervention. But, as the next chapter shows, the obstacles to organizing such a campaign were too great for most city agencies to overcome.

CHAPTER THREE

The State of Disaster

City Services in the Empowerment Era

Because city governments often fail to recognize the danger of extreme heat in time to initiate preventive care programs, disaster management during heat waves typically begins when paramedics and police officers respond to requests for urgent medical attention or reports of death. Victims of heat stress and heatstroke require immediate but simple interventions, such as immersion in ice or treatment with intravenous fluids, since the longer they remain overheated and dehydrated the more likely they are to die or suffer permanent physical damage. When officials in the Health or Fire Departments observe a dangerous climate or an unusual number of calls coming in to the emergency service network, they are expected to alert the city government's command center and, if necessary, ask for special support. In Chicago, as in many U.S. cities, the Fire Department manages the paramedics division and administers the city's emergency response programs.[1] Positioned on the front lines of the city service delivery system, workers in the Fire and Police Departments are often the first to see an emergent crisis. Their challenge is to convince high-ranking officials, opinion makers, and city agencies to recognize the problem and mobilize resources for an appropriate response. This process requires overcoming the enduring obstacles that stand in the way of public support for the most vulnerable citizens, many of which are visible in the political history of the heat wave.

Clark Staten, a retired Fire Department commander who had worked as a city paramedic for twenty years and participated in emergency response efforts during the 1983, 1986, and 1988 heat waves, remembers the 1995 disaster vividly. In 1995 Staten was directing the Emergency Response and Research Institute, a local think tank that evaluates emergency service programs and monitors Chicago's network of emergency care. He explained that many of the paramedics who worked during the heat wave view the city's emergency response as the worst expression of longstanding divisions within the Fire Department and systemic shortcomings of the city government's service delivery programs. "I was talking with friends of mine in Texas and Nebraska as the heat wave was coming towards us, so we were tracking the problem. I began to see that there were scattered heat deaths with the weather pattern, and then it came here and settled." On Thursday, 13 July, before the first heat-related deaths were reported, Staten's organization issued a press release to warn the public and city agencies about the encroaching trouble. "With the temperatures and humidity at dangerous levels, the air quality diminishing, and no end in sight, in some parts of the country, the Emergency Response and Research Institute is urging extreme caution. . . . The recent heat wave has already resulted in the untimely deaths of several people in the Midwest and Southwestern part of the United States and more heat injuries or even deaths can be expected."[2] Staten, who had served for two years as the public information officer for the Chicago Fire Department, issued the press release because his experience had taught him that "the city would react if the press picked up the story in advance. But when we told the press before Friday they essentially blew it off."

On Friday Staten stayed in contact with the paramedics and observed their response. The Fire Department handled more than one thousand calls that day, and when it was finished 188 Chicago residents had perished in the heat. According to Staten, "probably the first person to discover that there was a heat emergency was an Emergency Medical Services supervisor, because they got similar reports from several different teams. I was listening to the scanners, and they were saying, 'Sorry, there's no ambulance available. Sorry, there's no ambulance available. Sorry, there's no ambulance available.' And [the paramedics] were saying, 'Hey, we've got another DOA. Hey, we've got another DOA. Hey, we've got another DOA.' Then you hear, 'sorry, it will be a few hours before we can get a wagon over there.' Or, 'yeah, we're at the Medical Examiner's, and we're seventeenth in line.' "

The crushing demand for emergency services coupled with the logjam at Cook County Morgue to overload and delay the city's urgent care system. Observers of Chicago's health-care facilities have long warned that there are at least two problems with the local service infrastructure. First, the city's supply of fifty-six ambulances and roughly six hundred paramedics is inadequate to meet either regular or exceptional demands for care, and the typical response time of seven minutes often extends to twenty minutes or more in normal conditions.[3] Longstanding divisions in the Fire Department, where firefighters outnumber paramedics seven to one and emergency medical workers complain of second-class treatment from administrators and City Hall, leave paramedics with little capacity to obtain new public resources even though they handle 50 percent more calls than firefighters.[4] Second, the city's hospitals and trauma centers are concentrated on the North Side, creating a segregated geography of medical care that adds to the vulnerability of the relatively poor and polluted communities on the South and West Sides, where residents are most likely to need urgent or sustained medical attention. "We had been complaining about this for a long time," one paramedic explained, "partly because when hospitals go on bypass [whereby they close their emergency rooms to new patients] we're the ones who have to deal with the problem."

When the heat moved into Chicago, the city's supply of ambulances and paramedics proved insufficient to handle the crisis, and the Fire Department sent its equipment and firefighters into the streets to deliver health support. The city's medical centers filled their emergency care facilities beyond capacity and twenty-three of the area's forty-five hospitals went on bypass status, turning away people in need of urgent care even though the consequences of heatstroke are more severe when victims do not receive immediate medical attention.[5] The problems were particularly grave on the South and Southeast Sides, where residents who developed heatstroke or heat stress faced even greater obstacles to care than those to which they had grown accustomed. According to an Illinois state senate report, "With 23 hospitals on bypass status at various intervals during the period July 13–16, 1995, very few, if any, hospitals on the South and Southeast Sides of Chicago were available to accept patients delivered by emergency ambulance."[6]

Robert Scates, a deputy chief paramedic in charge of monitoring emergency services on the South Side during the heat wave, found it hard to believe what the city government was doing.

By monitoring the radio I was noticing that it was exceedingly busy, extremely busy. All of the sudden, you're getting call after call after call after call, and the fire engines and fire trucks are being dispensed to people's homes for calls. Paramedics would get in the ambulance and wouldn't see the firehouse until the next morning. Regular platoon goes from eight o'clock in the morning to eight o'clock the next morning. But some people worked 26-, 27-, 28-hour days. I mean, here you are in hundred-degree heat, and you're not getting any rest. Your air conditioner in your ambulance fails on you, but you're still ripping and run-

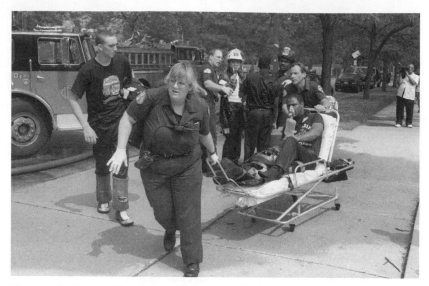

Figure 35. Paramedics assist a colleague suffering from a heat-related illness. Source: *Chicago Sun-Times;* photographer: Brian Jackson. Reprinted with special permission from the Chicago Sun-Times, Inc. © 2002.

ning anyway, and you're sweaty, and it's worse than trying to work out in a sauna.

Hospital workers throughout the city noticed the toll that such labor was taking on the personnel. "Paramedics that were coming in here [delivering patients]," said the clinical director of a North Side hospital, "were so dehydrated that they were very close to being patients"[7] (see fig. 35).

A thirty-year veteran who is now the director of emergency medical services for the local firefighters' union, Scates was well aware of what the emergency response system should do in the situation:

> This is what the Fire Department could have done. First off, what they could have done was institute a recall, they could have put everybody who was off duty back to work. And they could have put more ambulances out. At the time we had 59 ambulances, but 3 of them are steadily assigned to O'Hare Airport, so there's only 56 that actually work within the city limits. They could have put up an additional 15 ambulances. If that hadn't been enough, they had the ability to institute what they call a MABAS, mutual aid boxed alarm system, and get another 70 ambulances from the suburbs. They could have gotten 30 more from the Northwest Side suburban areas and 40 more from the Southwest Side. So we had

the capability to get a total of 145 ambulances out there. We could have put additional fire companies in. If nothing else, we had all kinds of sterile water and we could at least cool people down, but you need somebody to pull the trigger.

So what I did, because I was concerned, is call my immediate supervisor, the chief paramedic, and the deputy fire commissioner of emergency medical services, who had the power to make decisions to put in a recall and a MABAS response, anything like that. The fire commissioner, Raymond Orozco, was out of town at the time on vacation. So I got up to get ready to file a report to my field division, and I get a phone call back from the chief paramedic. He informs me that the deputy commissioner wants me to stop being so paranoid, that it wasn't as bad as I was blowing it out to be, and that he wasn't putting a recall into effect. So nothing happens, nothing, and next thing you know I'm hearing paramedics on the radio saying "we've got people who are critical"; "we just broke down a house, and we found a person dead from the heat." So I called back, and the chief paramedic said, "I'll try again." And I got the same reply: "Stop being so paranoid." So now, I call [a deputy commissioner] and try it myself. When I called him I said, "Commissioner . . ." [And he replied,] "Bob, I know it's you, and I'm not going to do it." And he hung up. Just that short and sweet.

The city's emergency response programs require not only that administrators trust the officers who report from the field, but also that they pass vital information on to higher levels in the command center. During the heat wave, paramedics complain, internal divisions within the Fire Department and an administration of firefighters with insufficient experience managing public health crises blocked the lines of communication and stalled the city's response.

Paramedics in the streets were never able to activate a greater city effort, but the public reports of massive mortality broadcast on radio and television captured the attention of Mayor Richard M. Daley's administration. "When complaints really started coming in" and the media began reporting on the death tolls, Scates remembered, "Mayor Daley called down and had Commissioner Orozco come back from Florida. But the thing is that some of those lives could have been saved [before then]. We could have had enough people to get them, to put fluids in them, to cool them down." Several problems slowed the response. The Fire Department had no centralized system for monitoring the number or the nature of the requests for service. The fragmented structure of the department, in which each unit operates independently and shares little data with top administrators, muted the many requests to sound an alarm. Moreover, several paramedics allege that the Fire Department leadership, which was dominated by firefighters at the time, would not issue a recall or request additional resources from the city government because they distrusted the reports coming in from field officers. "The question," Staten explains, "is whether they listened to the people who did recognize it, and the answer is 'no.' It's not clear to me that they took the EMS reports seriously."

High-ranking Fire Department officials told another story. During state senate hearings on the heat wave, the commissioner of the Chicago Fire Department stated plainly that the city's weak emergency response stemmed from failures among paramedics, police officers, and other street-level bureaucrats who, in his view, did not signal the crisis. "Nobody indicated that we needed more personnel or supplies," he told the senate committee. "Our field supervisors told us, 'we're holding our own.' We needed something to trigger the mechanism. Nobody pulled the trigger."[8] Few people outside the department have ever questioned this account, but it is clearly at odds with the testimony of several paramedics who worked during the week.

Robert Raica, an Illinois state senator and paramedic, dismissed the commissioner's line. "Instead of saying, 'we're in error,' they actually blame it on the people in the streets. It seems like there was a total breakdown in communication at the command level."[9] Perhaps the most serious charge of city paramedics is that Chicago officials and Fire Department leaders refused to call in additional ambulances and emergency health workers because the "reinvented" city government has cultivated an ethic of fiscal austerity among administrators that trumps even the most urgent requests for resources to combat a health crisis. Scates excoriates city officials for their concern with "saving money regardless of the expense to people's lives" and accuses the Fire Department administrators of "reckless indifference to the citizens of this city." Scates, Staten, and other paramedics complain that the city's refusal to update and expand its emergency care system, as well as its reluctance to recall off-duty officers and bring in additional ambulances during the heat wave, reflects a systemic prioritization of cost containment over life preservation. The philosophy, Scates says, is "We're not going to spend the money. We want maximum performance out of minimum manning, which is totally ridiculous in public safety because if you don't have the proper amount of people out there you're going to start losing buildings. The Fire Department believes in not filling at least 5 percent of the budget, [which] makes them look like good managers. You hold the line, you don't spend the money, you turn it back in, and the mayor pats you on your head." Scates and his colleagues are convinced that the practice has compromised the mission of their agency. "We're supposed to be in the business of patient care. We're the Fire Department."

According to then–Health Commissioner Sheila Lyne, though, the Fire Department's inaction had little impact on the city's emergency response. "Fire got blamed for the ambulances taking too long to get places," she explained. "But it wasn't going to matter. . . . I think the people were going to die anyway." Other city officials also speculated that there were few negative health consequences stemming from the problems with the city's emergency medical response system. Yet their position conflicts with recent epidemiological studies showing that prompt, appropriate medical treatment of heat-related illness can save lives and increase the probability of recovery from heatstroke. According to an article published in the *Annals of Internal Medicine,* during the 1995 heat wave Chicago health officials and physicians were insufficiently trained to treat heat illness properly, and many patients did not receive proper treatment upon admission to a health-care facility.[10] There were grave consequences for the city's failure to institute an immediate response. Without a warning from the Fire Department, which is in charge of disaster management, the city government did not recognize the crisis and failed to organize a multiagency emergency response before the death toll began to rise. A study by researchers from the U.S. Centers for Disease Control and Prevention indicates that a sweeping effort to contact and support vulnerable Chicagoans might have saved many lives. "A decreased risk of death was found among the people [city of Chicago social workers] contacted," but the city government did not put enough street-level workers into the streets.[11]

According to local journalists, Mayor Daley was vacationing at a family retreat in Michigan during the first days of the heat wave, and initially no one notified him about the heat wave casualties. "What could we have done about it anyway?" one "top Daley source" asked the press. "We were doing all we could."[12] Top officials in several other departments, including Health and Fire, were also out of town vacationing in the early days of the crisis, and they learned no more about the situation in the city than the public. As Health Commissioner Lyne recalled, no one put the administration on alert.

I was on vacation that week. I wasn't very far, though. I came back Friday evening to Chicago and I saw the news. *But I didn't get it.* I didn't get it

Friday evening. On Saturday I was here in my office. *And nobody called or said anything.* On Sunday I was in my office trying to get caught up, and somebody called me from the mayor's office about using an office as a cooling station. And *that* didn't strike me as too much. On Monday morning when I came in there was a note on my desk from our public relations person because then everybody knew that a great number had died. And I have to tell you that *I really still wasn't getting it at all.*

By Saturday, 15 July, the scene at the Cook County Medical Examiners Office had captivated the attention of the same newspaper journalists who had downplayed earlier warnings from the Emergency Response and Research Institute, and when city officials saw the stories they realized that they had to take action. By the end of the weekend the Fire Department had called in additional officers and ambulances, but much of the damage had already been done. Media reports played a crucial role in stimulating a political reaction. Although paramedics and police officers had been calling for support, a high-ranking member of the Health Department recounted that it was not until "the TV showed the lineup of patrol cars with the bodies at the morgue [that] everybody got serious about this thing." Even then, however, the city government's most public actions involved mounting a public relations campaign to deny the death attributions from the Medical Examiners Office, defend the service delivery system, and accuse other members of the metropolitan community—including the heat wave victims—of causing the crisis.

On Tuesday, 18 July, the *Chicago Sun-Times* reported that "the city apparently ignored its own guidelines for declaring a hot weather emergency, and waited until Saturday—when bodies began piling up at Cook County Morgue—to implement its heat emergency plan."[13] For although several officials were already arguing that no one in Chicago had realized the risks imposed by extreme heat, the city Health Department had established a model heat emergency plan several years before and had failed to follow it during the disaster. The sweeping problems with the local government's response infuriated some city residents, activists, and political leaders. Scates was so outraged by the Fire Department's refusal to meet its responsibilities that he accused the city of committing "murder by public policy" and, along with the department's chief paramedic, resigned his rank.[14]

The National Weather Service issued a more tempered, yet equally critical assessment in an official report on the disaster. "Despite timely NWS warnings, forecasts, advisories, and statements and effective media coverage of the event, the information either failed to reach or was not used effectively by the people who could have prevented heat-related deaths. . . . City officials had neither the experience nor the emergency response capabilities to translate the physical characteristics of the heat wave into human impact."[15]

Angered by reports from his colleagues in the Chicago Fire Department, one week after the disaster the paramedic and Republican state senator Robert Raica convened a public hearing to evaluate the governmental response to the crisis. The senate summoned representatives from the Chicago Office of the Mayor, the Department of Health, the Police Department, the Fire Department, the Transit Authority, the Housing Authority, the Park District, Commonwealth Edison (the city's primary electrical power supplier), private ambulance companies, the Illinois Department of Public Health, the Illinois Emergency Management Agency, and hospitals from Cook County to participate. Several community organizations and advocacy groups also had a chance to speak.

In his open letter introducing the committee's findings, Senator Raica wrote, "As a paramedic for the Chicago Fire Department and Chairman of the Illinois Senate Public Health and Welfare Committee, I became deeply troubled about the huge loss of life and thus felt it necessary to hold investigative hearings to determine what happened during the heat crisis. The goal of the hearings was to determine what steps were taken by government officials and health care providers during the heat crisis and what steps could be taken now to prevent such a tragic incident from occurring in the future."[16] The final report is a thin document consisting mainly of twenty-one enumerated situations uncovered by the committee as well as policy recommendations for addressing each of them in future heat disasters. In clear and pointed language, the list documents a number of gaps and shortcomings in the city's response to the crisis, portraying the local government as underprepared for the emergency and noting the extent to which city agencies failed to coordinate their efforts. The findings highlighted a number of problems with the city's service delivery and medical response system that were less apparent in other accounts of the trauma. The following passages from the report reveal the most urgent conditions.

- Some (city) departments, such as the Chicago Police Department, called in extra personnel on the weekend to help with the crisis. The Chicago Department of Health and the Chicago Fire Department both testified that they did not call in extra personnel.

• There was no crisis declared by the Fire Department and no extra personnel were called in because there is no mechanism in place to automatically trigger a crisis response.

• There were at least 55 instances of ambulance response times greater than 30 minutes, including one instance of a response time in excess of 70 minutes.

• During the period of July 13–16, 1995, 23 hospitals were on bypass status (the emergency rooms refused to admit new patients) for some portion of those days. Ambulances were diverted several miles out of their normal territory to deliver patients to hospitals not on bypass status, creating an even further stressed Emergency Medical Services System.

• During the heat crisis, 18 hospitals in the Chicago area were on bypass at the same time. The Chicago Fire Department testified that they were not aware that such a large number of hospitals were on bypass status simultaneously.

• During the heat crisis there were instances where public transit air-conditioned buses were requested by the Chicago Fire Department for use as portable cooling stations for school children and other persons. Those buses were often not available and arrived only after lengthy delays.

• The Chicago Department of Health was apparently not aware of the magnitude of the crisis at area hospitals over the weekend of July 15 and 16.

• The Cook County Medical Examiner was overwhelmed with the number of bodies his office was required to examine. The Chicago Police Department was asked to assist in transporting the bodies of victims to the morgue; however, officers in the field are not normally equipped for this type of duty.

Summing up these findings, the committee concluded that "there were significant individual efforts to protect the health and safety of Cook County residents. However, the system as a whole failed."[17] Reflecting back on the event, some city officials agree with this assessment. "Everyone was busy," explained John Wilhelm, the deputy commissioner of the Chicago Department of Public Health and the chairman of the Mayor's Commission on Extreme Weather Conditions. "The police were busy, fire people were busy, we were busy, human services (too). But it wasn't coordinated." Health Commissioner Sheila Lyne shared this observation. She recalled that when a press relations officer briefed her on conditions in the city, "I remember saying, 'you know, I don't think we did it right.'"

THE STATE OF DISASTER

If the city of Chicago's reaction to the heat crisis seems exceptionally flawed, what happened during the disaster is hardly surprising when it is placed in the context of the local government's typical mode of addressing deprivation and vulnerability in the city. The city's response expressed fundamental characteristics of the local government's methods for managing urban problems; several of these are particular to the era of reinvented governments, administered with techniques and system values honed in the private sector and recently adapted to public institutions. Situated in a competitive market for goods and services, the entrepreneurial state demands aggressive behavior from everyone in the system, including top officials, administrators, employees, contracting firms, and even the citizens who receive services. Chicago's city government in the mid-1990s was an exemplary case of an entrepreneurial state, as it was marked by (1) a concern with quality management and efficiency that pushed it to (2) outsource an unprecedented proportion of its services to private organizations, through which it (3) treats citizens as individuated customers or consumers in a market of public goods. This managerial strategy (4) demands that residents become "smart shoppers" of city services and (5) rewards consumers who have access to and mastery of information about state programs and policies. But it also carries the potential to (6) disproportionately empower residents who are already endowed with the forms of social and cultural capital necessary to navigate through bureaucratic systems while in effect (7) punishing people who are least likely to have the social skills and resources necessary to obtain goods and services that they are most likely to need. Operating in an age of intense media scrutiny in which managing public opinion is a key goal of governance, the reinvented local government is particularly concerned with its public image and that of the city's major public spaces. Public relations professionals and downtown planners play key roles in the local state, and their work is a crucial component in city politics.[18]

There is little reason to believe that Chicago's earlier modes of governance would have mobilized a more effective response to the crisis. The crucial comparison, then, is not between the reinvented government and the machine politics of years past, but between the current techniques of program management and the emerging risks to and needs of the city's vulnerable citizens.

In conventional accounts of disaster the government appears exclusively as a reactive institution whose involvement with the event begins after the catastrophe hits or as identifiable dangers approach. Yet welfare states are also stratifying agencies that help produce division and insecurity even when they aim to provide social protection, and states have historically played key roles in heightening as well as minimizing the risks that extreme environmental events will exact a high human toll.[19] Examining what different government agencies did or did not do during the heat wave uncovers only the most visible and immediate relationships between urban politics and the disaster. Understanding how the city shared or did not share accountability for the heat wave mortality requires placing its disaster management techniques within the context of Chicago's typical mode of governance and provision of social protection during the 1990s.

The heat wave of 1995 hit Chicago when the city government had gained local support and international praise for developing an exemplary set of reforms. The Mayor's Office had streamlined and downsized several agencies, with services long provided by full-time, in-house personnel contracted out to private sector organizations and reassigned to new programs; and Chicago had created an effective marketing campaign to promote the city to tourists, convention planners, and businesses. Though only embarking on the economic boom that would carry it through the 1990s, Chicago was beginning to show the signs of a renaissance. In preparation for the Democratic National Convention of 1996, the city government embarked on a massive beautification program to spruce up the streets, sidewalks, and parks around the downtown area, placing designer street lamps along roads and planters in the center of major thoroughfares. Daley, like his father before him, would make Chicago appear pristine and prosperous regardless of what was happening beneath the surface.[20]

Perhaps most important, Daley had initiated major reforms of the two largest city programs: the much maligned public school system, which the *Chicago Tribune* had labeled the "worst in the nation" in a book-length investigation published in 1992; and the Police Department, which would be subjected to an investigation from human-rights organization Amnesty International during Daley's term. In the true spirit of the entrepreneurial state, Daley named the new head of the school system the chief executive officer rather than superintendent, and subsequently downsized the agency by firing most of the top administrators. In March of 1995 *The Economist* ran a feature on "Da Manager," complimenting Daley for proving himself a capable leader, a fiscally responsible administrator whose reforms earned the city an upgrade in its Standard and Poor's bond rating system plus millions of dollars in revenues from privatized city services such as towing. As the summer of 1995 began, Chicago appeared to be a city that was back to work.[21]

Yet at a time when public programs were beginning to measure their effectiveness according to the number of employees they had cut from the rolls rather than by the number of people they had lifted out of poverty or distress, the local political climate had clouded out general concerns about Chicago residents who had not benefited from the boom. As the city poured millions of dollars into beautification programs around downtown, the local Policy Research Action Group argued that it was reducing the personnel budgets for " programs that are critical to addressing the economic and social priorities of low and moderate-income residents." According to 1990 census figures, roughly 396,000 Chicagoans lived in tracts with a poverty rate of 40 percent or above, making the city the third-largest site of concentrated deprivation in the United States. It was impossible for the city government to adequately address such inequality with the resources made available to it by the federal and state governments, and it would be unreasonable to expect Daley's administration to wage a full-fledged war on poverty on its own. But, according to studies by the Neighborhood Capital Budget Group, a local organization that monitors the use of the city budget and works on other issues of redistribution, during the 1990s the city government proved unwilling to make the fiscal contributions to the urban poor that it could have afforded. One study, for example, showed that forty-nine out of fifty wards in Chicago "will not receive sufficient funds to make even the most basic infrastructure repairs. . . . The City plans to spend nearly half of its economic development capital in just 10 wards . . . while the bottom 10 will receive less than 5 percent." Yet this news generated little attention or public concern when it was released. In the 1990s, it seemed, the method for dealing with urban inequality was to put it out of sight.[22]

The collective refusal to address poverty and isolation in Chicago during the prosperous 1990s was a crucial component of the cultural and political context of the heat wave. Chicago's commission reports and high-ranking officials have explained the city government's poor response to the heat emergency as the result of an acute failure to recognize the risks imposed by the climate. An effective public health response to any external threat requires awareness of the potential danger it imposes as well as knowledge about intervention strategies that will protect people at risk of harm; and administrators at several city agencies as well as the Mayor's Office maintain that—despite the warnings issued by national weather and public health agencies—they remained unaware of the risks facing the city. As one high-ranking official in the Chicago Health Department explained, "It never happened [before]. We didn't know." The National Weather Service study on the disaster found that the city government's failure to recognize the encroaching health threat did indeed render it unable to respond. "One reason for the general unpreparedness of the communities affected by the July heat wave," the report stated, "was that neither local officials nor the community at large recognized the potentially lethal nature of the extreme heat."[23]

There is no question that officials at the highest levels of Chicago's government did not understand the potential hazards generated by the blend of extreme climatic and social environments. But a closer look at the city's strategy for managing the crisis shows that structural conditions of the metropolitan government better account for the full political reaction to the disaster, which included the bureaucratic production of official knowledge about the heat deaths, a concerted effort to manage the public representations of the catastrophe, and conventional health work.[24] Five key features of the current mode of urban governance proved particularly consequential during the heat crisis.

1. *The delegation of key health and support services to paramilitary organizations,* such as the Fire and Police Departments, where administrative systems and top officials are not always attuned to the new demands for such "soft services."[25] This division of political labor creates an *organizational mismatch* between the capacities and responsibilities of government agencies that administer crucial health and welfare programs.

2. *The lack of an effective system for organizing and coordinating the service programs of different city, county, state, and federal agencies,* resulting in a complex but decoupled political structure that reproduces important functions and has no clear lines of accountability.[26]

3. *The lack of political will and public commitment to provide basic resources necessary for the protection of city residents* whose poverty or frailty renders them in need of support, but whose condition has become a normal, acceptable, and taken-for-granted feature of urban life.

4. *The expectation that city residents, including the elderly and frail, will be active consumers of public goods,* expert "customers" of city services made available in the market rather than "citizens" entitled to social protection. This market model of governance creates a systemic *service mismatch,* whereby people having the weakest capabilities and greatest

needs are the least likely to get them. In Chicago, it has also generated an everyday energy crisis for the elderly poor.

5. *The practice of governing by public relations* and relying on image-making projects for deflecting attention from city problems. In some cases, such as the heat wave, these projects take the form of official denial. Formal refusals to recognize the severity of various conditions both constrains city officials interested in addressing the problem and leaves the suffering citizenry more invisible and vulnerable.

This analysis of the politics of disaster is divided into two sections. This chapter examines how the first four modes of governance listed above compromised the city government's organizational capacity to provide effective support services to Chicago residents during the heat wave. Drawing upon fieldwork alongside the city workers who constitute the faces of the state, this account shows how everyday conditions of bureaucratic and service work in city agencies constrain the local government from providing the social protection expected of it. Chapter 4 scrutinizes the fifth mode of governance, politics by public relations, by tracing the city's representations of the disaster and placing its campaign to *spin its way out of the crisis* in the context of similar political efforts.

If the immediate political challenge posed by the heat wave concerned the problem of providing emergency care and support for vulnerable residents, the deeper question the disaster raises concerns the capacity of contemporary government agencies to protect an aging society of atomized and sometimes isolated citizens whose families, friends, and personal finances cannot provide for their social and medical needs.[27] Many of the emerging risks for today's urban elderly, such as lack of social support, family contact, specialized medical services, expensive pharmaceutical drugs, and flexible transportation, go beyond those that local and federal programs were designed to address.[28]

Finally, the political debates surrounding the heat wave suggest disagreement about the extent to which governments should be responsible for the protection and support of old and vulnerable citizens. In an era of sweeping "welfare reform," citizens of and officials in governments everywhere are being forced to rethink fundamental questions about the extent to which they hold states accountable for safeguarding the public health and welfare. For example, after floods in Nicaragua killed nearly ten thousand people in 1998, citizens gathered and screamed "murderer" to their president as he drove through towns to offer symbolic support for regions whose vulnerability the government had long tolerated. But in Chicago and other U.S. cities hit hard by crises, the dominant political culture of individual responsibility does not promote such understandings of disaster. Nonetheless, "the heat wave provokes a whole set of public health issues [we'll face] in the future because we have so many elderly people living alone,"[29] asserted Chicago resident Quentin Young, former president of the American Public Health Association. If trends of rising isolation, extreme inequality, family dispersal, and housing insecurity among the aged continue, residents of cities like Chicago will have to decide what kinds of risks they are willing to accept and what kinds of government protection they expect.

FACING THE HEAT: THE POLITICS OF ACCOUNTABILITY

According to many vocal Chicagoans, including prominent members of the local media, the idea that the city government shared any responsibility for the catastrophe was ludicrous, even corrupt. John Kass, the *Chicago Tribune* columnist who was working the City Hall beat during the heat wave, editorialized that critics of the government's response were merely projecting their own anxiety over abandoning their own responsibilities. "The bleating of city officials," he wrote, "obviates the guilt many feel while leaving their elderly to live alone. . . . Trying to blame the mayor for an act of God is not only unfair, it also does an injustice by wrongfully framing the debate. The question presumes not only that government could have done something, which is arguable, but should have done something to avert the disaster."[30] Cindy Richards, a member of the *Chicago Sun-Times* editorial board, took a similar position. "Time was," she opined, "that neighbors took care of each other. They kept an eye on the lady who lives upstairs. They bought groceries for the struggling family down the block. They took in their sister's kids when she couldn't care for them. Not so anymore. When scores of elderly residents succumbed to the sweltering heat, residents and community activists didn't ask how they could have worked to prevent some of these deaths. They asked why the city hadn't done more. Unfortunately, we have been conditioned through years of ever-burgeoning government to expect Big Brother will take care of all things. . . . It seems that neighborliness is a skill we will have to re-learn."[31]

There were few viable sources of opposition to Daley in 1995, and the mayor's stronghold on Chicago's public politics made it difficult for any strong voices of dissent to emerge. Political activists concerned about the disaster did not contest the argument that families and communities held great responsibility for protecting their vulnerable members. But in addition to insisting that their constituents worked assiduously to overcome the exceptional risks they regularly faced, a small group of dissenting political groups refused to let the city government off the hook. Community groups and activists representing the people most affected by the heat wave argued that there were, in fact, specific ways in which the city government had neglected its responsibilities to protect residents and preserve the public health. Their ability to make such a case was complicated by the disjuncture between the coarse vocabulary for referencing "the government" or "the state" that is readily available for citizens who make claims on the city, and the fine-grained distinctions between the numerous actors and agencies that constitute a governing regime.

In cities such as Chicago, the organizational complexity of a decentralized city government coupled with the bureaucratic slipperiness of overlapping city, county, state, and federal jurisdictions make it difficult to pinpoint the lines of political accountability. Moreover, as Charles Perrow has shown, such complexity is in itself a threat to public safety because it increases the probability that accidents and unexpected occurrences will result in disastrous consequences.[32] In the heat wave, for example, the Cook County Medical Examiners Office diagnosed the medical causes of mortality and established the official death reports; the Chicago Department on Aging opened cooling centers for seniors who needed relief; the Illinois state senate conducted hearings to investigate the nature of the city's emergency programs; and the National Weather Service issued extreme heat warnings before the disaster began. All of these actions were part of the government's response to the heat.

Working within such a complicated political field, groups that tried to assess the local government's accountability for the disaster shifted the terms of the debate from the generic question of how welfare states should protect residents to the matter of how specific government agencies and actors failed to fulfill their obligations. Metro Seniors in Action, an advocacy group for some ten thousand Chicago elderly, complained that city agencies had not only ignored their pleas to activate special support programs during the heat wave, but also turned down the organization's offer to provide the city with volunteer workers. Sidney Bild, an active Metro Seniors spokesperson, reported, "We were contacting the city to find out what it was doing and to urge them to reach out to seniors in every way that it could. More and more seniors are living on their own, so personal responsibility is a given. But beyond that, in an urban setting, there are certain things that people cannot do for themselves. There's very little that any civic organization can do in these circumstances. It has to be the efforts of the city to go to civic organizations and say 'we will work with you, how can we facilitate it?' A civic organization doesn't have a program. But we were willing to call people and we did." Bild argued that, despite the city's familiarity with dangerous heat and its extant heat emergency plan, no city leaders stepped up to direct a coherent policy response. "Coordination was attempted, but it was sort of like a Keystone Kop comedy," he remarked.

Metro Seniors was particularly upset over the Police Department's failure to utilize the trained and dedicated senior officers and neighborhood relations officers whom the agency had promised to place in every one of its twenty-five districts. According to Bild, "A senior officer means that he is assigned to seniors . . . to [look out for] the welfare, the safety, and the health of seniors. That is all the job is supposed to entail. That is a total duty." Metro Seniors' newsletter reports that during a February 1995 meeting with the organization, some four months before the heat wave, "the Superintendent [of police] promised that the Senior Citizens Unit would be fully reinstated. He promised to assign a trained senior officer to every district, to work only on senior issues. He promised that the senior officers would meet once a month. He promised that Sgt. Joseph Maratto would coordinate the officers' work. It turns out that the Superintendent was just trying to pacify us." Irene Nelson, chair of the Metro Seniors Crime Committee, explained that the heat crisis "confirmed our worst fears" because before the heat wave the organization had been warned that the Senior Units were not operating as promised. "We heard from some Senior Officers that regardless of the Superintendent's promises to us, there really was no Senior Unit. Many said they were still doing work unrelated to senior citizens and had never even met Sgt. Maratto."[33]

The organizational mismatch whereby the city assigned to the Police Department responsibilities that administrators as well as officers did not want to accept had created barriers to program implementation, the significance of which Metro Seniors struggled to make public. In its newsletter, Metro Seniors "claimed that had the Senior Citizen Police Unit been fully operational in July, hundreds of heat related deaths could have been avoided" because officers would have been in the streets spreading warnings about the dangerous environment and urging residents to contact their elderly neighbors.[34] But, as in the Fire

Department, which is another paramilitary organization that local governments increasingly use to provide health and social support services, no one in the police force activated an emergency prevention program. Metro Seniors was skeptical that the Senior Units were ever in place.

ORGANIZATIONAL MISMATCH: SOCIAL PROTECTION AND COMMUNITY POLICE

According to some critics of the local government, the Police Department's failure to institutionalize and activate senior officers to conduct preventive health and safety work expressed other problems with Chicago's Alternative Policing Strategy (CAPS, the city's system of community policing) as well. Police officers are the most prominent faces of the state on the streets and sidewalks of Chicago, the official agents who visibly represent the government and enforce its legal standards in the daily life of the city. The police have historically played important roles in the delivery of protective services to city residents and, as the historian Eric Monkkonen has shown, have been particularly involved in the social control and regulation of the urban poor.[35] Like the paramedics, in the heat wave Chicago's police officers were on the front lines of the city's response to the disaster. With hundreds of cases of mortality to investigate around the city and no other agencies available to deliver corpses to the morgue, Chicago delegated the difficult jobs of recording the deaths and handling the bodies to its police force. Officers involved in the disaster told me that it had been "one of the most difficult things [they had] ever done" and remembered it as "awful, gruesome work."

As it would during a routine death investigation, the Police Department dispatched officers to investigate each case. But during the heat wave the police were unusually busy. "I'll never forget that week," an officer working on the South Side told me. "I did a few of those calls, three, I think. There were apartments with the windows closed and the doors chained, no air-conditioning, no fans. The smell was foul, just death." When they reached the homes of the decedents, the responding officers followed the standard procedures of investigation, asking the neighbors or relatives when they had last seen the victim, inquiring about the person's social activity and medical history, and searching the rooms for signs of foul play. The police were responsible for recording their findings on official police reports, copies of which they would later turn over to the Medical Examiners Office.

Once they completed an investigation, officers were charged with bagging the body and delivering it to the morgue (fig. 36). This is

Figure 36. Storing bodies in refrigerated trucks at the Cook County Morgue. Many victims were delivered by the police. Source: *Chicago Sun-Times;* photographer: Bob Davis. Reprinted with special permission from the Chicago Sun-Times, Inc. © 2002.

Figure 37. Carting a victim into the Cook County Medical Examiners Office. Source: *Chicago Sun-Times* file photo. Reprinted with special permission from the Chicago Sun-Times, Inc. © 2002.

always a physically and emotionally difficult part of the job, but the condition of the corpses and the intensity of the heat made it even more unpleasant. The traffic at the morgue (fig. 37) added another layer of difficulty, since it could take hours to turn the body over to the medical examination staff and process the police reports. According to a reporter covering the scene for a city news wire, "we get homicides, some unusual cases, but never, ever, ever like this. The times that I've been there, I've seen police officers bring bodies. Maybe they're in and out for about 20 minutes, and they leave. Today, an hour and a half, or a line that wraps around the entire parking lot."[36] While they waited, most officers volunteered to help the mortuary staff load other cadavers onto carts and into the building. The work was interminable, but it constituted an essential part of the city's disaster management. If the Police Department's explicit function was to help dispose of the victims' remains, it also served the important implicit role of producing official knowledge about the conditions in which the victims died. This information would be crucial for the scientific and political investigations of the disaster.

But if the extent of the work assigned to city police officers was unusual, the nature of the work was not. For Chicago's Police Department, especially in the new system of community or neighborhood policing, is expected to do much more than enforce the law. During the 1990s, Chicago along with many other U.S. cities reorganized its police force around an elaborate community policing program designed to

Table 9. Full-Time Personnel for Chicago City Agencies, 1990s

Agency	1991	1995	1998
Police	16,243	17,441	17,752
Health	2,160	1,750	1,684
Human Services	1,074	580	474
Housing	345	255	195

Source: Alexander 1998.

appease both advocates for more law and order in government and grassroots community groups that had fought for police reform. Community Oriented Policing Services, a multibillion-dollar federal grant program that was part of the 1994 Crime Bill, provided ample federal resources for cities to use if they showed interest in and capacity for developing community policing programs. Thus while the federal government reduced funding for other city services and discouraged the formation or continuation of supportive programs for the poor during the 1980s and 1990s, it created new fiscal incentives for cities to expand their policing capacities and encouraged local governments to rebuild around their law enforcement agencies. The city of Chicago successfully tapped into these federal funds, bringing the Police Department's annual budget up from $629 million in 1991 to $817 million in 1995 and $923 million by 1998. In sharp contrast with other city agencies, which reduced their permanent staffs and outsourced their services in the 1990s, these resources allowed the Police Department to increase its full-time personnel by more than one thousand employees over the decade (table 9).

Although CAPS resembles many other new community policing programs, one distinctive mark of Chicago's system is the extensive service delivery and community relations responsibilities assigned to neighborhood police officers. CAPS is designed not only to make community police officers the brokers for basic city services such as infrastructure repair, closing and clearing abandoned buildings and empty lots, and removing graffiti, but also to provide more face-to-face contact between officers and residents. Under Chicago's program, all officers, and not simply special units, are part of CAPS; and in addition to traditional law enforcement work they are expected to be neighborhood organizers, community leaders, liaisons to other city agencies, and, if necessary, service providers. Central among these services is the protection of old and vulnerable city residents who needed special attention and support. The Chicago Police Department had operated special units designed to attend to the elderly since 1982, when it created the

Senior Citizens Services Division. But under CAPS the department pledged to establish closer ties with senior citizens and to look out for them during crises. The restructuring of police work so that officers are more familiar with the dynamics of the neighborhoods they patrol and more personally connected to neighborhood residents has played a major role in the political legitimation of CAPS. The myth of the community police officer as watchman or sentry, the contemporary equivalent to the precinct captain of Chicago's machinist past, is crucial to the program's popularity. The heat wave, which was the first major test of the program, offered an early sign of how difficult the reorganization of police work would be in practice; and subsequent studies have shown that the challenge remains unmet.[37]

Chicago inaugurated CAPS in April 1993, when it initiated experimental programs in four police districts. By December of 1994, six months before the heat wave, the system had been implemented in all twenty-five city districts. In theory, the city's community police officers, and the Senior Units in particular, should have been able to use their networks with neighborhood social groups and the local elderly to target assistance to the people most in need. "That's what CAPS should be all about," North Lawndale alderman Michael Chandler explained. "They could have city services checking up on these people. You've got seniors, don't just wait until there's a heat wave." During the disaster, however, none of the system leaders recognized the department's responsibility or capacity to protect vulnerable citizens by performing duties that fell outside the range of traditional law enforcement practice but were expected of the force in the new program. "We failed to pull the trigger because we just didn't see it," one CAPS leader told me in words that sounded strikingly similar to those used by the fire commissioner after the disaster.

During the heat wave the city learned that if community police officers are to succeed in their roles as service providers and community workers, they must be trained to recognize and react appropriately to dangerous social conditions that were outside their purview under conventional policing strategies. Chicago has already developed a retraining program for its officers in which it attempts to expand the scope of police practice. But, as the authors of the most comprehensive analysis of the program report, "virtually every sworn trainer we interviewed spoke negatively about the three-day skill-building sessions." Chicago officers were upset about community policing projects because most "just wanted to do 'what they signed up for.' Officers did not want to be 'pooper-scooper police,' and they said so. At the outset, dealing with peoples' concerns sounded too much like social work, and having all of the people's problems dumped on them sounded like too much work."[38]

Most of the police officers I met in my fieldwork are skeptical about the new duties assigned to them as community officers, and they have resisted the push to give up their old ways.[39] Officers often told me that they had joined the force because they wanted to "do something good" or "help the community," yet few had expected or desired to do the neighborhood relations work that they considered to be the soft labor of feminine social workers. Police organizations cultivate an ethos of masculine toughness and risk taking in its officers, and the introduction of community service responsibilities threatens this style. Indeed, once members of the department had been acculturated to the dangerous work of policing streets, they seemed unlikely candidates for the kinds of community work that neighborhood relations and senior service programming required. In the new system, officers feared that the jobs once reserved for the cops who could not cut it or for workers in the service sector would be assigned to everyone.

In practice, though, police personnel in Chicago's most violent and crime-ridden neighborhoods—precisely the areas that foster isolation and withdrawal among older and more fearful residents—found that the high demands of conventional law-and-order policing made it nearly impossible for them to do the neighborhood relations tasks expected of them. Even maintaining beat integrity (staying within a small area of a few square miles), which is the fundamental prerequisite for community policing, was difficult to achieve. Although there are great variations in the crime rates among Chicago police districts, the Police Department does not assign personnel to match the distribution of criminal activity, and it therefore leaves officers in high-crime areas with more policing responsibilities than they can handle. As one officer working around North Lawndale explained, "If we wanted to we could make arrests from the time our shift starts until the time it ends. But we can't keep up with the action here. There's too much going on."

Riding along, or sitting in the backseat as officers worked their regular shifts, I learned firsthand why it is so difficult for even the most well-intentioned members of the force to do the work of sentries and community leaders when they are policing the high-crime areas of the city. Problem-oriented neighborhood policing, the kind of practice that would allow officers to identify isolated seniors, people with special needs, and emerging local concerns, requires that officers have both sufficient time to work proactively and spatial boundaries that foster intimacy with a specific area and its residents. In police districts with high arrest rates, officers spent their shifts *reacting* to the crime reports and requests for emergency service that flow unceasingly from the command center to the patrol cars over the radio wires. As we drove hurriedly past the borders of the beats to which we had been assigned and responded to one urgent call after the next, it became clear that there was neither time nor space to fulfill the human service responsibilities assigned to community police officers. "In other districts," the officer riding shotgun told me, "they might be able to stay on beats a little better. But here we have to be all over the district based on the calls we get." We had responded to two calls from within our beat during the eight-hour shift, but we had spent the rest of the time outside the area.

There are, to be sure, other forums through which officers can do the neighborhood relations work of community policing. Primary among these are the monthly meetings held in each of Chicago's 279 beats, which have become the most consistent venues for mediation and collective planning between the city government and citizens or community groups, and the formal events sponsored by the department's Neighborhood Relations Offices. But recent studies show that the organizational culture and vocational challenges of police work make it difficult to cultivate enthusiasm for human service or sentry work among police personnel. As Skogan and colleagues report, "Many officers were not particularly interested in getting involved in non-crime problems and clung instead to a very traditional view of their job. To them, problem solving did not look much like 'real police work.' "[40] The failure of local officers and Senior Units to protect the isolated and vulnerable elderly during the heat wave was not simply a consequence of the Police Department's inability to recognize an acute problem and to activate an appropriate response. It was also a symptom of the underlying difficulties with the service delivery system CAPS was designed to implement in theory but had trouble achieving in practice. Like the Fire Department administrators who struggled to manage the paramedic and public health responsibilities now central to their organization, police officials forced to transform their paramilitary organization to meet new service demands were unable to adjust in time to ward off the crisis.

MALIGN NEGLECT: THE POLITICAL WILL
TO TOLERATE DEPRIVATION

While Metro Seniors voiced specific concerns about the Police Department, a group of South Side community leaders levied general criticisms of the city's response and argued that insufficient service delivery in their part of Chicago was a longstanding problem. Alderman John Steele, in the predominantly black Sixth Ward, complained that the city had neglected the health and welfare of residents in his area before and during the heat crisis; and U.S. Congressman Bobby Rush criticized City Hall for an "arrogance of power," claiming that "the lack of action by the city administration and the pass-the-buck mentality of Mayor Daley resulted in a gaping, bottomless hole in Chicago's safety net for the elderly. Cooling mechanisms were sitting empty while the elderly were dropping dead in their apartments because the city failed to activate any mechanisms warning of the severe danger of the heat."[41] The Task Force for Black Political Empowerment and a number of African-American politicians joined voices to denounce City Hall for its refusal to attend to the health crisis on the South Side. Robert Starks, a professor in the Inner-City Studies Program at Northeastern Illinois University, was outraged that city commissioners had not done more to provide emergency health services to the African-American elderly. In an editorial published by the *Chicago Standard News,* Starks opined that "the city's response to this crisis in our communities constitutes Criminal Neglect!" and called for the commissioners of several city agencies to resign.[42] In a subsequent discussion he argued that "it was simple callousness on the part of those who were responsible. They said that they didn't know what was happening, that they hadn't been warned. But everyone knew. We knew. The people in our communities knew. It's just that the city wasn't listening."

The South Side leaders were furious, but not surprised, by what they viewed as the city's disregard for the lives of African-American seniors during the heat wave. Such neglect, they argued, was typical of a government that refused to commit the resources necessary to protect an increasingly aged and isolated black population. They might have been surprised to learn that many officials and street-level workers at the Department on Aging agreed. According to Don Smith, who became department commissioner in 1989 and was still in office in 1995, in the mid-1990s the agency was struggling because its secure funding from the federal government was shrinking at the same time that the number of very old seniors and seniors living alone in Chicago was increasing, adding to the department's burden. Chicago's Department on Aging, which was among the first local governmental departments in the United States to focus specifically on the urban elderly, manages an impressive range of supportive and innovative programs. Yet its struggle to garner sufficient resources has made it impossible for the agency to meet the needs of a booming, aging elderly population.

City service workers commonly operate under difficult conditions and are typically unable to meet all the demands placed upon them. "Our department gets over eight thousand calls a month for case management requests," an Information and Assistance worker for the agency reported. "So you can understand how much we need to do."[43] Facing cuts in its secure funding, in the 1990s the Department on Aging was forced to increase its dependency on private foundations and other grant-making organizations for program support. In the middle and late 1990s, though, external funding for redistributive programs was in short supply, pushing some of Chicago's departments into fiscal shortages even though the state and federal governments were accumulating budget surpluses. As the Policy Research Action Group reported in its study of the city budget, "City of Chicago programs designed to address priorities of low-income communities, other than public safety, are extremely dependent upon grants from state and federal governments and foundations. Unfortunately, the level of grants coming to the City of Chicago that low and moderate-income residents depend on have declined substantially over the last few years."[44]

While the Police Department expanded to historic levels, the Department on Aging reduced its full-time staff and hired less expensive part-time and temporary employees. City governments have long contracted out many of their human services to private organizations, but in the 1990s Chicago and the Department on Aging outsourced more of their major programs to private and nonprofit institutions that agreed to do the work of the state despite the limited budgets available to them. As I spent time alongside social workers and home care providers for Chicago seniors, it became clear that underservice of Chicago's poor elderly is a structural certainty and everyday norm. The competitive market for gaining city contracts provides perverse incentives for agencies to underestimate the costs of services and overestimate their capacity to provide them. The agencies I observed had bargained themselves into responsibilities that they were strained to provide and taken on or inherited caseloads that required more resources than they could afford. "Most entrepreneurial governments promote *competition* between service providers," David Osborne and Ted Gaebler write in *Reinventing Government;*[45] and under certain conditions delegating more public services to the private sector can improve the level of support. But competition can undermine the working conditions for human service providers if it fosters efficiency yet compromises the time and human resources necessary to provide quality care. "My seniors love to see me," case manager Mandy Evers, an African-American woman in her late twenties, told me. "The problem is I never have enough time to get to them. You wouldn't believe how many people I have to keep track of here."

According to Mandy and a group of her colleagues at one of Chicago's largest social service organizations, the isolated seniors reputed to be unwilling to accept help are, most often, desperate for human interaction, attention, and support. While acknowledging that seniors who live alone are often wary of strangers and concerned about the possibility of scam artists and criminals who might prey on them, these social workers had developed strategies for gaining their clients' trust. Regular communication, if only by phone, was crucial for maintaining the lines of social contact and the loose bonds of trust. The problem was that their organization's contract with the city has left them with a small staff and, in the words of one case manager, "about two times more clients than we can possibly handle." Charged with the responsibility to visit their clients at least twice a year, most caseworkers I shadowed and got to know reported that they were managing to get to them once annually, at best. Seniors could receive more attention if they aggressively solicited it from the city or their service agency, but few of the people Mandy and her colleagues worked with were disposed to be so demanding.

Insufficient funding and staffing of social support organizations left isolated and homebound seniors on the periphery of formal assistance networks, but the standard operating practices of city and private service workers further marginalized elderly Chicagoans who lived in stigmatized African-American neighborhoods and housing projects. Like service workers in other Chicago industries and agencies, social workers and case managers for the elderly were generally anxious about making home visits to black residents of Chicago's most disreputable areas. In practice, these mundane concerns limited the city's capacity to support the most vulnerable and poor African Americans, particularly seniors and the disabled. What resources the local government committed to health and human services, in other words, were diminished by constraints in the street-level bureaucracies that enact policy on the ground.

Some of the caseworkers I got to know, including many African Americans, disliked working in these " no-go" areas because they believed that the risks to their personal safety were too high.[46] Although their agencies were mandated to serve everyone eligible for benefits in their districts, individual workers had some discretionary powers over which clients they would handle. If they had enough experience with the organization or a colleague who would help them out, social workers could avoid jobs they considered too dangerous to perform. Several social workers I met were willing to visit clients in Chicago's stigmatized areas, but only under special conditions. The general requisite was that the client be willing to accept a visit early in the morning. Every agency I visited had adopted an informal and unwritten policy of making rounds in predominantly African-American housing projects or very poor black neighborhoods before noon, and some workers tried to avoid them after 10:00 A.M. "When I'm going to this part of the city, I always leave by 8 A.M. at the latest," Mandy told me when I met her at that hour for a drive to some low-rise housing projects on the Near West Side. "I figure I can beat the gang-bangers and trouble-makers if I get out early. They're still trying to sleep off whatever they did the night before. But by lunchtime they're out again, and I try to be too."

When I observed the same practice of early visitation among other social workers, I asked the director of one city program if her department recommended that the staff make morning visits. "We certainly do," she responded. "We figure the bad guys aren't out of bed yet. And it works better." This service delivery strategy was understandable to Chicago seniors who had adopted similar routines for going out in their neighborhoods. Yet the mornings-only visitation policy constrained the options for service delivery and reception among residents of stigmatized black neighborhoods. The social distance between seniors residing in Chicago's most troubled areas and the state agents responsible for serving them helps to account for the gulf of understanding that separated city workers from isolated seniors during the heat wave. It also explains why political leaders on the South Side accused the city of neglecting the needs of their communities, and why some have not given up the case.[47]

SHOPPING FOR SERVICES IN THE EMPOWERMENT ERA

The rhetoric of abandonment and vulnerability used by Chicago's dissident political figures stands in sharp contrast with the language of empowerment and consumerism promulgated by the city government. City agencies promote themselves as purveyors of information about city services and programs to citizens who are expected to become smart shoppers of public goods. Driven by the logic that consumers of city services will not act effectively unless information enables them to make good choices, city agencies regularly hire expensive advertising and marketing firms to publicize their work.[48] As officials explain it, Chicago residents who need public assistance must also be able to activate support networks and make appropriate choices about the services they want and the programs they prefer. In principle, the concept appeals to city residents frustrated by old political bureaucracies, but many service providers for the elderly are convinced that the market model of government generates a *political mismatch* between service delivery programs that demand activist clients and an increasingly elderly population whose isolation and frailty hinder their capacity to claim the assistance they need.

Studies of urban politics and public health programs have consistently shown that local governments and the organizations that contract with them are more responsive to the demands of elite constituents than to citizens having the fewest resources and the least clout.[49] According to local social workers and case managers, Chicago residents with the lowest levels of education, the weakest ties to mainstream institutions such as government agencies and churches, and the least resources are also poorly prepared to claim the public benefits—from health care to prescription drugs to Social Security income—to which they are entitled. Cultural capital, in the form of skills necessary to hurdle complicated bureaucratic obstacles to care, and social capital, in the shape of networks of service providers and social support systems, are priceless possessions in the entrepreneurial government. But so, too, are other social characteristics that are atypical of the most frail and needy seniors: a disposition to aggressively demand public goods as entitlements, then to demand even more assertively after being turned away on the first try; and a social and spatial position that places one in sight of service providers and in reach of networks of information about available programs. Welfare historian Robert Halpern argues that "it has become a truism that those most in need of supportive services are precisely those least likely to have access to or to participate in them."[50] A system of service delivery that rewards the most capable threatens to make these inequities even more severe.

Stacy Geer, a seasoned advocate of Chicago seniors who spent much of the 1990s helping the elderly secure basic goods such as housing and energy, insists that the political mismatch between more entrepreneurial service systems and isolated seniors contributed to the vulnerability of Chicago's elderly during the heat wave. "The capacity of service delivery programs is fully realized only by the seniors who are most active in seeking them out, who are connected to their family, church, neighbors, or someone who helps them get the things they need," she pointed out. In some circumstances, the aging process can hinder seniors who were healthy and financially secure for most of their lives. Geer explained, "As seniors become more frail their networks break down. As their needs increase, they have less ability to meet them. The people who are hooked into the Department on Aging, the AARP, the senior clubs at the churches, they are part of that word of mouth network and they hear. I know, just from doing organizing in the senior community, that you run into the same people, and the same are active in a number of organizations."[51] City officials, including several members of the Department on Aging, agree that such active seniors are also the people most likely to go to cooling centers on hot summer days or to call friends or local organizations to request support. Yet seniors who are marginalized at the first, structural level of social networks and government programs are then doubly excluded at the second, conjunctural level of service delivery because they do not always know to—let alone how to—activate networks of support. Those out of the loop in their daily life are more likely to remain so when there is a crisis. This certainly happened during the heat wave, when relatively active and informed seniors used official cooling centers set up by the city while the more inactive and isolated elderly stayed home; and relatively protected residents of subsidized hotels received more attention and care than residents of most for-profit buildings.

THE EVERYDAY ENERGY CRISIS

During the 1990s, however, not even the best-connected city residents knew where to appeal if they needed assistance securing the most basic of primary goods: home energy and water. In Chicago, the combination of cuts to the budget of the federally sponsored Low Income Home Energy Assistance Program (LIHEAP) and a market-model managerial strategy for punishing consumers who are delinquent on their bills has placed the poor elderly in a permanent energy crisis. Facing escalating energy costs (even before prices soared in 2000), declining government subsidies, and fixed incomes, seniors throughout the city express great concern about the cost of their utility bills and take pains to keep their fees down. While the average Illinois family spends roughly 6 percent of its income on heat-related utilities during winter months, for low-income families the costs constitute nearly 35 percent.[52]

Poor seniors I got to know understood that their utility costs in the summer would be unaffordable if they had air conditioners. Epidemiologists from the CDC estimate that "more than 50 percent of the deaths related to the heat wave could have been prevented if each home had had a working air conditioner," and surely this would be an effective public health strategy.[53] Yet the elderly who regularly struggle to make ends meet explain that they could not use air conditioners even if they owned them because activating the units would push their energy bills to unmanageable levels. Along with the pressing needs for cash, the cost of electricity is a major reason that the beneficiaries of pilot programs to provide air conditioners to the poor have often sold the units rather than installed them. But the everyday energy crisis was pressing even during moderate temperatures. The most impoverished seniors I visited kept their lights off during the day, letting the television, their most consistent source of companionship, illuminate their rooms. Fear of losing their energy altogether if they failed to pay the bills has relegated these seniors to regular forms of insecurity and duress so fundamental, and yet so difficult for policy makers and the public to see, that their daily crisis goes largely unnoticed.

Initiated by the U.S. Department of Health and Human Services in 1978 and fully implemented in 1980, LIHEAP grants are made to the states, which develop their own criteria for determining eligibility and often supplement the funds. The LIHEAP budget peaked at $2.1 billion in 1985, at which time states used the funds to subsidize both home heating and cooling for the poor.[54] Beginning in the early 1980s, however, political support for the program, and in turn the money allocated to it, has diminished, falling to roughly $1 billion in real dollars by the year of the heat wave and finding its way back to the congressional cutting block. Illinois, like most other states with severe winters, not only has been unable to provide energy subsidies in summer, it also runs out of funding for winter support early in the season. According to Chicago Department on Aging workers, LIHEAP was the program that almost all of their seniors needed but could never get.

Programs such as LIHEAP fall into the category of conventional policies that provide rather than enable, so it is not surprising that critics of redistributive social protection policies, and Republicans in particular, have spent years campaigning to eliminate energy subsidies for the poor. During the week of 17 July 1995, as the heat wave deaths were still being counted, the U.S. Senate initiated a vote to end the LIHEAP program and finally settled on a compromise that skimmed 10 percent, or one hundred million dollars, from the budget. And on 19 July the Illinois Commerce Commission held hearings in which state officials announced that Illinois' funding for LIHEAP would be cut by 25 percent that winter regardless of the federal legislation. A few months later the U.S. House of Representatives joined cause with their congressional colleagues in the Senate, refusing to vote on a 250-billion-dollar funding bill for the Education, Health and Human Services, and Labor Departments unless they could eliminate LIHEAP entirely. The program ultimately suffered an additional funding cut but survived the congressional session. Ironically, as the environmental historian Ted Steinberg shows, during the same term that Congress trimmed its energy support for the poor it expanded the federal government's commitment to subsidize insurance companies and home owners who suffer property damage in disasters—even if direct reductions to social protection programs would be necessary to pay for the support. According to Steinberg, "What the new budgetary calculus means is that the poor will pay twice for natural disasters, as they continue to be left out of the relief equation and then are made to bear the costs of that very same relief effort through cuts in social spending."[55]

Already resigned to energy deprivation in 1995, during and after the heat wave an even more fundamental problem, loss of water, would become a pressing concern for Chicago's most impoverished seniors. Deprived of other methods of cooling, young residents in Chicago's low-income neighborhoods opened more than three thousand fire hydrants in the heat wave, triggering a militant response from local police officers. The city, which in 1995 had not yet installed special hydrant caps that release light streams of water, put police on order to crack down on teens who refused to accede to its repeated warnings. Soon thereafter local journalists declared that a "water war," in which more than one hundred crews roamed Chicago in search of open hydrants and police and young residents exchanged bullets in a battle for the most basic public good, had broken out in the streets.[56] The city Water Department was unable to maintain water pressure in the most affected neighborhoods, leaving clusters of residents without water for hours as the deadly heat seared into the streets. Similar water shortages plagued Chicago Housing Authority buildings, where electric water pumps shut down during the power outage and left the projects without energy or water. Residents of the Rockwell Gardens Projects on the Near West Side had no water for more than a day, and several people in the Randolph Towers on the South Side complained that their taps were dry for three consecutive days. Broken water pumps at a South Side station caused water outages around the area. "I'm very agitated and *hot!*" an African-American woman in the Morgan Park area told a local television reporter. "Look at us. It's ridiculous. We don't have drinking water. We can't flush the toilet. We can't do anything" (see fig. 38).

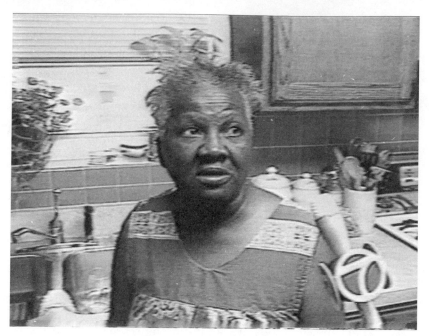

Figure 38. A frustrated Chicagoan shows reporters that her apartment has lost all water pressure during the heat wave. Source: ABC7. Courtesy of WLS-TV.

What no one in Chicago could anticipate was that, long after the city had restored its capacity to supply water, the local government would begin a policy of turning off the taps of Chicago residents who were unable to pay their water bills. Impoverished and ill seniors whose fixed incomes were too low to cover their water bills were not spared from such treatment. In the pure spirit of the entrepreneurial state, by the late 1990s the Chicago Water Department had decided that the most effective way to handle delinquent customers was to cut off their supply and punish them with heavy fees. City officials hoped that adopting a strategy similar to the one they used to collect parking fees—depriving debtors of the resource they have mishandled—would help turn the Water Department into a greater revenue generator for the city.[57] What they failed to consider, however, was that water, unlike a car, is a resource that people need to survive, and that the punitive policy would likely prove most devastating for the Chicago residents whose lives were already most devastated.

Predictably, the policy took a major toll on the city's poor elderly, including some of the seniors I had gotten to know. In a 1998 discussion, one Water Department employee who handles "shut-off" cases told me that he could not make a special exception and turn the water back on in the home of one senior with a severe illness whose doctor had called to complain, because the case was not unusual: "I get requests like that all the time. Constantly. I've got people coming to me everyday with stories like that. So what am I supposed to do?" For this administrator, if not for his department, the prevalence of shut-offs was a sign of irresponsible consumer spending rather than a signal that the agency's policy response had endangered the lives of the very people that the city government, with its special programs to support the elderly, promises to protect.

WELFARE STATES AND EXTREME EVENTS

Extreme events and disasters pose exceptional challenges for governments and societies, but their potential to cause physical damage and social suffering makes them crucial tests of social protection systems. As public health scholar Rodrick Wallace explains, "Extreme events— 'emergencies' . . . delimit and define our lives, both individually and in community. The ability to control both the occurrence and the consequences of such extremes is the hallmark of effective government, a government which retains the 'mandate of heaven.' "[58] When a government mismanages a crisis it can use its experience as a guide for building new forms of social protection, but doing so requires an open assessment of how its policies support or imperil its constituents. In the years following the heat wave Chicago has expanded its programs for supporting seniors during heat crises, developed a system for tracking isolated seniors and contacting them when there is severe weather, and continued its Benefits Eligibility Checklist and enrollment service. These programs will help to protect Chicago's elderly during future heat crises, yet they only begin to make up for other deficiencies in the city government's service delivery system.

In the meantime, the four features of urban governance explored in this chapter—(1) the delegation of key health and support services to paramilitary organizations that were not designed to deliver them, (2) the lack of an effective system for organizing and coordinating the service programs of different agencies, (3) the lack of a public commitment to provide basic resources, such as health care and energy, necessary for social protection of the vulnerable, and (4) the expectation that frail and elderly citizens will be active and informed consumers of public goods—will continue to create risks for city residents. Such organizational changes, political priorities, and market-based reforms are increasingly common in today's reinvented governments, and the story of the heat wave suggests that they deserve further scrutiny.

In Chicago, as in other cities, the popularity and legitimacy of these reforms is as much attributable to the city's capacity to manage its image through sophisticated marketing and public relations work as it is to the effectiveness of the programs. Whether in everyday city politics or extreme and unusual events, powerful image-making projects can compensate for shortcomings in other parts of the government's work. During the heat wave, as the next chapter shows, the city's most effective response to the dangerous environment was not a public health program, but a public relations campaign.

CHAPTER FOUR

Governing by Public Relations

hicago is a city of big stories, and one of the greatest legends of the modern metropolis concerns another recent disaster, the blizzard of 1979. Historians quibble over the political significance of the series of punishing snowstorms, which buried the city in powder and ice for weeks. But among Chicago residents there is consensus that the blizzard caused at least one casualty: the mayoral tenure of Michael Bilandic.[1] A recent study of Chicago politics provides a succinct representation of how the event affected the 1979 mayoral primary, in which Bilandic campaigned against the underdog Jane Byrne. "Until the very close of what had been a pleasingly uneventful administration, Bilandic was considered a shoo-in. However, when two huge snowstorms struck the city in January 1979, the response of city agencies was slow and quite erratic. At one point, the Chicago Transit Authority sought to maintain schedules on the Dan Ryan 'el' line by skipping stations on the black Near South Side, thereby excluding thousands of African-American commuters from the public system. Though Byrne's anti-machine credentials were always suspect, on primary day in February, she carried 15 of 19 black majority wards."[2] Chicagoans came to believe that mismanaging the extreme weather had cost Bilandic his job. When the heat arrived in 1995, everyone in City Hall knew that the stakes of the crisis could be high.

One reason that the snowstorm proved so politically damaging was that, unlike the heat wave, it blocked the circulation of people and goods in the city, shutting down businesses, closing schools, and inconveniencing the most powerful constituencies in Chicago as well as the disadvantaged. In other words, the blizzard was a universal disaster, whereas the heat wave created crises for only a small and politically marginal portion of the city. In addition, in 1979 Mayor Bilandic was mired in a mayoral campaign against a credible opponent, and his political rivals used the city's blunders to leverage their criticisms of the his administration. In the summer of 1995, however, Mayor Richard M. Daley had just completed a successful bid for reelection in a contest lacking any real risk of loss. The timing of the heat wave, coupled with the absence of a viable political opposition whose criticisms could threaten the legitimacy of the mayoral administration, minimized the political consequences of the catastrophe.

But the most significant difference between the politics of the heat wave and the blizzard is that in 1979 the Bilandic administration mismanaged not only the extreme weather problems but also—and more crucially—the public relations response. Bilandic and his aides proved incapable of responding adequately to community groups and local journalists, who demanded a forthright account of how city agencies were managing the snow. After the mayor insisted that the city had removed snow from several of the most affected areas, a series of investigative reports revealed that important sites listed as cleared remained covered in several feet of snow and ice. Chicago voters, furious that the mayor had tried to cover up his administration's wrongdoings, punished Bilandic at the polls for his deceit.

Since most of his constituents had access to air-conditioning in 1995, Daley did not have to worry much about damaging his reputation among the local elite. Yet more than any government in Chicago history the Daley administration had devoted its resources to the engineering of popular opinion that City Hall was working for the people, so negative publicity from a deadly heat wave threatened to tarnish the mayor's hard-won reputation. In the months before the heat wave Chicago was in the midst of a massive public relations campaign to regain the status it had lost after hosting the disastrous Democratic National Convention in 1968 and suffering an economic downturn that lasted through the 1970s and 1980s. In addition to launching a national marketing campaign designed to attract tourists and business travelers to the city, the local government invested heavily in promotional campaigns for its own social programs. Under Daley, Chicago budget expert Jacqueline Leavy argues, the city has made "a savvy, strategic investment in media, high profile ads" for many of its major initiatives, and built a "media machine that's been put in place to tell people over and over that Chicago cares." Many of Chicago's governmental agencies contract marketing or advertising services to major corporate firms, and some, such as the Police Department, offer their public relations programs as national models.[3] The results of these projects are visible throughout the metropolis: on the streets, which are lined with advertisements for public programs, and on local television, where the city manages a cable channel and employs a television production team to develop and broadcast programs that show off the government in action.

Strategic *symbolic* political action has long been an important value of governing urban regimes. But today, as political scientist Timothy Cook argues, "*every* branch of government is more preoccupied with and spends more resources on the news media today than it did forty years ago."[4] Since Douglass Cater coined the term in the 1950s, political scientists have used the phrase "government by publicity" to describe the role of *reporters* in the political process;[5] in the 1990s, however, governing by publicity was a standard practice of government itself. The news media are political institutions, but in an information age when governments have to manage and manipulate responses to constant journalistic scrutiny, political organizations are news institutions as well. Contemporary political regimes operate according to the principle that, as Harvard University public policy scholar Martin Linsky and his colleagues put it, "having policymakers who are skilled at managing the media will make for better government."[6]

Governments view public relations projects, which are crucial for defining or framing issues and generating public support, as essential for effective and legitimate political practice. But the relationship between good public relations and good government is not always apparent, since governing regimes can also use sophisticated image-making or promotional projects to advance their own interests and gloss over serious problems or dissenting positions. Such "staged and manipulated publicity," Jürgen Habermas claims, operates "under the aegis of a sham public interest," advancing the legitimacy of a dominant political group and "engineering consent" of the populace while repressing genuine criticism and concern.[7] An institutional knowledge of how to symbolically construct an image of an efficient, effective, and responsive city government proved especially valuable during the heat wave, when the encroaching public health emergency triggered an aggressive if unwieldy public relations campaign to avert a political disaster.

The city government benefited from its institutional position as a regular provider and creator of important news, using its organizational resources at the crucial framing and definition-setting stage of the public reporting on the situation.[8] Preserving the mayor's reputation in the face of such a massively deadly catastrophe would not be easy, though, in part because Daley had ascended in Chicago politics by explicitly pledging to protect the city from crisis and promising to stand accountable for problems that emerged while he governed. During his first successful campaign for City Hall, Daley the candidate boldly proclaimed, "We can't close our eyes to [Chicago's] problems any longer. Being accountable starts in City Hall. Because the responsibility for managing the city lies with the mayor. . . . I won't wait until disaster strikes."[9] If Bilandic had been removed from office because he left snow on the streets and deprived African Americans of transportation, what would happen to a mayor who did not prevent several hundred deaths and a public health breakdown on the South Side? Would city residents and journalists hold Daley and his administration responsible for the devastation? Or would accountability prove more diffuse?

The city is not the only political body with jurisdiction over Chicago. Cook County, the state of Illinois, and the federal government also contribute to the governance of the city, playing key roles in disaster management such as providing weather warnings, examining the dead, and distributing emergency relief funds for energy and infrastructure repair. Moreover, the city had some reason to believe that most of its constituents, steeped in the rhetoric of personal responsibility and individual determinism so influential in U.S. political culture, would not hold the incumbent regime responsible for the event. Yet in addition to the legacy of Bilandic's demise, Daley's administration had to face up to the widespread public notion that local governments are most accountable for local problems, so the city was positioned to receive more scrutiny for its role in the disaster than any other political body. The federal government (through the National Weather Service) and the state of Illinois (through the state senate) would indeed produce official reports on the heat wave after the crisis had subsided, and both would defend their roles in the disaster management while faulting the city for its failures. But as the political organization directly responsible for managing the city, the local government—and the Office of the Mayor in particular—faced the most public pressure to account for the catastrophic human damage. Despite its earlier promises to take responsibility for the city's welfare, when disaster did strike Chicago the Daley administration scrambled to avoid taking the blame.

DENY, DEFLECT, AND DEFEND

While the city neglected to follow its own guidelines for coordinating an emergency public health reaction to the dangerous heat, the administration accomplished a textbook public relations campaign to deny the severity of the crisis, deflect responsibility for the public health breakdown, and defend the city's response to the disaster. Mayor Daley often takes Mondays off during the summer, but with the heat wave death toll topping one hundred over the weekend of 14 July and Chief Medical Examiner Edmund Donoghue predicting that the city would discover more deaths throughout the following week, the mayor called in key aides and cabinet members for an 8:00 A.M. meeting on Monday, 17 July. Local journalists reported that Daley "went into a political damage-control mode" out of concern that the soaring mortality rates would create a public impression that the city was unprepared for the situation.[10] "Already," Health Commissioner Sheila Lyne recalled, "the press wanted to know what we were doing and why it happened." So the mayor and the cabinet planned their rhetorical response.

Daley's public relations team organized two media events for the day. First, the political entourage would visit a supermarket on the North Side where power failures had ruined food supplies (fig. 39) and announce the mayor's plans to conduct public hearings on Commonwealth Edison's electrical failures. The move, aides calculated, would focus attention on the utilities company and galvanize citizens who were already angry about their loss of power. Second, officials would hold a news conference at one of the five city senior centers, where they would dismiss any charges that the city had failed to organize a strong response and advise citizens on how to survive the heat.

The conference would also give Daley a chance to repair whatever damage he had done the previous Friday, when he had told reporters not to make too much out of the situation. "It's hot," the mayor acknowledged as the city registered its first heat-related deaths. "It's very hot, but let's not blow it out of proportion. . . . Yes, we go to extremes in Chicago. And that's why people like Chicago. We go to extremes."[11] Although the statement came before medical examiners understood the severity of the epidemic, the words made Daley appear callous once the mortality and morbidity rates began to rise.

The mayor opened the Monday press conference with a plea for understanding. "Let's be realistic," he implored. "No one realized the deaths of that high an occurrence would take place." Sounding a populist appeal, Daley castigated Commonwealth Edison for losing its power capabilities and failing to alert the city within the mandatory ten-minute window following a power outage. "People are angry," he acknowledged. "They're frustrated and they want to go back to normal living. My office has been in touch with Commonwealth Edison throughout the power failure, but I'm not happy with their response." "This is not over," the mayor threatened. He was ready to investigate.[12]

After Daley spoke, Health Commissioner Lyne, Human Services

Figure 39. A grocery store employee dumps spoiled food into garbage bins. The store lost its power during the heat wave. Source: *Chicago Sun-Times;* photographer: Brian Jackson. Reprinted with special permission from the Chicago Sun-Times, Inc. © 2002.

Figure 40. Mayor Richard M. Daley addresses a news conference in which he deflected criticism that the city administration did not do enough to avoid the high number of heat-related deaths during the heat wave. At left is Raymond Orozco, the city's Fire Commissioner at the time; at right is Deputy Public Health Department Commissioner Dr. John Wilhelm, who later became the city's Health Commissioner. Source: Reuters/Getty Photos; photographer: Sue Ogrocki. Courtesy Archive Photos.

Commissioner Daniel Alvarez, Fire Commissioner Raymond Orozco, and Police Superintendent Matt Rodriguez addressed the media, each making a strong defense of the city's response to the heat wave crisis. Faced with questions about the comprehensiveness of the effort, Rodriguez and Orozco surprised reporters by claiming that "their departments, though busy, were not overwhelmed by the heat wave."[13] Lyne, who moments before had made a backstage comment to a mayoral aide expressing concern that the city had mismanaged the situation, took a different official position. "We acted in an emergency alert," she insisted. "Get that straight. We did it all."[14] Her skeptical comment would remain backstage, however, since from the beginning of the crisis the city government had been scrambling to organize a strategy for averting a political disaster. Officials feared that self-criticism would encourage attacks on the city.[15]

The most powerful moment of the press conference came when Daniel Alvarez took the microphone. Like Daley, the Human Services commissioner had angered citizens with his comments on the previous

Friday. When reporters asked about the city's support programs for the elderly, Alvarez knew neither how many cooling centers the city had opened nor how the government would help the elderly access them.[16] Yet while Daley tried to curry favor from the public by sympathizing with their outrage at Commonwealth Edison, Alvarez boldly blamed the victims of the heat wave for their own demise. "We're talking about people who die because they neglect themselves," he declared. "We did everything possible. But some people didn't want to even open their doors to us."[17] Though it angered critics of the city and the families of heat wave victims, Alvarez's statement perfectly expressed the popular political position that individuals fall into trouble due to personal behavioral deficiencies that are beyond the government's control. The heat disaster, in the view of the Human Services commissioner, was a social catastrophe, not a political event.

Chicago officials had hoped that the crisis would disappear as the temperatures fell back to normal, but on Tuesday, 18 July, the city continued to receive reports of dead bodies being delivered to the Cook County Morgue. At the Cook County Office of the Medical Examiner, Chief Medical Examiner Edmund Donoghue announced that the heat-related death toll had reached 376. With more than one hundred bodies waiting to be examined, Donoghue warned that the number was certain to go even higher. In Springfield, state senators made their first public call for hearings to examine the political response, and reporters worldwide were coming to Chicago to cover the story of the summer. Although the city still faced a public health emergency, Daley and his cabinet were on the defensive again.[18]

By Tuesday it was clear that Alvarez's effort to blame the casualties on the victims had backfired, and the commissioner went before the media to apologize for his remarks. With journalistic attention focused on the hundreds of dead bodies being stored at the morgue, the city's new public relations strategy was to deny the Chief Medical Examiner's findings that the deaths were related to the heat. In a public statement that journalists considered Daley's "strongest comments to date," the mayor challenged the results of Donoghue's autopsies. "Every day," Daley told the media, "people die of natural causes. You cannot claim that everybody who has died in the last eight or nine days dies of heat. Then everybody in the summer that dies will die of heat."[19]

Chief Medical Examiner Donoghue, as we saw in the introduction, insisted on the validity of his assessments and refused to submit to the mayor's pressure to abandon his scientific principles for political expediency. Although he recalled that the recent Centers for Disease Control article listing techniques that governments should implement to prevent heat fatalities was sitting on his desk when the bodies started coming in to the morgue, Donoghue had made no criticisms of the city's emergency response and was not expecting any conflict with City Hall. He was surprised that the mayor, with whom he had always shared an amicable relationship, was suddenly questioning his authority and downplaying the crisis. Moreover, the medical examiner was among the first people to note the irony that city employees were authoring the official death reports for the heat wave victims at the very moment that their boss was pleading ignorance or trying to alter the record. "These bodies were being brought in by the Chicago Police Department," he asserted. "So we were working with the assumption that the city of Chicago was aware of the problem."

Donoghue remained diplomatic as the political pressure on his office intensified. "The mayor is entitled to raise questions. We would be delighted to have the figures checked. . . . But all of these people would have survived if not for the heat. . . . I think my criteria are absolutely fair. I think my criteria are excellent. The truth of the matter," he concluded, "is we probably have underestimated the number of heat deaths."[20] Medical examiners and heat disaster experts from around the country ultimately confirmed Donoghue's findings, as did officials from the CDC when they arrived to assess the situation. But for the public such arcane scientific squabbles were merely academic, and support for the Chief Medical Examiner's conclusions never received the media attention accorded to Daley's denials.[21] The mayor could not control the reporting on the crisis, but City Hall's symbolic power, access to journalists, and organizational capacity to frame the event made Daley's position the point of reference for the public and scientific debate.

At this point, a high-ranking city official remembered, "the mayor was nuts with Donoghue. He wanted him to shut up," and he refused to call the medical examiner's office and work out a plan. The debate with Donoghue and the struggle to establish a viable public position was making the city officials anxious. "The heat wave," a senior Health Department official reported, "was the only time during my tenure when we were having closed meetings with locked doors and signs saying 'No Press Allowed.' We were rushing back and forth between our office and City Hall, there were meetings all the time. We were forced to strategize to come up with a way of public speaking about the heat wave deaths." Despite such maneuvering, it was impossible for the mayor to sustain his critique of Donoghue's mortuary science once federal experts sounded their support for the medical examiner.

The same official recounted the meeting at which the Mayor's Office recognized the legitimacy of the heat wave death figures reported by the Medical Examiners Office:

> We were having a meeting with the CDC group that came down to do a case-control study, and soon after we started, the Mayor's Office sent a lawyer over to protect the mayor's position. The guy was in a difficult situation. Either he had to support the mayor's line, which was patently false, or he had to quit his job. Of course, the Mayor's Office was already furious about the heat-related death reports, and when I told him that the mortality was actually much higher he flipped. I explained the excess death concept to him, and he responded, "So we can't be 100 percent certain that these people died of heat. You can't prove it case by case? They all could have been killed by homicide, right?" And I said, "No, we don't have a confirmed cause of death in each case, but there is no other likely source of death and this is the way epidemiologists think. We know, anyway, that there weren't hundreds of homicides." Then the lawyer turned to one of the CDC people sitting in the room and asked, "Which one of us sounds right?" She told him that I did, and that pretty much ended the meeting. By the time I returned to the Health Department and went to see the commissioner, she had already received a call from the Mayor's Office with the instruction that no one was to see those numbers. We weren't allowed to say anything.

By the end of the week Daley declared that he was "not questioning anybody dying" and acknowledged that the surge in deaths must have been related to the heat. Yet the mayor never made a public correction of his initial denials or publicly announced an official death toll. Instead, his next move was to defend the city's response by embracing Donoghue's claim that the deaths were technically "heat related," a designation that emphasized the meteorological rather than the social or political determinants of the deaths. In a news conference at the John Hancock Center on Thursday, 20 July, Daley released a new heat emergency plan (almost indistinguishable from the one the city had failed to use) to address future crises, dismissed critics who charged that his administration had neglected to protect African Americans on the South Side, claimed that there was an equal number—but not an equal rate—of heat wave deaths among blacks and whites, and praised himself as well as other officials for organizing an effective emergency response. "My commissioners, my performance and city employees were excellent. I've got no criticism whatsoever."[22]

Although he expressed sadness for those who lost their lives,[23] the mayor reasoned that the "heat-related deaths" and natural disasters were ipso-facto caused by the weather. No one could seriously hold the city accountable for the heat; and, as one Health Department official explained, "government can't guarantee that there won't be a heat wave."[24] Of course, no one ever had blamed City Hall for the climate, but by emphasizing the natural and therefore uncontrollable character of the disaster Daley and other Chicago officials foregrounded a frame that deflected attention from the policy response and relieved them of responsibility for the crisis. Conventional language already categorizes heat waves and other extreme environmental events as natural disasters, and though the classification appears innocuous it suggests a powerful meaning for the event. Following Erving Goffman's work on frame analysis, political scientist Deborah Stone explains that "we have two primary frameworks for interpreting the world: the natural and the social. In the natural world we understand occurrences to be 'undirected, unoriented, unguided, purely physical.' . . . One cannot properly speak of action here, but only of occurrences. This is the realm of accident and fate. Politically, this is a good place to retreat if one is being charged with responsibility, because no one is responsible in the realm of fate."[25] Culturally, the natural frame was also a good place to fix official talk about the crisis, since the argument that heat caused the mortality was the default relationship and scientific explanation for the disaster.

Critics who wanted to argue that the heat wave deaths expressed some political or social failures, and therefore to move the event into the realm of management and control, had the onus of working against the ready-made framing of the event. Heat and energy, rather than politics and poverty, would become the objects of official concern. Accountability belonged to nature, primary power supplier Commonwealth Edison, and, if pressed, the families of the dead. Daley would continue to assert that the city government could do little if the families and neighbors of older residents neglected their own responsibilities to provide attention and care. In a news conference, he argued that "we have to appeal to all the family members of seniors to call, go over there, see your mother or father or aunt. That is a must." The comments prompted at least one journalist to report that Daley had "pointed a finger of blame at some of the families of senior citizens who died."

According to one top aide, the mayor "kept saying things like 'You've got to be watching your neighbor. That's the problem here. You've got to take care of them.' So he was spreading the blame in a sense, or spreading the responsibility. . . . But I'm sure he started it by deciding it was a good strategy to get them to stop blaming him for everybody's deaths." Some residents on the South Side, where water supplies were low and hospital emergency rooms were closed to new patients, felt wrongfully accused. The grandson of one heat wave victim told a local reporter, "I think the family members have a responsibility to check on each other. But I also believe that the city has a responsibility to hone in on those individuals who they know are alone to prevent the situation." "This is not only a neighborhood responsibility," a friend of the family added. "The city should be responsible for this."

To ward off such negative appraisals, City Hall would have to find a way to deflect remaining criticisms of its disaster response. One effective technique involved responding to specific criticisms of city agencies with general and politically popular statements about the limits of government and the need for individual and community accountability. The city also benefited from the passage of time, since the mayor's position dominated news coverage during the crisis; and once the bodies were removed from the morgue and the spectacular images disappeared from public view, the catastrophe lost its relevance. Republican state senators conducted a hearing on the heat crisis on Wednesday, 26 July, but journalists paid little attention to the investigation, and local papers buried the story in the inside pages of the Metro section. The most serious threat to the mayor's strategy of blaming nature and Commonwealth Edison for the crisis came from a group of Chicago aldermen who had called for City Council hearings on the disaster. An inquest set in Daley's own City Hall would surely make headlines, giving local leaders a dramatic occasion and visible forum for illustrating how various agencies, including the Office of the Mayor, had mismanaged the crisis. But it could also open the door for more-sweeping criticisms of the city's policies for supporting vulnerable seniors, providing emergency medical services, and managing community policing programs, and—more seriously—focus attention on a series of city problems that had been largely out of sight.

It is not clear exactly what happened between the heat wave and Tuesday, 1 August, but when the City Council met that day the aldermen who had vocally demanded hearings on the city's disaster response quietly dropped the matter. Bernard Hansen, the alderman of the Forty-fourth Ward who had called for city commissioners to explain their reaction to the crisis, reported that the inquiry was no longer necessary. "I don't know what a hearing would accomplish at this point," he said. "All the department heads have been questioned by the media. How much more public can you get?" The story of this surprising reversal received little media attention; it was left out of television reports altogether and relegated to the inside pages of the *Tribune*'s Metro section, where the headline "Rambunctious Aldermen Sideline Dog Law, Heat-Wave Probe" expressed its waning significance.[26]

Once the City Council cleared city department heads of official scrutiny, Mayor Daley moved forward with his plan to shift attention to Commonwealth Edison, the utilities provider that he had faulted for much of the damage. There was little question that Com Ed's generators broke down during the heat crisis. Encouraged by City Hall or not, residents throughout Chicago had blamed the energy company for leaving them without air-conditioning, refrigeration, lights, and television during the severe weather.

After the heat wave the Illinois Commerce Commission directed its staff to investigate the systemic and acute problems at Com Ed's local plants. The state hired Failure Analysis Associates to conduct the study, and in December 1995 the commission publicly reprimanded Commonwealth Edison for its role in the crisis. Within days, Mayor Daley urged the City Council to convene its own hearings on Commonwealth Edison. Although the aldermen had previously cancelled their investigation of the city government because other parties had already scrutinized the agencies, their standards suddenly changed. On Thursday, 14 December, a united front of business owners, residents, and aldermen met with the City Council's Energy and Environment Committee to provide five hours of testimony about the damage Commonwealth Edison had caused. The utilities provider was back in the spotlight, and City Hall was once again an advocate for the people.

Instead of holding hearings to investigate his administration's heat wave response, Mayor Daley organized his own commission to study the impact of the heat wave. Participants in the commission included some of Chicago's leading public health figures, a gerontologist, physicians, and a meteorologist, but no sociologist trained to analyze the social causes of the disaster. The mayor's aides invited at least one of the city's major news organizations to send a representative, but it declined.

The commission met several times in the late summer and fall of 1995, dividing into small groups to address different aspects of the crisis. The Mayor's Office published the final report in November, yet

Figure 41. The mayor's official report on the heat wave. The cover of the document makes no direct reference to the disaster, so few reporters or citizens noticed the publication.

only after designating the participants as the Mayor's Commission on Extreme Weather Conditions, rather than a commission on the heat disaster, and excluding any reference to the heat wave in the title of the document (fig. 41). Such euphemistic language provided an official account of the disaster without calling any public attention to the event. The familiar technique succeeded in helping the city to hide its most public statement on the catastrophe while ostensibly revealing it.[27]

The final report is, in fact, a rich but inconsistent document containing useful information for city agencies and service providers. It identifies the heat wave victims and enumerates a set of individual-level risk factors for vulnerability, yet the information about heat wave mortality pluralizes the death patterns and the relative impact on different groups, obscuring rather than clarifying the social structure of the disaster.[28] The executive summary offered by the Mayor's Office, for example, reports that "the numbers of African-American and white victims were almost identical," even though the death ratio and age-adjusted death ratio—which are included in a less prominent section of the document (page 12)—show that African Americans experienced substantially higher death rates than whites.[29] Similarly, the only neighborhood-level analysis presented in the summary explains that "nearly all community areas in Chicago were affected," which is analogous to saying that nearly all areas in the city are affected by poverty or crime, because it conceals the enormous variation in neighborhood mortality levels.[30]

The Mayor's Office, which controlled and edited the final publication of the report, showed little reluctance to use the document to advance an interpretation of the heat wave that absolved the city government from serious accountability for the crisis. The executive summary frames the disaster as "a *unique meteorological event*" and establishes the city's position that "one of the most valuable lessons of the heat disaster was that government alone cannot do it all," even though no critic had argued that it should.[31] These phrases—"government alone cannot do it all," "meteorological event," and "unique"—would become recurrent themes in the city's position on the event, and city officials used these very words in interviews about the disaster. Moreover, the report argues that vulnerable Chicago residents do not want more support from the city. "Research presented to the Commission," it claims, "indicated that those most at risk may be least likely to want or accept help from government."[32] Rather than recommending new programs, the commission exhorts individuals and communities to take care of themselves, calling for nongovernmental actors to begin "reaching out to those who are most isolated and fearful through the networks they already know and trust: community groups, churches and synagogues, ethnic associations and other community based organizations."[33] The Mayor's Office, in the end, was able to use the commission to promote a position that would have been more difficult to consolidate in a contentious city hearing.

SPINNING OUT OF THE CRISIS

In some respects the Chicago government appears unusually creative in its management of the potential political crisis imposed by the violent heat storm. City officials mobilized a diverse set of rhetorical strategies for defining and framing the disaster, and in the Mayor's Commission on Extreme Weather Conditions the Office of the Mayor found a powerful institutional mechanism for establishing a public record that would support its version of the event.[34] Yet when viewed within the history of government responses to cases in which political agencies are charged with condoning, contributing to, or failing to prevent casualties among their citizens, it is clear that the Chicago city government's reaction to the heat wave followed a predictable pattern of distancing and denial. Twentieth-century history has made us well aware that governments accused of overseeing or committing atrocities often engage in a sophisticated politics of denial to refuse responsibility. In his book, *States of Denial: Knowing about Atrocities and Suffering,* and in an article in *Human Rights Quarterly,* sociologist Stanley Cohen documents a range of specific techniques that states have used to deny involvement in cases where they are suspected of violating human rights or committing acts of violence.[35] Cohen's catalog of the common forms of denial includes the following:

- *Literal denial:* "The fact or knowledge of the fact is denied."
- *Interpretive denial:* "The raw facts are not being denied. Rather, they are given a different meaning from what seems apparent to others. . . . What is happening is really something else."
- *Implicatory denial, or denial of responsibility:* "To attribute responsibility to forces—named or unnamed—that supposedly have nothing to do with the government and are beyond its control."
- *Denial of voice, or silencing:* Using political authority to mute damaging reports.
- *Denial of realist language, or renaming:* "Using euphemisms to disguise meaning of the event. . . . These are everyday devices for masking, sanitizing, and conferring respectability by using palliative terms."
- *Denial of public record:* Using symbolic power of state to define official version of the event.
- *Denial of pattern:* Claiming that the event is unique and aberrant, historically isolated.[36]

Although the most severe critics accused the Chicago government of committing "murder by public policy," few would equate the soft violence of a failed emergency response to the heat disaster with outright homicide. The meaningful similarity, though, is not with the initial act

Table 10. Official Responses to the Heat Wave

Classic Form of Denial	Chicago Response
Literal denial	• Daley tells reporters not to "blow it out of proportion" and questions the Chief Medical Examiner's accounting.
Interpretive denial	• Daley refuses to accept findings of medical autopsies and challenges death reports: "You can't count everything as heat related."
Silencing	• Health Department official: "She had already received a call from the Mayor's Office with the instruction that no one was to see those numbers. We weren't allowed to say anything."
Denial of responsibility	• Mayor's Commission: "Government alone cannot do it all" and "those most at risk may be least likely to want or accept help." • City Hall and aldermen scapegoat Commonwealth Edison, holding hearings on the utilities provider but not on the city's response. • Mayor's Commission uses natural frame to define heat wave as a "meteorological event."
Blaming the victim	• Alvarez: "We're talking about people who die because they neglect themselves."
Euphemism and renaming	• Daley names the heat wave report the "Mayor's Commission on Extreme Weather Conditions: Final Report."
Isolation	• Mayor's Commission defines heat wave as a "unique meteorological event." • Wilhelm: "We are used to warm summers, but we are not used to what was truly unique. . . . We didn't recognize heat as a disaster until the summer [of 1995]."

Source for forms of denial: Cohen 2001.

of violence but with the public relations response for dismissing criticisms or denying accusations of involvement.

As table 10 shows, the city's official response to the disaster contained all the major elements in Cohen's list of denial strategies. First, Mayor Daley engaged in literal denial by calling for residents and reporters not to "blow it out of proportion" and questioning the death totals reported by the Cook County Office of the Medical Examiner. Second, when the scene at the morgue made it impossible to deny the deaths, the city used interpretive denial to refuse the association between the surge in mortality levels and the heat. Daley's argument that "you can't count everything as heat-related" provoked skepticism about whether the crisis was "really real" that continues to this day. Third, the city made several arguments that other parties or forces, including Commonwealth Edison and nature, were responsible for the crisis. This position remains the city's official explanation of the event. Fourth, a key official blamed the victims, "who died because they neglected to take care of themselves,"[37] and others chastised family members for leaving their relatives to die alone. Fifth, mayoral aides instructed officials in other departments to say nothing about the death totals they had discovered, thereby silencing scientific authorities who offered more information about the crisis. Sixth, the Office of the Mayor used the euphemistic title "Final Report: Mayor's Commission on Extreme Weather Conditions" to remove the immediate referent to the crisis and deflect attention from the city's formal analysis of the disaster. Seventh, and finally, city officials adopted the language of isolation and uniqueness, explaining that "we are used to warm summers, but we are not used to what is truly unique" and defining the crisis as a "unique meteorological event," to suggest that no reasonable person could expect the government to be prepared for a heat epidemic. Although this reasoning could not explain why the city had developed and then ignored its own heat emergency plan, it remained a key part of the government's public position.[38]

City employees responsible for monitoring Chicago's public health during the heat wave reported that another important consequence of City Hall's efforts to downplay the severity of the crisis and challenge the death reports is that it undermined their efforts to sound internal alarms and activate emergency programs. According to one key member of the Department of Health at the time,

> When Daley denied the Chief Medical Examiner's reports he defined everything that the city would do on this for the next six months. You have to understand, there were nine refrigerated trucks holding bodies in the parking lot of the morgue, a long line of police cars delivering more, and there is the mayor—mayor of the third-largest city in the United States—denying that people were dying, or later denying that the deaths had anything to do with the heat. Imagine what the mayor's position on the heat wave did for the morale of other city employees and city agencies, or how it limited their capacity to do their work. Once the mayor took the position that the death rates were overstated it became impossible for city employees to say anything else. We were forced to find all sorts of ways to reframe the issue or to talk around what was happening. We couldn't contest his position, and in this case that meant we couldn't be fully explicit about what we were finding.

The city's public relations campaign did more than influence public knowledge about the heat crisis. It also altered the local government's organizational capacity to address the encroaching health hazards by encouraging or enforcing bureaucratic denial in the very agencies that might otherwise have mobilized an effective response.

Policy scholars are surely accurate when they explain that media management skills are essential for contemporary political officials and administrations, yet there is little evidence for the argument that good public relations makes for better—and not simply more popular—government. "To be effective," policy scholar Mordecai Lee claims, "modern public administrators need to act as policy entrepreneurs, especially at the problem-defining stage of the policy process."[39] But, we may ask, effective at what? During the heat wave, leading Chicago politicians used their public relations skills to defend their agencies' legitimacy, engaging in a version of policy entrepreneurialism and problem-defining work that compromised rather than improved the city's emergency health response. Unlike the blizzard of 1979, the mayor and his administration suffered no major political consequences from the heat wave, so it appears that the city was extraordinarily effective in its campaign to deflect accountability and defend itself from charges of mismanagement or neglect. Governing by publicity allowed the city administration to stave off a political disaster but not to coordinate an adequate public health response.

There were other consequences of the city's successful public relations campaign. During the crisis, the codes of silence and the multiple forms of political denial undertaken by public officials prevented city agencies from activating emergency programs to address problems requiring rapid intervention. Would the Fire Department have issued a mutual aid boxed alarm system alert and called in more paramedics and firefighters if City Hall had sounded emergency warnings rather than muted the mortality reports? Would the Police Department have activated its Senior Units and Neighborhood Relations programs if the city had worked to coordinate an interagency response? Would the Health Department have issued more aggressive calls for help if the Office of the Mayor had not demanded that the agency repress its estimated death figures? City employees in each of these agencies believe that the answer to these questions is yes; if they are right, the political history of the heat wave illustrates dangers of governing by public relations that deserve more serious scrutiny.

Yet the second consequence of the successful public relations campaign in the heat wave is that it has blocked the very process of social and political analysis that a more searching investigation into the disaster might have generated. By publishing its heat wave report under a euphemistic title that disguised the content of the inquiry, the Office of the Mayor moved to close off the public discussion about the significance of the trauma rather than open it up. The content of the executive summary also appears designed to deflect attention from the political implications of the event. The commission is surely accurate when it claims that citizens, families, and community organizations need to look out for and support one another, particularly the most vulnerable, and that "government alone cannot do it all" when it comes to protecting city residents from heat waves. But such rhetorical positioning obscures what might have been the disaster's most significant revelations: first, that the city government's social protection systems are undermined by the mismatch between the format of its programs and the risks that its most vulnerable residents, including the emerging population of isolated seniors, face; and second, that when societies and their governments fail to provide basic protection for the health and welfare of their most vulnerable citizens, external forces beyond their control can be uncontrollably dangerous.

Finally, the city's public relations campaign to manage the disaster had an impact on the journalistic coverage of the heat wave. Once the Medical Examiners Office announced the mortality figures, news agencies everywhere sent journalists to Chicago to get the story. If the heat wave represented a potential disaster for Chicago's citizens and officials, for news agencies the event marked a major opportunity to reach the public. Disasters always rank among the most popular forms of news content, and the spectacular scene of refrigerated trucks and dead bodies at the morgue provided journalists with especially dramatic images for their accounts. The political maneuvering at City Hall and the emergence of a conflict between the mayor and the Chief Medical Examiner established a second source of intrigue, thereby orienting journalistic attention toward the official debate over whether the deaths were "really real" and away from other possible subjects and frames.[40]

In theory, journalists are supposed to act as little more than mediators of information for a public that has time for and interest in only a select number of current events. But in practice, journalistic mediation takes the form of a professionally structured process through which news reporters and their sources play major roles in symbolically constructing issues and events.[41] The newsroom, then, is a key point of production for the symbolic life of the city. In the heat wave, as in normal times, what happened inside city news organizations shaped the ways that audiences perceived and did not perceive the catastrophe around them. So it is to the newsrooms of Chicago that we turn next.

CHAPTER FIVE

The Spectacular City

News Organizations and the Representation of Catastrophe

O n Wednesday, 12 July, the late-night newscast on Chicago's ABC television affiliate opened with a dramatic close-up of a full moon ablaze in orange and yellow light. The sweltering city dwellers below could be excused for mistaking the sight for a second sun. Although it was close to midnight the heat index was above one hundred degrees, and there was no sign of relief. It was "a summer sizzler on a moonlit night," anchorman John Drury announced as the camera panned to shots of people walking the streets. "On the ground, residents are seeking relief any way they can. . . . The heat is on, and tomorrow will be the hottest day of all." After a quick series of shots between the news desk and overloaded air-conditioning units, the cameras turned to a live view of Marquette Park on the South Side, where a group of children rejoiced in the shower of a powerful water fountain and defied the evening heat. Standing before them, reporter John Garcia began to recount the city's struggle to keep cool (fig. 42). First the screen showed disabled generators at a Commonwealth Edison plant, and then the face of an elderly woman who explained that without power, she "had to go to the basement where it's cool." Next the footage moved to the inside of an appliance store, where anxious Chicagoans clad in shorts and tee shirts scrambled for air conditioners and loaded the heavy units into their cars. "I can't take the heat," a shopper told Garcia, and then a grinning store manager assured the newsman that the customer was not alone. "It's going great. I'm happy to see it," the merchant exclaimed. The store had received a new shipment of air conditioners a few hours before, and already they were selling out.

Garcia's report continued and the camera moved again. Suddenly there was daylight and a panoramic view of bikinied swimmers at North Avenue Beach, where some ninety thousand city dwellers descended to treat themselves to what the reporter called "nature's air conditioner";

Figure 42. ABC7 reporter John Garcia gestures toward children playing in water. "High lows" (elevated evening temperatures) made the climate exceptionally dangerous during the heat wave. Source: ABC7. Courtesy of WLS-TV.

then a shot of Human Services Commissioner Daniel Alvarez, who was perched in front of the Chicago city seal, advising people with respiratory problems to stay indoors; finally, back to the newsroom, where meteorologist Jerry Taft summed up the conditions. "It's pretty amazing," he said. "The heat index, right now, makes it feel like one hundred degrees—at ten o'clock at night. . . . Tomorrow will be a dangerous day, actually, for a lot of people, although uncomfortable for most."

The Thursday evening broadcast began similarly. Producers led the news with footage of the sun setting in a smog-filled sky and radiating the number 104 in burnt-orange figures on the screen. Drury, again at the anchor's desk, noted the record temperature and warned that "the heat isn't over yet." The cameras skipped to a public swimming pool crammed with dozens of children, then to a street scene of dozens more dancing in the spray of a fire hydrant, one of three thousand illegally opened that day. The image of young people frolicking in water had already become an emblem for the heat wave coverage (see fig. 43). It would recur throughout the week, seamlessly woven into video sequences containing shots of dead bodies, exhausted relief workers, city officials, and weather maps to make a surreal mosaic of the steaming city.[1]

Figure 43. A standard image in the heat wave coverage: young people playing in the spray of an open fire hydrant. Source: ABC7. Courtesy of WLS-TV.

"With the heat," Drury announced, "a serious water problem. . . . Some communities, at times, have lost water pressure completely." The newscast grew somber as coanchor Diann Burns reported that "tonight there's word that the heat wave has now turned deadly in Chicago." Chief Medical Examiner Edmund R. Donoghue said that two men, one eighty-six years of age, the other thirty-two, were the first casualties of the heat; a South Side hospital listed another man in critical condition with a body temperature of 108 degrees. Next Burns introduced reporter Paul Meincke, who narrated footage of irritated African-American residents in two South Side neighborhoods. Open hydrants there had caused water pressure loss serious enough to deplete water supplies, yet the Water Department had not repaired the problem. The contrast between the dry apartment taps and the drenched streets below was striking.

As Chicagoans awaited relief, the national and international news media picked up the story. Cable News Network assigned correspondent Mark Leff to report on the Midwestern casualties, animal and human, and to track the heat storm moving toward the East Coast. On National Public Radio's *All Things Considered,* Chicago-based correspondent Ira Glass reported the air-conditioning crunch story along with an account of two men who tried to sleep outdoors but were driven back inside by police, beggars, and bugs.

As the environment grew more dangerous the two major Chicago newspapers, the *Chicago Tribune* and *Chicago Sun-Times,* organized the most comprehensive efforts to cover and reconstruct the story. When the Chief Medical Examiner announced the rising death rates the journalistic production teams changed gears. The heat wave shifted from a light feature about the weather to a sensational disaster story demanding extensive coverage. There was no shortage of raw material. Dead bodies were piling up at the Cook County Office of the Medical Examiner and police officers were delivering more every hour; political officials were beginning to bicker and City Hall was organizing news conferences to manage the complaints; Com Ed generators were failing and thousands of residents and businesses were stranded in the heat; hospitals were closing their doors to patients seeking emergency care and ambulances were circling the region in search of empty beds; city workers were hosing down children like cattle; concrete roads were buckling. Journalists had all the ingredients to render the heat wave as a spectacle of dramatic proportions (see fig. 44).

Figure 44. The spectacular city. Source: ABC7. Courtesy of WLS-TV.

NEWS AND DISASTERS

Like city agencies, news organizations have standardized routines for managing disasters, so when editors receive reports of an exceptional event in their area they are supposed to trigger their mechanisms for producing expanded coverage.[2] During crises governments often rely on major local media outlets to provide citizens with important information, including public health tips and suggestions about available sources of support. The media's public service obligations are limited, though: in practice, journalistic organizations structure their reporting according to their own professional standards and interests. Disaster stories rank among the most popular forms of journalism, and U.S. news agencies are known to feature them prominently.[3] But events such as the heat wave present newsmakers with difficult challenges because such occurrences exacerbate the tensions between informing and entertaining, analyzing and sensationalizing, explaining and dramatizing, that have become so prominent in news culture.

According to one of the most influential theories in the sociology of the media, accidental news events such as the heat wave are also important because they disrupt the routines through which journalists and the key sources on whom they habitually rely construct the news, thereby forging a division between those who promote the event as news and the parties who are responsible for the occurrence. In their article, "News As Purposive Behavior," Harvey Molotch and Marilyn Lester argue that an unanticipated event in which this customary social order breaks down not only opens possibilities for disruptive parties to compete in defining the story, but can also "foster revelations which are otherwise deliberately obfuscated" because "the suddenness of the accident and its unanticipated nature means that event makers are initially not ready and thus the powerful could give uncoordinated, mutually contradictory accounts."[4] Molotch and Lester explain that not all accidents become public events, but those that do give the resulting news coverage great potential to illuminate conditions that are otherwise difficult to perceive. In this way, such news events often serve as pivotal historical phenomena.

The 1995 Chicago heat wave fits many of Molotch and Lester's criteria for an accidental news event. The disaster was an unanticipated occurrence in which several hundred city residents died, and it quickly became a major local and national news story. Key officials had not prepared for the crisis, and they did, in fact, make incompatible and deceptive claims about it. A few unfamiliar groups and marginal political players attempted to use the disaster to promote their agendas; and, after the heat subsided, city officials made a sustained effort to restore order and impose their analysis of the event as its official record. Yet several elements of the disaster did not live up to the predictions Molotch and Lester proffer. Despite the "inherent drama, sensation, and atypicality of accidents [that make] it . . . difficult to deny their existence," public officials generated widespread skepticism that the deaths were "really real," sparking a debate over the impact of the disaster that lingers to this day. Although "typically unimportant groups can more easily hold sway in the temporal demarcation process" through which events are defined, during the heat wave marginal political players and community organizations, such as Metro Seniors in Action and the Task Force for Black Political Empowerment, received little attention in the mainstream media. And, if the public silence about the conditions that made the heat wave so deadly is an appropriate barometer, the event did not "provide the local public . . . insights into the everyday functioning" of the city that make accidents and disasters "a crucial resource in the empirical study of event-structuring processes."[5] Far from initiating a serious inquiry or probing public discussion about the social or political conditions contributing to the lethal nature of the event, most of the reporting framed the heat wave as a natural disaster and social spectacle, a novel and engaging human interest story but not a revelator of emerging or emergency concerns.

WHAT'S NEWS?

What were the professional responsibilities of the reporters and editors who worked on the heat wave stories for various news outlets? According to conventional theories of the news media, and especially those advanced by journalists themselves, "the essence of real journalism . . . is the search for information of use to the public."[6] "Prevailing wisdom," Jay Rosen writes, holds that journalists "give us timely information about matters of common importance; they entertain and enlighten us with compelling stories; they act as our surrogate and watchdog before the high and mighty, asking sharp questions and demanding straight answers; they expose wrongdoing and the abuse of public trust; and they put before us a range of views, through opinion forums marked as such."[7] But in practice, news audiences have always demanded that journalists do more—or maybe less—than provide them with information that will help them act as responsible democratic citizens.

Journalists themselves disagree about the kinds of roles they should play in reporting public events such as the heat wave. During the crisis local newsrooms became the sites of conflicts between editors who wanted to generate large audiences through spectacular human interest stories and those who wanted to produce more substantive news reporting. But even the combatants in these disputes took for granted that the news coverage would employ standard journalistic material such as sensational visual images, provocative headlines, and dramatic story leads that cause little controversy in the newsroom and exert great influence over the content of the coverage. News audiences expect the media to entertain them with spectacles that animate the world. As Daniel Boorstin writes, "we have shifted responsibility for making the world interesting from God to the newspaperman,"[8] and most journalistic organizations are designed to serve this role. Yet the major news organizations, particularly reputable and award-winning papers such as the *Chicago Tribune*, are generally committed to a professional ethic that values rigorous and serious journalism. Balancing the market's demand for novelty, drama, and spectacle with the journalistic imperative to produce quality news is one of the great challenges of the news team.[9]

We have already seen how local officials managed to spin the heat crisis in terms that would block insights into the social and political features of the event. This chapter examines how journalists—particularly those at the news organizations that produced the most thorough and multifaceted disaster coverage and are known for maintaining high standards—contributed to the symbolic construction of the disaster.[10] Scholars of social problems typically conduct surveys of news coverage to assess how journalists represent issues or events for their audiences, but they rarely analyze conditions in which reporters and editors produce their accounts. One consequence of this research strategy is that most social scientists do a more convincing job of *showing that* news organizations *distort* their coverage or omit key issues from their stories than of *illustrating how* journalists come up with such representations. Another is that, without sifting through the messy world of journalistic practice, social problems scholars tend to analytically unify the media and even individual news companies in the same way that they unify the state, treating "the media" as a monolithic actor rather than as a differentiated set of institutions. This chapter begins with a content analysis of the major news reporting on the heat wave. But then, rather than speculating about the reasons journalists constructed their stories as they did, the focus shifts to the newsrooms and newsmakers who, through an elaborate process of cultural production, transformed the disaster into a mediated public event.

Although Chicago political officials worked vigilantly to frame the heat disaster in favorable terms and aggressively used their resources for shaping news coverage, the journalistic production of the heat wave news was not a mere "'exercise of power over the interpretation of reality.' "[11] Media critics often speak of major journalistic organizations as conveyors of dominant positions and viewpoints, but news agencies do not *reflect* the perspectives of powerful actors and event makers so much as they *refract* them through a layered set of institutional processes and reporting techniques.[12] When the heat settled into Chicago, for example, news teams began their typical process of discovering and selecting the news during an unexpected situation, determining which events were newsworthy, choosing the appropriate frames in which they should be cast, and assigning reporters, photographers, and copy editors to the stories. As always, reporters and editors quickly referred to other media accounts, placing themselves in a closed network of credible information in which the relations among different media and media organizations shape the kind of stories that various news teams produced. Once they began their reporting, journalists had to select the sources who would provide the expert commentary or opinion that animated or directed the reports. Editors had to determine where to place the stories in the paper or broadcast, thus designating whether the heat emergency would receive prominent attention from its audience or get buried out of sight.[13] Editors and copy editors had to produce headlines and story titles that attracted audiences whose attention was rarely assured. And once the heat had subsided and the death toll had been tallied, news organizations had to judge the event's significance and decide whether to produce or publish a retrospective account. By looking at the social and organizational processes through which journalists symbolically produced the heat wave as a public event, we can assess the exogenous pressures and internal constraints that affected the disaster reporting.

As the heat wave ran its course, local and national news companies produced hundreds of stories about the disaster, with the Chicago newspapers probing deepest into its nature and causes and integrating the broadest range of editorial content and opinion into their coverage. Relative to local television news, the printed media offer more space for extended and varied treatment of important issues, so it is not surprising that the papers produced more depth, diversity, and detailed reporting in their packages of heat wave stories.[14] Newspapers produce more content than do television or radio, and the multisectioned structure by which they are organized allows editors to present conflicting ideas or opinions in forms that managers in other media do not make available. The *Chicago Tribune,* for example, published roughly 119 news stories, 13 editorials and letters, and 11 news briefs during and immediately after the crisis; the *Chicago Sun-Times* printed 99 news stories, 12 news briefs, 14 editorials and letters, and approximately 30 assorted reports and commentaries. No other news organizations matched the amount of research and reporting that went into the newspaper projects or contributed so much to the public record of the event.

Despite its relative depth and diversity, however, the newspaper accounts of the disaster necessarily focused on the particular sites, issues, and images that made for good copy while marginalizing others. As the newspaper content analyses presented in tables 11 and 12 show,[15] the representations of the heat wave stories in the major local papers

Table 11. Content Analysis of Heat Wave Stories: *Chicago Tribune* (July 1995 to July 1996)

Frame	Text	Title	Image
Deaths and morgue	58	52	35
City government responses	37	28	14
Individuals and coping strategies	36	34	45
Meteorological conditions	29	50	30
Political scandal and death debate	26	24	4
Aging	10	6	12
Isolation	9	8	4
Poverty	3	2	NA
Crime and safety	2	2	NA
Ethnoracial issues	2	2	NA

Table 12. Content Analysis of Heat Wave Stories: *Chicago Sun-Times* (July 1995 to July 1996)

Frame	Text	Title	Image
Deaths and morgue	37	51	23
City government responses	38	36	10
Individuals and coping strategies	42	41	19
Meteorological conditions	23	35	9
Political scandal and death debate	21	20	2
Aging	11	8	7
Isolation	8	8	4
Poverty	4	3	3
Crime and safety	2	2	NA
Ethnoracial issues	0	0	NA

emphasized the deaths and scene at Cook County Morgue, the natural or meteorological conditions, the coping strategies of individuals trying to stay cool, and the city's rhetorical and institutional responses to the health emergency. Photographic images of the dead bodies, the morgue, and the use of water to combat the heat were especially prominent. The content analysis also shows that local news organizations de-emphasized some of the social conditions that affected the impact of the disaster. There were relatively few stories or images focusing on aging, poverty, isolation, crime and fear, and the ethnoracial or gender distribution of mortality, morbidity, and access to care.

The overall distribution of news stories and images should not imply that the papers neglected to provide any in-depth reporting about the social etiology of the disaster. Indeed, amidst the dominant frames of natural disaster and massive mortality, both the *Tribune* and *Sun-Times* published exemplary pieces of news reporting about people who died alone and those who managed to make it; neighborhood conditions that made some areas especially vulnerable; and emergency city programs that were not mobilized. These stories were marginal parts of the overall package, though, and often were buried in the back sections and inside pages that fewer readers see. Analyzing the content of newspaper articles helps to establish the general economy of the heat wave coverage, but explaining how and why local journalistic organizations framed and focused their coverage on some issues at the expense of others requires shifting attention from the news stories themselves to the newsrooms where the stories were produced. There is no better place to do this than the *Chicago Tribune,* the city's most renowned and respected news organization, and by many accounts the source of the most thorough and serious heat wave coverage. The story of the *Tribune*'s heat wave reporting, reconstructed from the written record as well as interviews with many of the editors and reporters who worked on the catastrophe, provides a window into the conditions of contemporary news work that helped transform the disaster into a dramatic spectacle and public event.

DISCOVERING DISASTER

On Saturday morning, 15 July, veteran reporter George Papajohn was filling in for an editor on the *Chicago Tribune* Metro desk.[16] By journalistic standards, the amount of newsworthy activity during summer weekends in Chicago is low. Local officials seldom hold weekend news conferences, many businesses are closed, and the public relations teams that feed news organizations with information slow the pace of their work.[17] As Papajohn explained, "generally the Saturday shift is a fairly quiet one. Obviously the government is shut down; the paper has spent all week producing its giant piece of journalism [the Sunday edition] and the stories are generally enterprise stories that you have to play around with. But you're there, editing, to fill in some of the news and update the stories."

Papajohn began his workday by taking up his routine for generating story ideas. He had been following the heat wave coverage closely, watching the television news reports at home and listening to radio while driving to work. In the office he looked over the daily papers, scanned both the national and the City News Bureau wire reports, skimmed the large pile of faxes sent to the *Tribune*, talked with the paper's bureau chief, listened to voice mail, and chatted with fellow reporters. Papajohn soon began to realize that something unusual was happening.

> I was coming in and I had heard on the radio . . . that the Medical Examiners Office was looking into a number of deaths that they thought could be associated with the heat wave. . . . We were still in the mode of gee, it's really hot, you know. What does that mean? . . . However, it seemed to me that, just based on what I heard on news radio, that we ought to make sure we were pursuing the other thing, and that we shouldn't pursue anything else until we made sure we didn't have a major news story on our hands. And then, the other sort of routine thing to do is you sign on the computer and the City News Bureau wires are there,[18] and they're sort of the local AP,[19] they're the people out there who send things out over the wires. You look at that every day. Twice a day they update the Medical Examiner's list of deaths they're investigating. This is normally a list that could be anywhere from five to ten names, but on this day it was just an incredibly thick list that not only was thick, it went on for three thick paragraphs. . . . That was when *I became very certain that we had to just completely shift gears.* . . . And it sort of fell into place after that.

Lou Carlozo, then a suburban reporter who worked the Saturday afternoon shift downtown, was in the newsroom when Papajohn decided to change the focus of the heat wave coverage.

> So I'm on the desk on Saturday and George is looking through the wire reports. And George is shaking his head and he's like, "Something is not right." There are all these people dying and he says, "I wonder if we have the makings of a catastrophe here. Because it is hot, it has been hot. If this many people are being brought to the morgue, who knows how many

people are out there waiting to be discovered?" So immediately . . . he made a couple of us go in pool cars. I was one of the people. He said I want you to go, go to these addresses. Find out everything you can, talk to as many people as you can, learn about these people.

The *Tribune* had originally reported the heat wave exclusively as a meteorological event, describing it with little detail and placing it in the weather section of the paper. On Wednesday, 12 July, though, the temperature matched a Chicago record and the *Tribune* editors were impressed enough to make the heat a front-page feature, the kind that newspapers conventionally publish on days when the climate is extreme enough to affect normal conditions. In the story, which was printed in the Thursday edition, two reporters crafted a light account of residents' coping strategies out of interviews with a number of city visitors and nonnatives who spoke about the heat in their home cities. The article implored Chicagoans to stop complaining about their discomfort. Headlined "If You Can Stand the Heat, You Must be Out-of-Towner" and set beneath a photograph of a park worker hosing herself down, the piece opened, "Stop your whining. So what if it got up to 97 degrees on Wednesday, tying the record. . . . Even though tens of thousands of Chicago-area residents probably suffered through the first day of an anticipated week-long heat wave, for many others, Wednesday's weather was just a walk in the park."[20] Continuing to frame the heat wave event as a humorous feature, the *Tribune* editors next sent a reporter in search of air conditioners, taking up the same theme used by local and national television news reports. The article was also scheduled to make page 1, but when Papajohn and the other editors learned about the ominous death toll on Friday, they realized that they had to change the frame of the story as well as the practical work of producing it. From then until the city cooled down, the *Tribune* would make this coverage its top priority.

George Papajohn had substituted as an editor enough to develop a system for learning about the news on the days in which he "worked the desk," a routine similar to the one he kept as a reporter. He depends heavily on other news media to generate story ideas, with radio broadcasts playing a prominent role because radio reporters can produce fast journalism and late-breaking news by simply reading wire stories as they come into the studio. Little production work or time is necessary for these broadcasts, and although the reports are thinly written, print journalists can use them as points of departure for more-developed accounts. Television news stories, especially now that Chicago and many other cities have local twenty-four-hour news television stations, usually provide the first visual images of events, yet they are seldom longer than a few minutes.[21] Other newspapers suggest additional angles to stories that the *Tribune* staff is likely to have already covered or considered covering. Only occasionally do papers scoop each other on daily news reports in an era when the news cycle has exploded into a twenty-four-hour-a-day news cyclone.

The newsroom itself is saturated with other mainstream news media. Part of the reason that newsmakers in the major media employ conventional frames and themes, such as the story of city residents looking for air conditioners or the image of children playing in water, is that by continuously reading, watching, and listening to their colleagues' reports they internalize a set of routine story types that are easily reproducible in the time constraints that organize journalistic work.[22] The formal and informal training journalists undergo is only a small part of their socialization into the profession. Like other professionals, they are continuously trained on the job and their approaches to the news are regularly reinforced when they consume, critique, and mimic the work of their colleagues. Although journalists write or produce information for the public, they are one another's most important and responsive audience; indeed, several reporters explained that colleagues are their most vigorous critics and supporters. If it is true that, as Manuel Castells argues, members of most contemporary societies "live with the media and by the media," daily journalists live *in* the media, forming a subculture and a "vicious informational cycle" that affirms the importance of issues that interest other journalists but excludes alternative ideas that might otherwise be considered newsworthy.[23]

At the *Tribune*, for example, news stories from other local organizations played a key role in switching the focus of the early heat wave coverage. Hearing the radio reports and reading the other papers helped Papajohn recognize that as the story changed from a weather report to a breaking and continuing feature on a local catastrophe, the *Tribune* had to shift its journalistic strategy and devote more resources to the event. The feature on air conditioners still ran on Sunday, as did a women's fashion piece instructing how to stay cool in the heat and headlined "Gimme Swelter! It's the Height of the Steamy Season, But the Heat Doesn't Have to Sap Your Style. Here's How to Ward Off Wardrobe Wilt and Make-up Meltdown." But neither story made the front section, which featured more serious news reports on the mounting death count.

By Saturday afternoon, 15 July, the editors had decided to increase their coverage of the deaths by sending reporters to the Medical Examiners Office and to the addresses of the deceased, which were included in the mortality lists released by the office. The problem was that the paper generally produces little news on Saturday and Sunday, and some of the weekend staff lacked the experience and the skills that the news editors considered necessary to adequately cover the big story. As one experienced reporter explained, "You have to understand how the *Tribune* works on weekends. There's really not a lot of people here, and a lot of the people who work here on the weekends are the younger staff. So we have a lot of "one-years" [junior reporters hired on one-year contracts] and interns. And they have varying abilities. And most of them don't know the city."

The timing of the disaster on the weekend affected the manner in which the *Tribune* covered it in the first news reports. The shortage of staff was particularly severe on Sunday, the first day that everyone at the paper knew how serious the disaster was, because most of the experienced editors and writers were attending the annual editorial picnic. Yet as a daily procedure, including weekends, the editors on duty have a list of reporters and editors whom they can call if they need additional staffing for a breaking story. During the heat wave they could not have produced the paper without it.

Cindy Schreuder, one of the lead science writers at the *Tribune*, was working on a special project during July and was therefore not involved in production of the daily paper at the time. That Sunday she happened to be heading into the office to work on her series when she was asked to help with the heat wave coverage. The editors had decided that the story needed a medical and environmental perspective, and they wanted a senior science writer to oversee the reporting. Schreuder recalled,

> I was almost walking out the door [when] my telephone rang and it was the Metro editor, and he asked me if I could go downtown and help coordinate the coverage of the heat wave. [He] said, you know, the people we have on this are mostly one-years and he was a little concerned that they just didn't have the experience for what this might turn out to be. When I went down that day I talked to some of the others to find out what they were doing, whom they were calling. Later in the evening there was some sort of discrepancy in the stories we were getting from people in different places. I got a little concerned so I started making some calls. The original lead that I had on that first story was a soft feature. But as the night wore on it was clear that there were a lot of deaths

and that was totally inappropriate. So I started making more calls and I suddenly realized that what we had on our hands was a really large death toll. It became clear that I was going to have to dump [my project] and report on this story."

At the picnic, the editors remained worried about their paper's coverage of the emerging crisis. They were vexed by the reports from the Medical Examiners Office and by the early statements from City Hall that expressed skepticism over the coroner's findings. The situation provoked a conflict among the editors, with some of them sympathetic to Mayor Daley's initial claims that the mortality figures were overstated, while others were convinced that the city was experiencing a genuine catastrophe.

News organizations, with their large editorial and reporting teams and their rigid division of labor, are not unified actors but participants in a field of institutional players that operates collectively and relationally. Within the *Tribune* there are daily competitions among the various reporters and section teams, all of whom vie for the front-page spots and big headlines that make and mark the significance and success of their work. There are boundaries that limit the range of editorial content and opinion that will be produced by any given journalistic organization. Pierre Bourdieu argues that, in fact, "competition homogenizes when it occurs between journalists or newspapers subject to identical pressures and opinion polls, and with the same basic cast of commentators. . . . Just compare the weekly newsmagazine covers at two-week intervals and you'll find nearly identical headlines." News production is a collective process, and "journalists—who in any case have much in common, profession of course, but also social origin and education—meet one another daily in debates that always feature the same cast of characters. All of which produces [mental] closure."[24] Within these constraints, though, journalists experience real and intense conflicts over how news will be covered and placed, as well as professional pressure to produce original and distinctive work. Reporters and editors who engage in such daily struggles over the form and content of their work discount the argument that mainstream media stories are orchestrated by higher powers of elite groups and vested interests. But many journalists, including an increasing number of prominent figures, recognize that the insular professional networks and the institutional structure of the field have homogenized news production and limited the vitality of the public sphere.[25]

During the heat wave the initial disputes among the editors, reporters, and producers at several Chicago news organizations were notably acute. Meteorologist Paul Douglas, who was reporting on the crisis for a local television station, newspaper company, and radio station, recalled a conflict he had had with a television producer about whether to frame the coverage as a human interest story or as a public health warning and news story:

> I came in early on the worst of the days, when it got up to 106, and our executive producer came over, and we were very proactive. We went to the producers and we said, "This is going to be a major story. People are going to be dying. This is something you'd better hit very, very hard. What can and should we be doing at other times of the day? Should we be interrupting programs with heat alerts?" And I believe that afternoon we did interrupt programming, even before the news began. We had a couple of cut-ins, where we talked about the extreme heat and the extreme danger. But I'll never forget, [the executive producer] kept coming over to us she kept asking, she wanted to do a live shot with some place in the United States that would be hotter than Chicago. She kept talking about wanting to do a live shot with a meteorologist in Phoenix. . . . You know, basically making it more of a *featury,* lifestyle kind of cutesy—"hey, let's have the dueling meteorologists try to figure out who's hotter"—story. . . . And I kept pleading with her and telling her, "You're missing the point. We should have people at the hospitals, we should have people at City Hall." And it degenerated into a shouting match in the newsroom. She started screaming, "You don't get it, you don't get it! This is television!" And I said, "I do get it. I understand. This is a dangerous situation for Chicago. We are the hottest spot. People will be dying later today. That's your story."

Douglas was pleased with his producers' decision to clear time for public service announcements before the news, as well as with the placement of the weather stories early in the news broadcasts. The human interest frames and feature stories seemed inappropriate to him given the danger of the situation, but the television program accommodated the inchoate streams of light images and heavy ideas that blend together to make the news exciting and fresh. The producers, who are ultimately responsible for the broadcast, decided that the human interest stories made better television, and therefore better news.

The early reports of rising heat-related mortality convinced most news organizations to shift the direction of their coverage, but the mayor's public skepticism about the Chief Medical Examiner's scientific methods was another influence on their decision. At the *Tribune,* some editors had been persuaded by the city government's criticisms of the heat-related death measures and the attributions reported by Ed Donoghue, the Chief Medical Examiner. According to Paul Weingarten, the editor at the Metro desk, his colleagues were initially skeptical of the heat wave death reports: "It was a little unclear at first if this was a normal thing, if there was a re-categorizing somehow, or whether this was truly a cataclysmic event. Because, you know, it had been hot in Chicago before, and we were all saying, could one day have killed so many people?" Schreuder felt the tension even from her office. "There was a little disagreement among the editors on the staff. What was going on here? Was this *really real*? Is there really more [mortality] or are people more aware of it? That was the question that was being raised about this. Were deaths that would normally have happened anyway being attributed to the heat wave? Were these people who might have lived only a week longer, or only three days longer, how sick are they?" One key question, reporter Graeme Zielinski explained, was "whether the coverage was being driven by the event or the event was being driven by the coverage. The heat wave had become a cliché almost as soon as it began. Here in the newsroom people were making fun of it, because people make fun of clichés in newsrooms. And 'the heat wave' [he intoned in an anchor's voice] was something that was real present and really real to a lot of people and yet it didn't seem real. It just seemed, it seemed, propped up somehow. There were some editors who were insisting that it was a much bigger deal [in the media] than it was and others who were worried, really worried that we were pushing this thing way too far. You know, that there was overkill." Zielinski's comments express a reflexive awareness of his own role in constructing the heat wave as a public event. But they also show that the process of transforming the disaster into a news spectacle had confused the same journalists who were in charge of clarifying the nature of the occurrence.

WHOSE NEWS? OFFICIAL SOURCES AND JOURNALISTIC ROUTINES

Some of this confusion stems from the distribution of journalistic labor, because general reporters have to cover such a broad range of events and issues that it would be impossible for them to develop expertise in many of them. Key sources, particularly the local officials and large organizations that employ public relations professionals to generate and manage media interest, play an influential role in helping journalists get the "inside scoop" on political matters and thereby in shaping the substance of the reports.[26] Although not all public officials possess public and media relations skills, media-savvy official sources often cultivate relationships with reporters that heighten their trustworthiness during difficult situations. As communications scholar Phyllis Kaniss notes, journalists are sometimes "reluctant to criticize a source who has provided them with information in the past, for fear of alienating the source and stopping the flow of information."[27] They, too, are embedded in symbiotic relationships of accountability, reliance, and trust with their informants. Journalists learn to understand and gain sympathy for the perspectives of their intimate professional contacts, and when regular sources are also officials, reporters are more likely to present their observations as "facts." Occasional sources they find for specialized stories and issues are unknown and less dependable, though, and consequently reporters are disposed to treat their statements or observations as "allegations" that have to be verified before taken seriously.[28]

The early heat wave reporting was especially difficult because few of the city-beat reporters knew where to turn for reliable information that would clarify their questions or settle the emerging dispute between City Hall and the Medical Examiners Office. They had no choice but to seek reports from city agencies even more than usual because the government offices had unmatched access to morbidity and mortality figures and were the only official information sources capable of centralizing knowledge about the diffuse event.[29] The heat-related death controversy became a major theme in the news coverage in part because journalists depended on the organizations generating the conflicting public statements to produce a unified account of the disaster.

Reports from editors and journalists in Chicago indicate that another reason the debate over the death toll became a major news story is that *journalists themselves* were fascinated by the issue. At the *Tribune,* where staff members were engaged in their own internal debate, reporters and columnists began covering the death attribution issue the day after the city administration's first major news conference and continued to press the matter even after medical examiners had collectively moved to support Donoghue's findings, thereby ending the politically charged discussion. On Tuesday, 18 July, for example, the front section of the paper contained two articles questioning the mortality figures. One, authored by the celebrated columnist Mike Royko, was headlined "Killer Heat Wave or Media Event?" The other, a cover story provocatively entitled "Coroners Don't Always Agree on When Heat Kills,"[30] explained that medical examiners did not have a unified set of criteria for classifying deaths as heat related but quoted only one coroner, Barbara Cook from Lake County, who was critical of Do-noghue's findings. Where, then, was the scientific debate? In the fol-lowing days a number of medical examiners and national experts voiced their support for the validity of Donoghue's heat-related death criteria, and when Cook reversed her position only Chicago officials were left to challenge the findings. Nonetheless, journalists dutifully reported the administration's criticisms of the autopsies and wrote as if the scientific debate remained undecided. On 27 July federal officials from the Centers for Disease Control and Prevention confirmed the Chief Medical Examiner's mortality figures, and the *Tribune*'s John Kass wrote that the endorsement was "at least temporarily ending a public debate between Mayor Richard Daley and Dr. Edmund Donoghue."[31]

Two months later, when a study conducted by Chicago public health officials showed that the excess death toll was 733, more than 200 deaths above Donoghue's figure, the *Tribune*'s report implied that CDC officials were skeptical about the science used to arrive at the figure. According to the paper, "a CDC epidemiologist said Wednesday that federal scientists were 'shocked' by the 733 figure compiled by city pub-lic health officials. 'The number is very high,' said Dr. Jan Semenza, who was in Chicago for a month recently to study the heat death toll. 'It was definitely unexpected. We were all surprised.' Semenza said other scientists will have to review the Health Department's method for calcu-lating excess deaths. 'I can't judge whether his methodology was appro-priate to do that.' "[32] The article went on to quote other experts who endorsed the public health study, but it explicitly used Semenza's com-ments to set up another heat wave mortality debate. The problem, how-ever, was that Semenza claimed he never questioned the public health study, and that the scientific conflict was nothing but a journalistic fab-rication. In a letter addressed from the U.S. Department of Health and Human Services to Steven Whitman at the Chicago Department of Pub-lic Health and dated 25 September 1995, Semenza wrote:

I would like to clarify my position in regard to the article that was pub-lished in the *Chicago Tribune* on 9/21/95 concerning the heat wave. Spe-cifically, I would like to rectify the alleged statements on which I was misquoted.

1. The reporter asked me whether I was shocked to learn that 733 people died during the heat wave. I responded: "it is fair to say that we were all surprised at how many people died during the recent heat wave. It was definitely unexpected that the heat would take such a big toll in Chicago. The number is very high. Such a big disaster has never

happened in the history of Chicago." At no point did I question the results of your calculations as the *Chicago Tribune* subsequently conveyed. I stated that I was 'surprised' by the impact of the heat wave in Chicago, not about your calculations. I am confident that the number 733 has been calculated properly.

2. In response to whether your methodology was appropriate, I answered: "I am not in the position to judge whether this methodology is appropriate since I have not seen the results in writing and, furthermore, am not a mathematician. Other people would be in a better position to judge that." I did not say that your methods for calculating excess deaths have to be reviewed by other scientist [sic]. I simply stated that I was not in a position to comment on your methods. . . .

In conclusion, I am neither "shocked" (I never used that word) by the number you calculated nor do I think that the method for calculating excess mortality needs to be reviewed by other scientists.

I am extremely displeased that the *Chicago Tribune* grossly misquoted me and inappropriately used my words to discredit the work of a colleague of mine.

Sincerely yours,
Jan Semenza, Ph.D., M.S., M.P.H.[33]

Semenza's letter effectively accused the *Tribune* reporters of transforming his interview into the source for a false debate, one that only journalists and the political officials who promoted it took seriously. He had good reason. No journalist I interviewed reported that they had focused their attention on the death attribution debate because of a conscious desire to generate or perpetuate a scandalous public contest. But the regular practices of daily news reporters attune them to conflicts that will make for good copy and dramatic reporting, and the Chicago journalists who followed the heat wave stories became so deeply absorbed in their own debates about the death figures that few noticed their own role in promulgating it. All subcultural and professional groups develop their own biases and dispositions, but journalists are unique in their capacity to project their own ways of seeing and thinking into the public sphere, where their ideas often set the terms of broader debates. Despite the efforts of several medical and public health figures, during the heat wave most news consumers had little access to the dominant scientific perspective that the death attributions were legitimate and fair. The journalistically endorsed skepticism over the attributions was available everywhere, though. In part because it was so dramatic, and it part because news outlets never featured the scientific reports that affirmed the Chief Medical Examiner's findings as prominently as they did their own cynical reaction, the legacy of calling the heat wave death figures into question continues to this day.

ALTERNATIVE VOICES AND THE SPACE FOR DISSENT

Epidemiologists and public health scholars were hardly alone in their struggle to reframe the journalistic coverage of the disaster. Outsider activists and community organizations who criticized the city for failing to secure the health of its most precarious residents, and community leaders who demanded more assistance for their constituencies, also received little coverage in the major media; they had no choice but to turn to the smaller, community papers to publicize their positions. A *Tribune* story headlined "Residents Leave Cooling Centers in Cold," for example, quoted Daniel Alvarez, the commissioner of Human Services, Matt Rodriguez, the Police Superintendent, and Mayor Daley as saying that Chicagoans were failing to take advantage of the city's official cooling centers. During the weekend Metro Seniors in Action and other community groups had criticized the city for not providing special transportation to the centers, yet no one other than city officials and a single health care worker was quoted in the article and none of them expressed this position. Other city news agencies treated the story similarly. The *Chicago Sun-Times*, which gave its front-page piece the headline "116 Die; Few Using City Cooling Centers," cited only city officials in its account of the empty centers, but quoted a medical officer from the St. Louis County Health Department who explained that "personal action is the most important thing."[34]

When critics of the city's response to the disaster did appear in the major papers and television news reports they were often relegated to the slot in which journalists, whose professional ethic is to appear objective and neutral and to show both sides of a story, place the dissenting view. Typically, this slot is small enough that the oppositional case is not expressed as completely as are the authoritative views of key sources, which also tend to frame the coverage.[35] On Wednesday, 19 July, for example, the headline for the front-page story in the *Sun-Times* read "The Shocking Toll: 376: Daley Vows to Revise City's Emergency Plan," and Daley provided the lead quotation: "The city did a very good job, but we could have done better." The article, which focused on the city's own effort to assess its emergency response to the heat, outlined several problems that officials had acknowledged. But Daley's spin—"the city did a very good job"—was not challenged by a dissenting voice until the last column of the six-column story, where state senator Robert Raica called the mayor's promise to evaluate the city emergency plan "totally ludicrous" and a Metro Seniors spokesperson explained that "we expect more from [the city]."[36] Although the criticisms are strongly worded, their placement at the back of the story rendered them not only less prominent, but also less challenging to the frame—responsible reaction to a difficult situation, rather than neglect of vulnerable citizens—that organizes the story.

Other news organizations treated dissident voices similarly. In a *Tribune* article headlined "Daley, Aides Try to Deflect Criticism," John Kass, the City Hall beat reporter at the time, quoted city officials repeatedly and followed the administration through a day of news conferences, giving the mayor and city commissioners the space to explain their positions and define the controversy in their own terms. In the twenty-fourth paragraph of the twenty-eight-paragraph story, Commissioner Alvarez affirmed that the city "did everything possible, everything possible." Only after this, in the twenty-fifth paragraph, did the article state that "Metro Seniors in Action, a politically active seniors group, said City Hall failed to provide transportation for seniors to cooling centers, that some centers were inadvertently closed and that the administration should have done more to stress the physical dangers of excessive heat."[37] Not only was the dissenting position buried in the back of the article; there was also no voice from the oppositional organization, nor from any other nongovernmental agency, appearing in the piece. City officials can speak for themselves in the news report, but those who challenge them are often *spoken for* by the media.

The voices of outsiders and activists received more space in the specialized and less influential city publications, such as the *Chicago Defender,* the city's largest African-American paper, and the *Daily Southtown.* On 23 July, for example, *Daily Southtown* published a story entitled "Experts: Daley Won't Feel the Heat for Long," in which reporter Rick Bryant quoted a political consultant about the fallout from the city's incapacity to manage the crisis. "I don't think this will stick," the consultant explained, because "most of the people who were hurt have no organized spokesman. They were the isolated, the dispossessed, the incommunicado, which is why so many of them died." The same edition of the paper also contained an article reporting that twenty-eight of Chicago's fifty-nine ambulances were idle at some point during the heat crisis, along with an interview with an advocate for local seniors who opined that poverty and fear of unmanageable utility bills left the elderly vulnerable to the heat.[38] Yet relatively few Chicago residents or other journalists read these stories, and the perspectives that the alternative sources offered were unlikely to affect either the local political debates or the national coverage of the event. Most of the local news magazines and weekly papers simply ignored the heat disaster. *The Chicago Reporter,* which is the leading local publication on race and poverty issues and an excellent source for rich investigative reporting on inequality in the city, did not recognize the heat wave as relevant to its concerns. When I asked a staff member whether the magazine had reported on the hundreds of seniors who died alone, she responded plainly, "You know, we don't cover stories like that. We deal mostly with race, poverty, and injustice." The natural framing of the disaster, it seemed, had structured the editors' own perceptions of the crisis.

ASSIGNING THE STORY

The organizational structure of the news companies orients their attention and resources to the places and institutions that regularly produce newsworthy events, as does their routine process of framing issues and occurrences as particular story types. The *Tribune,* like the other major city news agencies, has a number of beat reporters who regularly report on a region, an institution, or an issue, as well as a pool of general reporters whom they can use for any kind of story.[39] Events such as the heat wave can disrupt the paper's regular routines for covering the news, but the regular routines and the distribution of human resources also shape the coverage of such crises. Paul Weingarten, the Metro editor in charge of assigning city reporters to the heat wave stories, explained how the organizational structure of the *Tribune*—in this case the presence of beat reporters committed to specific issues or locations—influenced his efforts to cover the crisis:

> I think this is a big story so I start thinking about the kinds of sources of information we're talking about. The Cook County coroner. We have a Cook County beat person, so he or she would know the coroner, would have a relationship with this person and we'd send them over to talk to him rather than someone he doesn't know. You know who your better street reporters are; you know who's better in certain communities; you know who knows the City Hall structure and you've got a City Hall beat, so if it is a matter of deploying forces they are in some cases already out there. You call your reporter in City Hall and say, "What is Daley going to do about this and what is the city doing about the people and cooling centers?" You call your county reporters and say, "Let's go over there and talk to them, what's going on?" Your police reporter, "What are the cops doing?" And just down, down the line.

The *Tribune*'s coverage of the catastrophe was distinctive because the editors not only instructed their specialty writers to follow their beats, but also sent a team of reporters into the streets. Weingarten explained that the editors wanted to interview "survivors and victims' families and to try to figure out who are these people and what were they doing and why did they have to die." This required that general reporters, such as Carlozo and Zielinski, drive to places where people died or lost power and water and search for the human experience and social life of the disaster that would be inaccessible from standard news sites. During the heat wave coverage the editors took responsibility for selecting the kinds of sites, if not the exact locations, that staff reporters would visit, as well as the general questions that reporters would ask. After Papajohn saw the list of deaths on Saturday he sent a team of reporters, each with a list of addresses where people had died, in a pool car that brought them to the death sites. Carlozo recalled,

> It wasn't like I had to go looking for people. I already went out with a name and an address in my hand. . . . I was sent out to a person's home and I think it was up on Milwaukee Avenue maybe just past the Polish part of town. And there was an apartment building and this woman lived on the top floor, which was like the third floor of this very short apartment building. It was blazing hot when I got there, and I went in the building. It had to be easily 120, 130 degrees in there. And the person I interviewed, I believe, was sort of like the liaison for the landlord. She was the caretaker for the building and also for this woman. And she lived there, and I remember her telling me that she had seen the woman earlier, she was very concerned about her and she wanted to see if she needed a fan or anything like that.

The team of reporters with whom Carlozo had been sent out dispersed to find scenes similar to this in different areas of the city. They phoned the editorial desk to convey their discoveries in the field and to receive the next set of directions. At this point in the investigative process the editors, as well as the lead writer for stories involving multiple reporters, had an opportunity to shift or deepen the investigative coverage based on the other information that they had gathered. "Most of the time," Papajohn noted, "we tell reporters on breaking news that they should call from the scene before they come back. Because they're going to tell you something, and maybe you heard something over the wires, or you have an idea and you're going to need them to follow up on that out there. You don't want them to come all the way back." Editors felt pressure to monitor their reporters in the streets because the newspaper's tight production schedule allowed little time for them to coordinate the coverage of a breaking news event.

In addition to assigning field reporters to cover the heat wave, *Tribune* editors selected a few senior staff members to act as the main writers for the larger stories. Like many other large papers, the *Tribune* employs what is generally considered *magazine-style* production practice, in which one lead writer constructs a story based on information generated by a group of reporters, for stories that require substantial reporting. "When we have a big story," the Pulitzer Prize–winning reporter and frequent lead writer Louise Kiernan explained, "we send out fleets of reporters. There's one person who's the lead reporter and the coordinator, which is what I was for [the heat wave] story." Lead writers do some of their own research and although sometimes they may not do any of the reporting, they often participate in all parts of the process. Their main responsibilities are to coordinate reporters, distill their notes from the field, and clarify questions that emerge as they reconstruct the story. The job requires considerable writing and editorial skill, so editors entrust the task to only the most experienced journalists and proven writers on their staff. As lead writers often work on stories in their areas of expertise, during the heat wave the editors asked Schreuder to produce the initial medical and scientific stories and subsequently gave the task to Kiernan, who had been writing features about urban poverty. The most senior general writers also contribute to major stories, regardless of the topic, acting both to polish and edit high-profile pieces. During the heat wave several of the *Tribune*'s veterans served this function.

The process of magazine-style story production expands the amount of information available for a piece. But it can also be frustrating for both the writers and reporters because writers have little time to go out into the streets and get a feel for the issue or event, so reporters worry that the writer will not recognize the significance of their findings. More important, many reporters argue that the writers' distance from the subject matter increases the probability that they will trust and follow their preconceived understandings of the situation when they are skeptical of a firsthand report from the field. Routine and conventional frames become more entrenched when writers have limited access to the people, places, and conditions that might call them into question. "It's hard when you have so many people talking to one [writer]," a reporter who worked the heat wave pointed out. "You don't know whether your voice is being heard because there's no way to see the finished product that's coming out in the paper before you contribute to it. So sometimes you tell a story that you saw and the person who writes it has a preconceived idea of what they're going to write before they write it. Changing their assumptions is a lot harder. And I think that happened a little bit in this [heat wave story]."

FAST THINKING

On breaking news stories, lead writers also face intense time pressure. As Schreuder noted, "It's not a perfect process and in everything we're doing we're dealing with the clock. Bang. Bang. Bang. Bang. Bang. And the clock just goes on all night until the story runs. [The reporter at] the Medical examiners Office would call in periodically and talk, and I would ask him questions about what I wanted to know to write the story. I would say to him: 'Who are you talking with? How many medical examiners are there? How long are they working? Are they talking to other hospitals?' So there's a lot of back and forth going on between me and the person at the site."

According to Carlozo, there is also a lot of communication among the reporters in the field, even though they, too, have limited time to do their work. Journalists who went out in the pool car spent roughly two hours going to their sites, conducting their interviews and observing the scenes, and reporting to their editors via telephone. This is typically the amount of time budgeted for reporting a breaking city story, Carlozo explained, and sometimes reporters have even less time to scour the streets. The hurried process allows little time for thinking critically or analytically about the interviews or the event, and if reporters revert to conventional frames and story ideas when they write their articles or submit their notes to lead writers it is in part because the system of daily news production constrains their capacity to make sense of the conditions they see. Invoking a journalistic truism, reporter Robert Becker contended that he and his newspaper colleagues do not try to provide definitive answers to difficult questions because "what we do is write rough drafts of history. Someone will come in after us and finish the job." "We didn't do a lot of charts and statistical data," recalled Gerould Kern, an associate managing editor during the heat wave, "because it was not a scientific study and we weren't presenting it as that." Instead, Kern explained, *Tribune* writers tried to depict the heat wave as "a human story and a medical science story," so they were "looking for good storytelling" more than systematic knowledge. Yet in practice, daily news reporters often shift from storytelling to expository writing, and they rarely preface their analyses by reminding their audience that the conclusions presented are provisional or incomplete.

The most common form of slipping from description to explanation involves the journalistic invocation of the official rhetoric and preconstructed folk wisdom that is readily available to account for an event. During the heat wave the frames of natural disaster and climatic causality advocated by city officials and some meteorologists proved particularly appealing to local reporters. One journalist wrote a series of news articles probing the reasons for the heat wave's deadliness, but neglected to consider any social or political causes of the crisis. According to the headlines of a front-page story in the *Tribune*'s Chicagoland section, "Exceptionally High Humidity Proved to Be Real Culprit" in producing the record mortality. "Basically," the article explained, "it all comes down to this: it's not the heat, it's the humidity." A few days later, the lead story of the Chicagoland section elaborated this logic. It is not merely heat, but "humidity, pollution, wind direction and other factors—such as the way the concrete and asphalt turn cities into heat-retaining islands—[that] are now known to be as important as temperature in determining if the weather is dangerous."[40] The articles would have carried different connotations if they had been modestly framed as inquiries into the weather, but instead they were presented as authoritative explanations that the catastrophe was a climatic occurrence and not a social event. Reporting organized entirely around the natural and meteorological frame, which was common during the heat wave, played an important role in naturalizing the disaster.

Another common analytical practice among journalists involves conducting solid reporting but then reaching beyond the information at hand to make rushed explanations and assessments. Take, for example, the *Tribune*'s first major story about the characteristics of the heat wave decedents, which exemplifies a typical mixture of thick, detailed street-level journalism with thin, speculative analysis. The article appeared on the front page of the Tuesday 18 July edition under the headline "Casualties of Heat Just Like Most of Us: Many Rejected Any Kind of Help." Coauthored by Zielinski and Louise Kiernan and supported with reporting by seven other contributors, the story begins with descriptions of several deaths: "Some died simply because they didn't like the fans, didn't want to run their air conditioning, or were afraid to open their windows to the threat of crime."[41] It is reasonable to presume that the authors had solid evidence for this account. In fact, the second page of the article contains rich material gathered by the reporting team, including descriptions of nine decedents for whom reporters could find friends or family members to interview; quotations from several of the bereaved; a list of the names, addresses, and ages of the decedents (both the *Tribune* and *Sun-Times* would produce several such lists during the crisis); and a map plotting several of the heat wave deaths in the city. The basic reporting that grounds and animates the article establishes important information, but the framing statements that organize this material are based on less reliable findings.

On the first page of the story, the section most likely to capture readers' attention, Kiernan and Zielinski provide a summary of the decedents' manner of death that they surely could not support. There were 179 official heat-related deaths when they wrote the piece on Monday, and the Medical Examiners Office had predicted at least one hundred more. No one had analyzed the death patterns to learn about the conditions in which the decedents had perished, yet in the second paragraph Kiernan and Zielinski maintain that "[the decedents] weren't, for the most part, the second-hand victims of loneliness, collapsing in their dark, silent, humid homes because no one cared enough to offer the help that would have saved them."[42] But aside from the staff's few hours of reporting, during which journalists looked for sources close enough to the victims to provide information about the conditions of their deaths, there was no basis for this claim. Not only had the authors generalized on the basis of a small number of reports; they also disregarded the probability that their reporting method, which was based on interviews with friends or relatives of the decedents, oriented their attention toward people who had contacts nearby and away from those whose isolation made it difficult to learn about their lives or whose identities the Medical Examiners Office had not yet confirmed. Yet there it was on the front page of the *Tribune:* an unqualified summary of the mortality patterns claiming that most of the victims perished with friends and family around them.

Newspaper reporters have no choice but to work under firm deadlines that limit their access to information. They can, however, avoid quick judgments and hurried analyses when they have limited facts or time to think. But in the contemporary division of knowledge, officials and news audiences expect that major news organizations will provide a grounded interpretation of key events, and journalists—whether in their own reporting or in their roles as pundits, critics, and columnists—often seize this opportunity to establish the terms of public debates. In a rush to establish a powerful and provocative front-page story, though, the editors and reporters of the Tuesday edition framed the heat disaster in flagrantly misleading terms. The headlines were even farther off the mark.

HEADLINES AND VISUAL IMAGES

As communications scholars have demonstrated, the central frame for news articles is not established in the stories that reporters write, but in the headlines and graphic or photographic images that draw readers' attention, introduce main issues in the accompanying article, and summarize the article's content. Headlines are important because they both organize the substance of news publications in ways that allow for selective reading and because they suggest which events and issues matter most. Few people have time to read an entire newspaper, but many scan its headlines and photographs as part of their daily routine. Headlines and photographs also serve a marketing function: when used provocatively, they can lure readers to buy a paper they might otherwise ignore, or to pay attention to stories that they might otherwise neglect. At the *Tribune,* as at many other papers, copy editors are responsible for generating most headlines; reporters and editors are seldom involved in the process for stories that do not make the front page. At times this process produces headlines that are not substantiated by the content of the stories, misleading the reader rather than summarizing the articles. When Kiernan and Zielinski submitted their piece for the Tuesday edition, for example, they did not know that the copy editors would title it "Casualties of Heat Just Like Most of Us: Many Rejected Any Kind of Help." The headline, which was the largest and boldest text on the front page that day, is not only manifestly wrong, it is also plainly contradicted by the substance of the reporting as well as by the accompanying graphic. Not far beneath the headline that characterizes victims as "just like most of us," the article text states, "Most of the heat victims were elderly. Many were ill or weak. A number were poor. A few drank or acted a little strange, or otherwise inhabited the dim pockets of society." On the next page, in a caption for the map showing the distribution of heat-related deaths, copy editors—perhaps the same ones who wrote the headline—explained that "[a]lthough the number of heat-related deaths in Cook County increased to 179 Monday, addresses are known for only 60. *Most of those victims were men aged 60 years or older living in Chicago's poorer neighborhoods.*"[43] Why, then, did the copy editors produce a front-page headline claiming that the casualties were typical Chicagoans?

According to one of the copy editors who worked on the heat wave, they had a simple reason for producing the headline. They wanted, he said, "to broaden the appeal of the article to readers and get them into the story." The headline, in other words, was designed to interest readers who are more concerned about people like themselves than they are about poor old men. As one journalist explained, this was a common practice for newspapers and magazines during the 1990s, when market research showed news companies that readers were most likely to pay attention to publications that had the words *you* or *your* on the cover or in article titles. Having reinvented marketing principles as journalistic norms, copy editors could compromise accuracy so long as they gained attention.[44] News reporters and editors had no opportunity to check the work.

Similar pressures shape the journalistic process of illustrating newspapers and other news media with visual images. News editors and producers expect photographers and camera operators to illustrate stories with material representing crucial information that words convey less effectively. But in practice, news agencies use photography and video footage to dramatize their coverage, selecting the images that are the most sensational and unique even though this convention focuses attention on the exceptional rather than the typical features of an issue or event. Extraordinary images are journalistically valuable when the shots capture meaningful social action or unusual occurrences, and news audiences expect to see the highlights rather than the mundane features of newsworthy events. Yet catastrophic situations such as the heat wave offer news organizations so many possibilities for spectacular image making (figs. 45, 46) that the news can easily transform crises into visual spectacles concealing the deeper social and political features of events.[45]

When the heat wave first moved into Chicago it posed a visual challenge to photographers and camera operators because heat—unlike hurricanes, tornadoes, blizzards, or floods—cannot be represented directly and contains little dramatic action. The standard solution to this problem—which is apparent in the early television and newspaper images of children playing in open fire hydrants and city residents at the beach—is to express the heat through shots of people cooling down with water. The visual frame of water combating heat, or nature versus nature, dominated the initial reporting of the disaster. When the heat wave became deadly, though, photojournalists could obtain new and even more powerful visual material. News audiences expect to see dramatic images of death and suffering displayed prominently in their television news programs and newspapers. The Cook County Morgue, with hundreds of dead bodies, a parking lot full of refrigerated trucks containing even more corpses, and frenzied emergency workers, was a spectacle waiting to happen. It was also easy to cover, since journalists interested in capturing the image did not have to scour the city in search of the scene. They could simply wait in the morgue parking lot (see fig. 46) and be confident that a perfect image—shocking, dra-

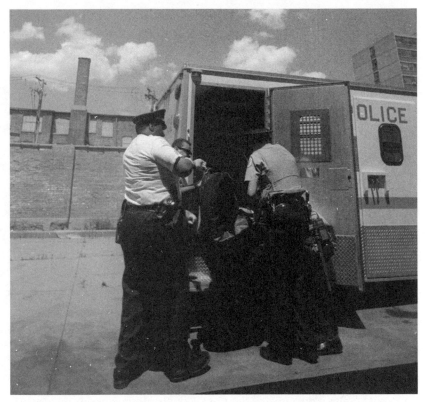

Figure 45. In their heat wave coverage, newspapers ran photos of decedents in body bags. Source: *Chicago Sun-Times;* photographer: Brian Jackson. Reprinted with special permission from the Chicago Sun-Times, Inc. © 2002.

matic, morbid, and different—would come to them. Producers and editors, certain that there would be "good color" for their broadcast or publication, sent other staffers into the neighborhoods to capture on photographic or video film police officers carrying dead bodies out of homes and residents coping with the heat. As the content analysis of newspaper graphics for the heat wave coverage shows in tables 11 and 12, after the shots of coping strategies, images of the dead bodies and the morgue were among the most prominent visual features of the news coverage. Photographs depicting the conditions in which the victims had lived and died were not featured in the reporting.

News organizations devote substantial resources to producing and displaying visual images, and the process of planning the look of a segment or story is a fundamental part of journalistic work. Television news, which is the most visual journalistic medium, is most explicitly

Figure 46. Camera operators at the Cook County Morgue, where spectacular images were readily available. Source: Office of the Medical Examiner of
Cook County; photographer: John A. Kelley.

organized around the production or acquisition of dramatic footage,
and reporters working for television are always concerned about making their stories visually rich. Paul Douglas, the meteorologist who covered the heat wave for radio and newspaper as well, explained that
even on television weather reports,

> you're constrained by pictures and [the question of] how do you make
> a heat wave story visual and interesting. I know that we hit the whole
> "survival tips" hard with special graphics, and so we tried to build graph-
> ics that would tell the story. You spend a majority of your time on [plan-
> ning] what visuals you are going to show. And one of the inherent frustra-
> tions with being a television meteorologist is that so much of your day
> is spent pondering pretty pictures. I don't spend nearly as much time as
> I'd like actually looking at maps and forecasting, because a majority of
> my time is spent producing the show.

Douglas has ample support for his belief that the producers' emphasis on planning and arranging graphic images structured the news coverage of the disaster and compromised his time to do conventional reporting. At the *Tribune,* which is relatively less beholden to visual material but still dependent on dramatic shots and powerful graphics to animate its stories, Schreuder summed up her colleagues' positions:

> There's an emphasis [at the paper], much more than ever, on graphics. This [the heat wave] was in many ways a very visual story, and that influences how our editors think we should cover it. . . . So some of the time that you're writing the story has to be spent with the graphics team, talking to them about what we're doing, so that they can add and not simply repeat. But also, as a reporter, you are providing some reporting information for graphics, which is a whole new layer [of production]. And sometimes the information that you provide for graphics isn't necessarily what you would provide for your story. Photography is a whole other layer. Because generally speaking, at this paper, the reporters fill out the photo assignments. And what this means is that you are responsible for figuring out when a photographer can come, figuring out how to get there, telling them what the story is so that they take pictures that go with the story. You're always supposed to be thinking as a reporter, what can photo do?

The photo editors at the *Tribune* played an active role during their paper's heat wave coverage because it demanded extensive visual material. But news reporters and writers remained involved in the image-making parts of the news production process and looked for the extraordinary sights that might move their story to a more prominent place in the news.

STORIES, IMAGES, AND NEWS PLACEMENT

Photographs and graphics play an even greater role in what is perhaps the most important editorial decision that the news staff makes: the placement of a story or segment within the newspaper or broadcast. Editors and producers are always looking for dramatic images for the front-page or lead story, which is explicitly designed to hook audiences into the coverage. At the *Tribune,* photography and graphic design editors often play a key role in the daily editorial meeting to determine what goes on the front page. If there is no clear choice, dramatic photographs or graphics will often determine the story selection. Sometimes editors place provocative images on the front page even without an accompanying story, or, similarly, delay the publication of an excellent story that has no good visual accompaniment.

Most local and national news organizations that reported on the heat wave displayed prominent images of victims in body bags or the chaotic scene at the morgue. The *Tribune* placed a photograph of autopsy technicians moving corpses from refrigerated trucks into the Medical Examiners Office on the front page of one edition of the 17 July paper, and a shot of Chicago Police Department wagons waiting in line to deliver "freshly discovered casualties" in another. The 18 July front-page photo was similar: an exhausted police officer in the Englewood neighborhood is shown resting against a car after removing a victim's body from an apartment; one pair of gloves remains on his hands, while another lies at his feet. The 19 July front page led with a graphic displaying the record fatalities on a bar chart, and the accompanying story contained a photograph of funeral workers loading into their minivan a body discovered in a Chicago Housing Authority building. The front page of that day's Chicagoland section was almost identical: four police officers remove a victim from a single room occupancy dwelling on the South Side in one shot, and in another CHA residents look out their window, awaiting the removal of a deceased neighbor. A similar sequence ran in the *Sun-Times*. On 17 July the front page showed an overhead shot of trucks at the morgue alongside a close-up of autopsy technicians loading a body into a vehicle; on 18 July photos of Daley, Commissioner Alvarez, and the unused Chicago Heat Plan made the cover; and on 19 July there was another exhausted morgue worker on page 1. Dramatic images of dead bodies, refrigerated trucks, and wilting emergency workers dominated the heat wave coverage across the media, making for a memorable week of news. But there is little evidence that the photographs helped audiences to understand the sources of the trauma that was happening around them or to establish connections between the social and political conditions in the city and the emerging public health crisis. It is more likely that the sensational accounts and images of death and disaster produced by journalists detracted from the journalistic goals that, in theory, news organizations are designed to achieve.

FRAGMENTATION OF AUDIENCES AND TARGETED NEWS

If the spectacular representations of the heat wave story obscured the social conditions contributing to the disaster, editorial decisions regarding which aspects of the event were relevant to which news audiences rendered some features of the crisis invisible. The most fundamental decisions for all journalistic organizations concern questions about what issues or occurrences are *newsworthy* for their audience, and several institutional routines and professional standards shape these choices.[46] Newspaper companies such as the *Chicago Tribune* once produced a single news product that reached their entire readership, so editors made judgments about story selection and placement in the publication with respect to the diverse interests of their constituents. In 1995, however, the *Tribune* used advanced publishing technologies to produce eight zoned editions of the daily paper for different regions of the metropolis, with specialized Metro sections and some front-page stories "swapped" with others and targeted for particular readers.[47] News from the center city remains the key part of the *Tribune*'s local reporting, and most of the heat wave stories were important and dramatic enough to appeal to audiences throughout the larger metropolitan region. But most suburban readers, who tend to be more affluent than city residents, did not face the social and economic hardships— much less the lack of air conditioning—that made so many Chicago residents vulnerable to the heat. Editors knew that suburban readers would be interested in and entertained by the major stories and the spectacular images from the city, but they were less certain that the audience outside the city cared about the details of the social and political nature of the event.

The zoned production and distribution system allowed the *Tribune* staff to target their coverage of the disaster, and as the heat wave took its course editors at some of the suburban bureaus did choose to eliminate, edit, excerpt, or reposition certain heat wave coverage for their readers. In the 17 July Metro sections, for example, some suburban editions of the *Tribune* carried "Finding the Mane Attraction," a long feature about a horse photographer, on the front page, instead of the Chicagoland section's lead story about problems with city cooling centers; an image of a horse replaced the photograph of an elderly Chicago woman suffering the loss of electricity.[48] The basis for this decision was simply that editors believed the information about city residents struggling for relief and government agencies scrambling to make the cooling centers viable would be less important or relevant to suburban readers than the story about equestrian matters.

Another technique for targeting news audiences through swaps is to change the graphics and photographs so that the paper's visual images resonate with particular readers who want news about people like them. This process often involves substituting images of one ethnoracial group for another and, more specifically, swapping photographs of African-American or Latino residents in the city-zoned editions for shots of white residents in the suburban ones. The front-page photographs of the different 14 July Metro sections, for example, show four Latinas— Christine Hernandez, Yolanda Ortiz, and Esperanza and Erica Hernandez—in the urban Metro Northwest edition (fig. 47), and five white children—Doug Wisner, Greg Homuth, Paul Mroz, Alex Auvenshine, and Ashley Bedore—in the suburban Metro McHenry edition (fig. 48).

Editorial choices that displaced the cooling center story or changed the ethnoracial composition of a news photograph may not have dra-

Christine Hernandez, 4, (at right) gets a dousing from a hose held by her mother, Yolanda Ortiz, at their Elgin home. Ortiz (above) also cools off her niece, Esperanza Hernandez, 1, who shrieks. She is held by her cousin Erica Hernandez, 9. Rocky the German shepherd gets a drink in Elk Grove Village.

Tribune photos by Chuck Berman

Figure 47. This photo of young Latinas ran on the front page of the *Chicago Tribune*'s 14 July urban Metro Northwest edition, reflecting the newspaper's strategy of targeting news audiences of particular ethnoracial groups with its heat wave coverage.

It's frying time again

Figure 48. The *Chicago Tribune* targeted its suburban news audience with this front-page photo, which ran in the 14 July Metro McHenry edition.

matically altered the public representation of the event. But small, everyday decisions similar to them shape the production and distribution of city news by adding a layer of informational segregation to metropolitan communities that are already socially and physically separate. If various *Tribune* readers viewed the heat wave differently, this is in part because the news organization provided resources for them to do so.

THE NEWSWORTHINESS OF DISASTER: THE RISE AND DEMISE OF THE MAJOR STORY

After the heat subsided and the Medical Examiners Office counted the last of the victims, some of the *Tribune* reporters and editors assessed their coverage of the disaster. Bill Recktenwald, one of the paper's revered senior editors and writers, believed that the *Tribune* had failed to tell the human and social side of the story in its reporting. The victims remained mysterious, the conditions of their deaths obscure. As one reporter who had worked on the breaking stories explained,

> The coverage didn't show as much of the life of these people—and these people had really ugly lives. It was just like poor people, crazy people who lived in squalor and had suffered and were in pain for a lot of their lives and died. There is a routinization, there's a routine when you report on poor people dying. There's a tone that's taken and it's almost a car-

toonish image of these people. It's journalism shorthand, how you cover poor people, and it's easy. It's hard to write about it without blaming the victim. You've got very specific things that you describe when you write about poor people. It's very moralistic, but it's not necessarily accurate.

The journalist had good cause for his discomfort with the coverage because his reporting, which he believed to be full of evidence about the hardships and dangers of poverty and isolation, had been used for the story subtitled "Most [victims] Rejected Any Kind of Help." But several of the reporters who had worked on the initial heat wave stories also expressed frustrations with the coverage, and even a few of the editors felt that the paper had treated the heat wave victims superficially when they wanted to do something more.

Recktenwald had been in Chicago long enough to recognize the significance of the catastrophe, and he added his voice to those requesting that the *Tribune* return to the story and pursue the angles it had missed when the heat wave was breaking news. "Afterwards there was a big question about what we could do," he said. "This is one of the biggest events that had ever taken place. As many people died here as in the *Eastland* disaster, almost as great as *Eastland,* and let's look at that." According to Recktenwald, then–Managing Editor Ann Marie Lipinski came up with the idea of sending out a large group of reporters to investigate the victims and write profiles about their lives and deaths, and he took charge of the project from there. The plan was to use about ten reporters, each of whom would go into a neighborhood in which a large number of deaths occurred, to learn everything they could about the people who died. With the help of Gerould Kern, another of the more experienced *Tribune* editors, Recktenwald developed a standard questionnaire for reporters to use in their inquiries into the lives of the decedents. Both men were convinced that they had a major story on their hands, and they wanted to make sure that the reporting for the project would help them see whatever patterns of death there were to find. The reporting, Recktenwald and Kern hoped, would produce profiles of roughly one-quarter of the dead, which they would use for a major story about the disaster. As Recktenwald recalled, "We wanted to get a list [of the victims] and to look at maps. I mean, this is awesome, so I was able to convince the bosses to do a quarter— I think it was a quarter of the city—black areas, Hispanic areas, white areas. I work with the reporters so I had an idea of who would be more inclined to go out and climb the stairs and knock on doors. You want to put the right people in the right areas."

Recktenwald assembled his reporters, a group that included Carlozo, Zielinski, Becker, and Kiernan, as well as Michael Martinez, Melita Marie Garza, Janita Poe, Jerry Thomas, and Paul de la Garza. Over a three-week period they produced roughly one hundred hard-won profiles. "I just went to the addresses and knocked on doors," Zielinski explained, "pretty traditional reporting. I ended up in some of the poorer neighborhoods . . . because all of the people that were dying, most, or the majority that we covered, were poor. But I ended up on the West Side [and] in the State Street corridor, some of those [public] housing units there. I was just collecting anecdotes, collecting any stories, you know, trying to put a face on the big story." When the reporting was over, the team had a huge amount of information about the victims and was prepared to write a major piece. Recktenwald also obtained an exhaustive list of the dead from the Medical Examiners Office, which he used to map the deaths. Amidst what one reporter called "a whole lot of numbers and statistics that in themselves reflected certain facets of the heat wave but didn't point to any absolutes," Recktenwald discovered that "the overwhelming numbers of deaths were in the poor areas and the poor areas are normally black or Hispanic." He and his colleagues were ready to produce a powerful and provocative set of stories about the disaster, to make explicit the inequities that the initial coverage had inadequately explored.

But before Recktenwald and the reporters began writing they ran up against a set of substantive commercial considerations that the news team had not expected to see. "By the time we got done [reporting]," Carlozo recalled, "it was September, and it was a very serious decision as to whether people were still interested in this story." Originally supportive of the project, some editors now worried that the story would not work. "There was a perception that our readers didn't care. . . . When it starts to become fall or winter in Chicago, how many people are going to read about a summer thing?" The heat wave had been reframed once again, this time as a "summer story," a particular kind of human interest piece that is appropriate for one season alone.

Ultimately, the top editors concluded that not many readers would care to read a summer story during the fall. Despite the large amount of resources they had committed to the project, they decided that rather than printing the major story Recktenwald had planned, they should run only a brief narrative of the event followed by about eleven short vignettes about individuals who died. The final story was published on 26 November as a front-page story. Headlined "The Heat Wave Victims: Joined in Death" and adorned with a photograph of a North Side rooming house, the article was based on a draft written by Louise Kiernan but never finished because the *Tribune* decided to print it when she was on vacation. Although Kern and Recktenwald had done considerable work to sort out mortality patterns, the story contained no systematic analysis of the deaths and showed little evidence of the extensive reporting that went into it. "I wrote a draft in story form from the information that we gathered. Then I went on vacation for Thanksgiving, and while I was gone they decided to run the story," Kiernan explained.

"It was not a happy project," she remembered, in part because she did not think that the reporters uncovered anything new about the victims, and in part because she never had a chance to finish the article. One editor admitted being "extremely disappointed" with the final product, and some of the journalists who worked on the piece felt that they had wasted their time on the piece. "We could have had a fantastic story," Carlozo lamented, but good reporting and a deadly crisis of historic proportion was not enough to make the news once the city edged toward winter and the disaster receded into the past. In the end, the major story that the editors had planned proved to be as forgettable as the heat wave victims have been themselves.

Emerging Dangers in the Urban Environment

O n 29 July, less than two weeks after the deadly heat wave passed and long before the last victims were buried, a new hot-air mass moved into Chicago and threatened the health of the city again. The intensity and duration of the extreme climate were less severe this time, but the recent trauma had sensitized residents and officials to the risk of disaster, and the collective response was tremendous. Not only did Chicagoans make special efforts to protect themselves, assist their neighbors, and check up on their family members, but the same city agencies that initially disavowed accountability also implemented and executed a comprehensive emergency plan to assist the old and isolated residents most likely to need support. Belying its own public position that the government cannot take responsibility for securing the health and welfare of its citizens, the city declared an official heat emergency and spent several million dollars on support services and programs.

Under the leadership of Mayor Daley, the government's sweeping effort to protect its constituents included establishing a hotline that Chicagoans could call if they needed special assistance or if they wanted information about cooling centers and other available city services; opening a phone bank with some eighty employees and volunteers whose explicit task was to call seniors and check on their well-being; and managing a Heat Command Center with a staff of two hundred workers, including several professional nurses, and hundreds more city employees on call. The local government also added sixteen ambulances to the Fire Department for temporary use during the heat wave; contracted with local cab companies to make several hundred taxis available to seniors needing transportation to cooling centers; extended the hours of senior community centers; distributed brochures with instructions on how to keep cool; and paid outreach workers to go door to door and check on residents in areas with high numbers of seniors living alone. Finally, city agencies arranged to monitor the emergency rooms of local hospitals, as well as 117 nursing homes, for cases of heat-related illness and level of admissions; place vehicles on standby to transport residents to cooling centers; open seventy cooling centers and extend open hours at beaches and public pools; work with local media to broadcast heat emergency warnings, encourage families and neighbors to check on one another, issue instructions on how to "beat the heat"; and publicize procedures for handling heat-related illnesses. It was, by any measure, an extraordinary and comprehensive response.

The second heat wave was shorter and less dangerous than the first. The temperature and heat index peaked at 94 degrees and 104 degrees, respectively, and the nights cooled down even further. Variation in the climate and the recent loss of hundreds of fragile residents two weeks earlier make it impossible to know exactly how many lives the city programs saved, but after the heat abated Chicago reported only two heat-related deaths. Local critics agreed that the city's response was exceptionally strong only because local officials feared a reprise of the disaster that remained prominent in their memories. Still, some of Chicago's leading opinion makers were unimpressed by the city government's efforts to ward off a second crisis. Although there was good evidence that the city had failed to respond adequately to the first heat wave, the *Chicago Tribune* editorialized that "once again . . . the majordomos at City Hall appear to be overreacting in ways that are not only wasteful of taxpayer dollars but harmful to the preparedness they are trying to achieve. . . . It's also questionable whether the city employees ought to be doing the telephoning when a better and more cost-efficient job could be done by church and community organizations."[1] The official heat emergency response, deemed wasteful, inefficient, and even dangerous to the local culture, was already a controversial program. It was uncertain that city agencies would have public or media support to mount such an effort again.

By the summer of 1999, though, Chicago was even better prepared for extreme summer weather. Pamphlets about heat risks were everywhere in the city, and the media issued frequent public warnings about the dangers of the summer climate; the local government established a registration system allowing any Chicagoan to request phone or personal contact during all weather-related emergencies and constructed a World Wide Web site devoted exclusively to the threat of heat; the Department of Public Health developed a system for coordinating emergency medical services; and the Department on Aging expanded its network of isolated seniors and used its senior community centers to educate participants about seasonal survival strategies.

When a heat wave that meteorologists characterized as "somewhat less intense but longer lasting" moved into Chicago during the end of July and beginning of August in 1999, the city embarked on an active effort to look after isolated seniors and other vulnerable residents.[2] Once again, Commonwealth Edison's generators could not handle the demand for electricity. The major North Side substation that failed in 1995 went out in 1999, too, and roughly ten thousand city residents had no power for three days.[3] Water shortages were common as well. Although the city was unable to sustain the exceptional level of services and support that it had offered in August of 1995, it utilized the heat emergency plan and encouraged families and community groups to look out for anyone who might be at risk. The Midwestern Regional Climate Center summarized the city's response:

> Chicago activated its Extreme Weather Operations Plan and opened a Central Heat Command Center on the 22nd [of July]. Strongly worded press releases were issued to the media to remind everyone that 700 had died in the 1995 heat wave. The city designated 34 cooling centers, provided free bus service to anyone needing to reach a cooling center, and announced plans to check on the elderly and public housing residents. The Chicago Fire Commissioner was put in charge of the city effort. On the 23rd, the city of Chicago opened 31 schools to provide more cooling centers, and police officers augmented the other city workers going door-to-door checking on the elderly living alone. . . .
>
> On the 25th, the fifth hot day, the city, through the broadcast and news media, urged people to go to cooling centers after finding low attendance since the 22nd. Inquiries showed many were afraid to leave their residences, fearing robbery of their homes. Efforts to reach out to the elderly resulted in over 30,000 persons being visited during July 21–25. . . .
>
> The heat wave conditions returned abruptly on July 29th, as was forecast previously. The city re-opened its Heat Center on July 29, and reactivated its Extreme Weather Operations Plan. . . . The city urged the elderly to call 311 for assistance, and sent out hundreds of employees to check the elderly again. . . . Over 1,200 people were brought to cooling centers in Chicago during the heat wave. About 50 of these people were taken directly to hospitals due to obvious signs of dangerous heat stress.[4]

Despite these extensive efforts, Cook County recorded 114 heat-related fatalities—a high toll by historical standards but not close to that exacted in the 1995 event. According to official records, more than 70 percent of the victims were discovered dead or dying in stifling hot apartments, and more than half the dead were men.[5] Roughly one-third of the decedents were aged sixty years or younger, a clear sign that the dangers of extreme heat and isolation are not exclusive to the elderly.

The climate accounts for only part of the difference in the mortality levels between the two disasters. According to researchers at the Midwestern Regional Climate Center, "in Chicago, conditions during the peak of the 1999 heat wave were very similar to those during the 1995 heat wave peak, especially the extreme nocturnal conditions of temperatures and humidity. Therefore, it seems unlikely that the reduction in the heat wave death toll in Chicago from about 700 in 1995 to 114 in 1999 is due solely to climatic differences between the two heat waves."[6] Instead, the Climate Center team finds, a "pro-active," "timely and vigorous" response by the Chicago city government that was "in marked contrast to what happened during the 1995 heat wave" played a major role in promoting public awareness about the risks of heat-related problems, thereby reducing morbidity and mortality levels. The finding is consistent with research showing that well-executed heat wave response systems in other cities have reduced mortality during extreme summer weather.[7] "We ought to give the city an A-plus for their efforts," Chief Medical Examiner Edmund Donoghue told the media. "But we shouldn't rest on our laurels. We should continue until there are no heat-related deaths in the summertime, and that's doable."[8]

Yet Chicago's experience in the 1999 heat waves suggests that Donoghue might be underestimating the severity of the social conditions that make residents susceptible to the summer climate, and that a comprehensive heat emergency plan is a necessary but insufficient element of disaster protection. In 1999 a sensitized populace and an aggressive policy response helped to reduce the number of fatalities in the city, yet roughly one hundred people were isolated and vulnerable enough to slip through the cracks and die alone. A severe heat wave could have an even greater impact on a city with comparable social and economic hardships but fewer political and cultural resources to mount a prevention plan—or even on Chicago in a foreseeable future when residents and officials are less attuned to the dangers of summer.

According to many environmental scientists, more devastating summer hot spells are likely on their way, and their impact will be dire even if the weather is not as severe as it was in 1995. The Intergovernmental Panel on Climate Change, for example, recently projected that there is a 90 percent to 99 percent probability that there will be "higher maximum temperatures, more hot days and heat waves over nearly all land areas" in the twenty-first century. The likely consequences include an "increased incidence of death and serious illness in older age groups and urban poor," and a greater reliance on the same air-conditioning systems that contribute to the production of heat waves and the warming of the earth.[9] Although climatologists skeptical about global warming argue that a weather system as intense as the one that hit Chicago in 1995 is unlikely to recur soon, meteorologist Paul Douglas is in good company when he argues that the story of Chicago in 1995 "is just a preview of coming attractions." Heat waves have long been America's most deadly environmental events, and they are likely to become even more devastating.

In recent years an increasing number of cities have learned from heat disasters such as Chicago's and implemented more sophisticated programs for proactively combating the dangers imposed by extreme summer weather. Yet there is less collective commitment and political will to develop comparable programs to proactively combat the everyday crisis, the slow death from social suffering rampant among poor and isolated urban residents. In fact, during the late 1990s—the very years that U.S. city governments adopted advanced heat warning and protection systems—Congress advanced its campaigns to eliminate the Low Income Home Energy Assistance Program and remove federal energy support for the poor; the city of Chicago lost more affordable housing for low-income individuals and families; and governments at all levels did little to assess the challenges and address the needs of an emerging population of seniors living alone. These policies work at cross purposes, since no severe weather plan can adequately compensate for the extreme vulnerability that we collectively produce in other domains. It might be practical to limit disaster prevention planning to warning and response programs. But the health risks of future heat waves will continue to grow so long as there are no strong public policies to address the social, ecological, and physiological conditions that make everyday life so precarious, and extreme events so treacherous, for the rising population of vulnerable city dwellers. The isolated, to paraphrase Chicago's disaster commission, cannot do it all alone.

THE FORMULA FOR DISASTER: TYPICAL DANGERS
OF EVERYDAY URBAN EXTREMES

The heat should not be our only concern. This book has shown that extreme exogenous forces such as the climate have become so disastrous partly because the emerging isolation and privatization, the extreme social and economic inequalities, and the concentrated zones of affluence and poverty pervasive in contemporary cities create hazards for vulnerable residents in all seasons.[10] Analyzing the Chicago heat wave is useful because the event expressed and exposed conditions that are always present but difficult to perceive. Yet if the primary value of a social autopsy is to deepen our knowledge about the social processes that help produce isolation and death, its deeper contribution is to expand our understanding of conditions in which urban residents continue to live. I conclude, then, by identifying the emerging conditions that constitute a formula for disaster in Chicago, and other cities similar to it, even in the absence of the heat.

First among these is *the rise of an aging population of urban residents who live alone,* often without proximate or reliable sources of routine contact and social support. Advances in medical science, health care, and private and public pension programs for retired workers who had long and stable careers have extended the typical life span for most Americans, but our society has not moved apace. The elderly, especially isolated men and those who outlive their social networks or become homebound and ill, often suffer from social deprivation and role displacement in their later years. Older women, who are more likely than men to be poor, sick, and living alone in old age, tend to be less isolated but are by no means insulated from the challenges of aging alone. If these seniors face greater risks of death than any other group during heat waves, they also endure invisible crises and unspoken indignities in normal times. There are no easy solutions to the challenges posed by the aging and individuating of society, but the current vocabulary for addressing these issues represses troubling anxieties about living and dying alone that deserve more rigorous scrutiny.

Recent debates about social capital—the networks and reciprocal relationships that help people gain access to resources, information, and support—have neglected to take seriously the obstacles to civic and social engagement for the millions of seniors who live alone or suffer from health problems. But the increasingly narrow and technocratic inquiries into the significance of social capital have also diverted attention from what might be the key finding in decades of network research: that, contrary to much folk wisdom, poverty and duress, including physical injury and illness, tend to strain rather than sustain social bonds. People with pressing anxieties about making ends meet, avoiding proximate dangers, maintaining vitality in manifestly unhealthy environments, or losing informal sources of support are likely to express stress in their relationships and, in turn, pull apart the social ties that they need to preserve. As they become more isolated, poor or old people lose access to information and the capacity to mobilize resources that might help them reconnect. Current strategies to build new forms of social protection by "empowering" the poor or the elderly with choices in the market of goods and services, or with new opportunities for affiliation in local groups, will be undermined by the everyday pressures of poverty and aging. If we are to devise a collective response to the specter of isolation, and to the particular risks for the elderly who slip into the margins of society, we will have to confront them directly.

Perhaps the greatest obstacle to such a collective endeavor stems from the second element in the formula for disaster: *the increasing spatial concentration and social separation of the affluent and the impoverished,* who cluster in exclusive or excluded parts of the city at the expense of the expendable, discarded people. As Douglas Massey argues, the new ecology of U.S. inequality inhibits the growth of a political movement to protect the vulnerable because the middle and upper classes inhabit "a social environment that [is] far more homogeneously privileged than at any time in the previous twenty years." Although economic growth and population increases provide some cause for the glib rhetoric about urban revitalization in the United States in recent years, a crucial, enabling condition for this collective belief is the secession of the successful who opt out of environments in which they must face stark deprivation and suffering. According to Massey's report on the major demographic trends at the end of the twentieth century, "in their daily lives, affluent residents of U.S. urban areas were increasingly likely to interact only with other affluent people, and progressively less likely to interact with other classes, especially the poor."[11] If the affluent benefit from their exclusive and segregated environments, concentrated deprivation and abandonment compounds the risks of crime, disease, violence, and isolation for the poor while putting impoverished people and regions out of sight. As we have seen, recluses and shut-ins who abandon cities that have already abandoned them are not the only casualties of these socially produced and spatially organized inequalities. But their fate in Chicago signals the dystopic possibilities in a city of extremes.

One crucial question raised by Chicago's experience in the heat wave is whether contemporary techniques for removing disadvantaged people and their problems from the sight lines of most urban and suburban residents have transformed the terms and covered over the tensions of social and political life, banishing the experience of misery and desperation to the realm of television entertainment and news spectacle. How much of the discourse about pervasive prosperity or the successes of welfare reform is founded on a widespread refusal to consider the living conditions of millions of isolated, impoverished, overworked, or even incarcerated people whose existence has become distant, irrelevant, and easy to ignore? What would happen to the glib sentiments about the rise of a "network society" of constantly connected cosmopolitan actors if we looked closely at what Manuel Castells calls the "fourth world" of people alienated from the flows of goods, services, and information that their fellow city residents take for granted?

Taking their mandate from the same citizens and constituents who have sequestered themselves in zones of concentrated affluence, it is no surprise that *the government agencies best positioned to redress these inequities and protect the most vulnerable urban residents have done little to help.* The federal government's simultaneous expansion of disaster relief efforts to subsidize property holders—often at the direct expense of social programs for the disadvantaged—coupled with the reduction of national programs to provide home energy support to the poor, is perhaps the most egregious example of how the welfare state has protected the privileged while leaving the vulnerable to fend for themselves. But there are numerous ways in which the absence of political will to provide basic goods such as energy and health care, or to assist the poor more generally, expresses itself in public policy and local governance.

The social autopsy of the heat wave points to four important but seldom discussed problems with current political approaches to social protection. First is the organizational mismatch created by increasing *delegation of key health and support services to paramilitary governmental organizations,* such as the fire and police departments, where administrators and officers are rarely committed to "soft service" work and the department infrastructure is poorly suited to the jobs. A second problem is *the expectation that city residents, including the elderly and frail, will be active consumers of public goods,* smart shoppers of services made available in the market rather than "citizens" entitled to social protection. This market model of governance creates a systemic service mismatch, whereby people with the weakest capabilities and greatest needs are the least likely to get them. Third, *the social distance between city adminis-trators and the disadvantaged people they serve is increasing*. As governments operate more like professional firms, commissioners become CEOs, agencies subcontract more services out to private companies, and po-lice officers replace aldermen and precinct captains as the community sentries, political organizations risk losing contact with citizens and— as in the heat wave commission report stating that isolated residents do not want support—failing to understand their needs. Fourth, *govern-ments increasingly use public relations and marketing programs to spin good news stories about the success of their programs.* Responsible governments can use such image-making campaigns to inform citizens about public programs and resources that are available to them, but the campaigns can also be manipulated to become *mechanisms for denying* the severity or persistence of problems that might concern residents and compro-mise their political support.

The final condition highlighted by the social autopsy concerns *the role of news institutions in the symbolic politics of cities.* There are two signifi-cant trends to consider: first, the transformation of journalistic organi-zations to meet advancing cultural and economic pressures to make news more entertaining for audiences and more profitable for news companies; and second, the rise of news delivery systems that use mar-keting principles to segregate audiences so that consumers receive less information about collective metropolitan matters and more news about themselves. In recent years prominent journalists and media crit-ics have called attention to the ways in which "the corporate takeover of America's newspapers," in the words of former *Tribune* editor James Squires, or the rise of "the media monopoly," according to Ben Bag-dikian, have compromised the integrity of news organizations.[12] Under the management of large corporations whose concerns about the bot-tom line and stakes in intense competitions for market share often conflict with editors' commitment to professional news values, major journalistic organizations—reputable newspapers as well as local televi-sion stations—now scramble to balance demands for different kinds of content. The heat wave offered editors and reporters opportunities to provide a blend of spectacular coverage and serious, street-level re-ports. But several of the most probing and insightful accounts were overshadowed by prominent and sensational photographs, dramatic but misleading headlines, and false political debates that obscured the social aspects of the disaster. According to several *Tribune* staff mem-bers, the most in-depth reporting on the heat wave victims never even made it onto the printed page because the "summer story" no longer seemed relevant in the fall. How many other stories about deprivation and suffering in the city are dismissed for the same reason in the everyday world of the newsroom? When there are other, less dramatic or camera-ready crises for the urban poor, how will we know?

Advanced systems for targeted news production and distribution make these questions all the more relevant to contemporary metropolitan regions. We have seen how local news organizations covering the heat wave matched the ethnic group represented in one photograph to the audience receiving the product and replaced a detailed story about the city's cooling centers with a feature about equestrians for some suburban county editions. Urban news outlets will continue to provide suburban audiences with dramatic stories from the city, but journalistic organizations are already developing better techniques to differentiate their products for narrow market segments and symbolically segregate communities that are already separated geographically.[13] If the editorial decisions made in the heat wave expressed media managers' view of what kinds of city stories interest suburban audiences, there is good reason to believe that urban scandals, spectacles, and tragedies will always be newsworthy to every audience.[14] But consumers who prefer not to know about more mundane urban problems will be spared such information, and the unpleasant features of life and death in the city will fade from view.

THE SOCIAL AUTOPSY

In the nineteenth and early twentieth centuries, scientists such as Rudolph Virchow and William Osler fought to legitimate and institutionalize the autopsy as a technique for identifying causes of mortality and, in turn, increasing the effectiveness of medical care. The subsequent successes of biomedical models of analysis and intervention not only revolutionized medical science, but also transformed our cultural vocabulary for making sense of life and death. Today we have more precise technologies for examining the body than ever before, and researchers in several fields promise even greater advances in the future. Our faith in biomedical explanations for all kinds of conditions knows few limits.

But medical science can tell us little about the social conditions that affect the course of our lives and the context of our deaths. Excessive use of the medical microscope obscures or makes invisible the social pathologies that generate illness and disease. Recently a growing number of critics, many of them physicians and scientists, have argued that a fixed orientation to clinical and medical knowledge has left modern societies particularly unsuited to understand the most consequential of all health events: death. All agree that repairing our cultural estrangement from the processes of death and dying requires deepening our knowledge about the social organization of our lives. But our long-standing reliance on medical diagnoses and the official reports that back them up make it difficult to conceive a social autopsy, let alone conduct one. However unsatisfying, the monopoly of the biomedical model is difficult to break.

The looming threat of catastrophe and the quotidian crises that mark our time make this an opportune moment to develop new humanistic and social scientific approaches to the study of life and death. The project, as this account of disaster in the city illustrates, is far more than an academic task.[15] As with all autopsies, then, this examination of the 1995 Chicago heat wave closes with the hope that by studying death we have improved our capacity not only to understand life, but also to protect it.

Together in the End

lthough occasionally Chicago residents or journalists refer to the heat wave of 1995 when summer steams into the city's pores, the disaster has failed to take on the mythic significance ascribed to other major catastrophes, including many that have wrought far less human damage. The institutional histories and popular memories of the heat wave matter because collectively they constitute the evolving mythology of the disaster and establish the terms and ideas through which we interpret its meaning and significance. Myths about extreme events often serve as key resources for organizing historical knowledge about the period in which they occurred and motivating action once the event has passed. The Great Chicago Fire, for example, became a source and symbol of the city's capacity to remake itself and renew its splendor, an inspiration to emerge from the ashes as a great modern metropolis, and an impetus for political reform.[1] Similarly, the urban riots of the 1960s became cultural markers of longstanding ethnoracial antagonisms and class cleavages that many Americans had taken for granted. Accounts of the uprisings helped to produce new recognition of what journalists and officials suddenly considered an "urban crisis," and stimulated social movements, cultural products, and policy measures that directly addressed the problems of urban inequality.

Events change the order of things, but how they do so depends on the empirical resources and cultural schemes that actors use to make sense of what happened.[2] The heat wave may be a completed historical experience, but its status as a subject of history and myth will never be settled. Insofar as this book has aimed to identify unexplored dimensions of what happened in July of 1995, it represents a contribution to the record of the catastrophe and a call to reconsider its meaning. The great Chicago heat wave, I have argued, can serve as a barometer of contemporary urban conditions that shape the way we live and die even when we are not aware of them. For now, however, the trauma stands as a nonevent in the grand narrative of affluence and prosperity that dominates accounts of U.S. cities in the 1990s, and public discourse about the summer of 1995 lacks the insights into the condition of the city that the disaster might have exposed. In my informal discussions with people in Chicago and elsewhere, I find that few remember the scale of human devastation during the heat wave. The bodies at the Cook County Morgue, the debate about heat-related deaths, the power outages and the problems at Commonwealth Edison—these are the images that dominate the public imagination. Most estimate the death total at around one hundred; the official figures never fail to surprise.

If the heat wave's popular obituary conceals the social conditions and processes that produced its effects, though, the story of its largest funeral (fig. 49) speaks its deepest truths. Far from being the great equalizer, the deaths of the Chicagoans for whom no one came only reinforced and perpetuated the degradation of their lives.

By August 1995 Chicago had moved on to other matters and journalists had turned their attention to new scandals and events. But the bodies of forty-one heat wave victims remained unclaimed at the county morgue. More than a month had passed since the deadly week in July, and county officials recognized that they would have to inter the decedents in a potter's field. On 25 August the county buried the remaining cadavers, along with twenty-seven other unclaimed bodies that had accumulated during the month, in a mass grave at the suburban Homewood Memorial Cemetery. The independently owned cemetery, which is a forty-minute drive from downtown Chicago, held the contract to bury the unclaimed dead in Cook County for most of the 1980s and 1990s. Joseph Ledwell, the longtime pastor of the nearby First Presbyterian Church, volunteered to administer services for the indigent deceased during this time. "I keep my own records of the people buried there," Ledwell told me. "I don't have all the names, but I did a count in 1996 and there were at least four thousand adults since 1980. I've done almost all the services by myself, alone. They are short, dignified services. And I say the same prayers I would say for anyone else."

The county keeps the cost of the burials low by using a simple, unfinished plywood box for each corpse, marking the case with an identifying number on a brass tag and a disposable paper note, then placing the caskets together in a single trench. "It's based on economics and efficiency," cemetery general manager Kevin Vaughan explained. "It would take a long time to bury, in this case, sixty-eight individual

Figure 49. Together in the end: mortuary workers bury the unclaimed victims of the heat wave in a mass grave outside the city. Source: Reuters / Getty Photos; photographer: Scott Olson. Courtesy Archive Photos.

graves."[3] In general, Vaughan said, the least expensive burial costs at least one thousand dollars. But the mass burial comes out to about one hundred dollars per body, and workers can dig out and replace the broad swath of dirt in a matter of hours.

On the morning of the mass interment a score of journalists arrived at the cemetery to witness the event. Only two civilians, local Homewood historian Elaine Egdorf and her young granddaughter, showed up for the service. Elaine recalled the occasion in brutally clear terms, and her account of the funeral is worth quoting at length.

> I remember it very, very well. It was Friday morning. I had the radio on, and I heard an announcement that the burial of the heat victims was going to take place in Homewood that very morning. And when I heard that, I thought, "Well, how did I not know about that," and then I thought, "Oh, for many years, the Homewood Memorial Gardens has bid on the contract to bury the unclaimed bodies from Cook County, and Reverend Joseph Ledwell always volunteered to do a service over these unclaimed people, and it would happen about once a month." It was always my understanding that it would just be the truck drivers and the cemetery personnel and Reverend Ledwell, and that's all that was ever there, because no one ever cared about these people—or, maybe they did care but they were just unclaimed. And I thought, "Well, as the local historian, I need to go out there and bring my camera." But I also thought, "This is my opportunity to just be a witness to history."
>
> It didn't occur to me until we pulled into the cemetery that there would be media there. There usually isn't. This happens all the time, I know. At that cemetery, they'll maybe bury every thirty days, every sixty days, whenever they get a truckload of bodies. You live near a big city and a lot of people don't have close friends who check on them, and it happens.
>
> I think the number of boxes made it really hit home. It was a little bit overwhelming to see so many wooden boxes in a row. To think that there were so many unclaimed people, and after a certain period of time they had to do something with the bodies. It would be one thing to see five or ten, but to see this long, long row, and what flashed back in my mind were the newsreels of the nineteen forties, of the mass burials with wooden boxes in Europe, because of war. Well, this wasn't war. This was right here. This was where I live.
>
> [The grave site] was at a barren spot, way at the edge of the cemetery, right next to the quarry. It wasn't underneath the trees, because you had to have such a big site, and when they have to do a mass burial like this

they usually use the perimeters of the cemetery. You had to have a big area. You just couldn't do, you know, one or two at a time. It wouldn't be economically feasible for them.

Well, they just dug a trench, a long, long trench, and put the wooden boxes in, and usually they rent a truck and bring the bodies, so the truck was still at the north end, and during the summer time, many times the cemetery then hires extra personnel. Many times they're just teenage kids. "To think," you know, "You witness all of these things, but when you get to a certain age in life, you think, okay, well this is life, this is a fact." But that long, long trench . . .

And then chills ran up my spine, as hot a day as it was, because there weren't any families there like my family, to cherish them and mourn them as they were being buried. I felt sad that these people didn't have—even though they had Reverend Ledwell and these other people, they didn't have family to mourn them as they were being laid to rest. It was just like there was nobody there caring about them.

But this whole thing was very, very long, because apparently they were waiting for other clergymen to arrive, and I don't know if the time had changed for some of them, but I think it was Reverend Ledwell who said a few words, and then there were some late arrivals, apparently from the city, after Reverend Ledwell was done.

Meghan and I were the only civilians there. So the media converged upon us wanting quotes because we were the only people to interview. [Looks over a photograph of reporters at the cemetery] Well, just in this one picture, one-two-three-four-five-six-seven-eight-nine-ten-eleven-twelve-thirteen-fourteen—fifteen [journalists] in this one photograph. And that probably was a fraction of the people who were there. There were cameramen, camera crew, drivers, the reporters that actually appear on camera, there were print media. There was all this media there and nobody to interview. It was almost as if we became symbols for the mourners, the family that wasn't there.

But you have to do that to make yourself feel better that these people maybe were neglected or didn't have family or, "Gee, I should have brought them a fan," or, "Why didn't I bring them some food?" I think the world kind of felt like they needed to show—whether it was the memory of these people or the rest of the world that were not really like that—we don't neglect people, we really care about them, so we need to bring flowers or we need to have a monument or whatever. I'm not exactly sure, but that's kind of the feeling that I got. We need to do this, you know, for our own sake, that makes us feel better, that we're going to remember these people, even though we didn't know them, or maybe some of them really did know some of these people and they felt badly.

When you think of how many people died because of the heat . . . these were just the unclaimed ones. The heat wave, when you think of it [pauses], how could this really happen?

Due to the unusually high number of unclaimed bodies to bury and the public nature of the heat wave deaths, the county and cemetery staff had arranged to have several religious officials administer the funeral. Yet long after the service was scheduled to begin, two of the ministers who had promised to attend had failed to arrive, and the ceremony began and ended without them. As always, Reverend Ledwell led the service, and the man accustomed to handling the occasions alone found that the presence of so many journalists and the constant clicking of cameras made the countless other burials he had done seem all the more tragic. "It's sad that we only get interested in this when there's a natural disaster," he remarked. "I did a service just before the heat wave and no one was there."

Another religious official, a stranger to the potter's field, found the discordance of the gruesome event in a city brimming with pride and confidence to be too much to bear. "You always hear about mass burials around the world, in war and disaster," he lamented. "And this was home. This was Chicago." At the time of the service, the large grave, which is more than 160 feet long and 10 feet wide, had no tombstone, no sign, nothing to show that the bodies buried therein testify to the expendability of life on the margins of a major American metropolis at the moment of its greatest prosperity. In the summer of 1996 a group of private citizens led by the late Earl Lewis helped to erect a four-foot-high granite monument to adorn the burial site; the stone now stands as the only durable marker of the bodies lying beneath.

I last visited the burial grounds in the summer of 2000, a little more than five years after the heat wave. It was a quiet, cloudy morning, and there were few other visitors at the cemetery. I drove toward the grave with one of the cemetery managers, parked at a shed near the road, and trudged up a slight incline until we reached the vast and empty place. A small American flag, its canvas worn from exposure, lay in the dirt at the base of the monument. When I asked the manager how often visitors came to the cemetery, she answered as if she had considered the question many times before. "Some reporters come from time to time, but that's it. We've never had a family member come for any of the heat victims. Not once. People from Chicago don't come either."

Homewood is not far from Chicago, but it is not surprising that the mass grave and the people interred therein matter so little to a city that had no place for them in life or in death. Almost no one is interested in a reminder of what is otherwise so easy to forget. For some people in Chicago, though, the glimpse of isolation afforded by the city's deadly summer week proved too powerful to ignore. As he carried the bodies toward their final resting place, one of the young mortuary workers paused to consider the human tragedy that he was helping to bury. "It's so sad," he remarked, and then summoned the words that so many had pondered but so few had spoken as they watched the urban disaster unfold. "I hope what we all hope: that we don't end up this way."[4]

Notes

PROLOGUE

1. Official city reports list two different heat-related mortality totals for the month of July: 514 and 521. I use the latter figure throughout this book. The excess death measure, however, is the more accurate count.

2. National Weather Service 1995, x.

3. Whitman, et al. 1997, 1517.

4. Bachelard [1934] 1984, 104.

5. Farmer 1995, 5.

6. Park [1916] 1969, 126.

INTRODUCTION

1. Laczko's story was initially reported by journalist Michael Lev (1995), and I extended the inquiry into his case by examining files at the Office of the Cook Country Public Administrator. According to public investigators, the practice of collecting junk is common among people who live and die alone.

2. City of Chicago 1995, 2.

3. This will not to know about U.S. social problems was the subject of Philip Slater's "toilet assumption" in his best-selling book, *The Pursuit of Loneliness* (1990). Slater's provocative claim is that Americans live with the hope that ignoring the noxious social byproducts of the world they have created is a means of making them go away.

4. Weather systems such as hurricanes, tornadoes, earthquakes, and floods not only make a direct and recognizable physical impact on the people and property in their paths, they also provide graphic and spectacular images for the news media to display. Television, newspaper, and magazine reports feature such disasters prominently, making them the focus of local and often national attention even when their human toll is slight (Gans 1979; Singer 1987; Sood, Stockdale, and Rogers 1987).

There is a long line of epidemiological and public health research that establishes an association between heat wave mortality and poverty, old age, sex, and ethnoracial status, with poor and elderly black men being most vulnerable (Applegate, et al. 1981; Jones, et al. 1982; Martinez, et al. 1989; Oechsli and Buechley 1970; U.S. Centers for Disease Control and Prevention 1995a). In addition to the nearly annual review article on heat-related mortality published in the *Morbidity and Mortality Weekly Report,* medical and public health scholars typically analyze unusually severe heat disasters and report their findings in professional journals.

5. Scholars often make inquiries into other disasters as a way of revealing otherwise imperceptible conditions in organizations (Das 1995; Vaughan 1996), cities (Davis 1998), communities (Erikson 1976), and politics (Molotch and Lester 1974, 1975). Yet reporting on heat waves tends to conceal the social conditions that make them so deadly. Social scientists, whose studies of disasters in the United States generally focus on the stratified impact of extreme events, have largely ignored heat waves, thereby confirming as well as contributing to the insignificance of heat wave victims. Indeed, a survey of major U.S. disaster studies reveals that heat waves receive scant if any attention despite their severe human impact. Recent studies by Erikson (1994) and Davis (1998) trace the impact of numerous forms of disasters but say little about extreme heat; Mary Comerio's (1998) study of housing and disasters reviews the significance of architectural vulnerability in tornadoes, hurricanes, and earthquakes, but does not mention the impact of housing conditions on human victims of heat waves.

In its effort to broaden the scope of social research and contemporary politics by redefining nature and highlighting exposure to hazardous environments as an important but underanalyzed form of inequality, environmental justice research has established new ways of conceiving the forms of modern social division (Cronon 1995; Szasz and Meuser 1997). According to most of this research, environmental dangers such as proximity to hazardous waste storage facilities and polluting industries, unsafe water sources, and unsanitary residential conditions are largely distributed according to the class, group status, and political power of communities. In their attempts to denaturalize nature (Steinberg 2000), environmental justice scholars have noted the possibility of treating catastrophes as social events, and this study helps to establish a problematic that belongs at the center of environmental sociology.

In the social sciences, though, most recent disaster studies have shifted the focus from environmental to technological catastrophes, and scholars interested in what Kai Erikson calls "the new species of trouble" increasingly draw firm distinctions between "technical" and "natural" disasters (Erikson 1994; Freudenburg 1998). As these terms reorganize the field of disaster research, they produce a gulf between the new environmental sociology and the sociology of disaster, which often affirms the idea that environmental catastrophes are natural phenomena and neglects to establish that social exclusion and deprivation render certain communities vulnerable to the elements. An obvious distinction exists between environmental disasters, such as heat waves and floods, and catastrophes, such as plane crashes or factory explosions, which stem from industrial or technological mistakes and malfunctions. But the category *natural disasters* naturalizes, and therefore renders necessary and inevitable, the damage that is induced by the climate but organized by societies and their governments. In his book *Poverty and Famines: An Essay on Entitlement and Deprivation,* Amartya Sen (1981) shows that a series of catastrophes such as sustained droughts, long considered to be caused by natural forces, were in fact produced by political and social systems that deprived people of the purchasing power they needed to avoid starvation. The risk that an external pressure such

NOTES TO PAGES 17-19 • • • 245

as the heat will induce massive social suffering and death hinges on the "risk positions" in which vulnerable segments of societies are situated (Beck 1992); and, as Sen argues, these positions, as well as the levels of vulnerability that they represent, are shaped by the systems of entitlement and social protection that help define but also differentiate modern societies.

6. Mitchell 1999, 2.

7. Erikson 1976, 12.

8. See Kiernan and Zielinski (1995) and Fornek and Steinberg (1995). It is common for political commissions, journalistic reports, and popular myths to cover up the stratified impact of disasters and other major traumas, often through accounts that simplify and pluralize suffering or mortality experienced primarily by the most vulnerable groups. In his study of the *Titanic* disaster, Steven Biel (1996) calls attention to the myths of social consensus that masked the extreme class differences in the *Titanic* mortality levels. One minister observed that "'[t]he rich died and the poor died alike' . . . which was probably true in individual cases though not in the aggregate" (Biel 1996, 45). The anthropologist Veena Das (1995) recalls a similar story in her analysis of the Bhopal disaster in India.

9. Throughout this book I use the term *ethnoracial* to describe the basis of identities reputed to be based on "race" or "ethnicity." There are particularly compelling reasons for refusing to use the term *race* outside of quotation marks so as to deny it status as an analytic term; for although "race" is a social fact of modern life, the term carries with it the historical resonance of a scientific fact rooted in biology even though such ideas have been largely refuted. All categories are real constructions, classifications realized in theory and practice regardless of their foundations. The concept of "ethnicity" carries much of the baggage contained within the concept of "race," but scholars have treated it more kindly because it refers to historical experience rather than the body, and because it is viewed as a less pernicious form of division. The concept "ethnoracial" brings the two ideas in tension and purposely calls attention to the peculiar, conflictual, and often unexamined ways we classify people and groups. The term is not intended to serve as a solution to the problem of classification, but as an incitement to deeper consideration of modern dividing practices.

10. See Whitman, et al. (1997) for the most comprehensive assessment of the death rates for different Chicago groups. In a memorandum from the Chicago Department of Health dated September 1995, city epidemiologists cautioned that the rough equivalence of African-American and Caucasian heat-related deaths should not be interpreted as equivalent heat-related death rates: "The number of deaths among Non-Hispanic Black people (n = 253) and Non-Hispanic White people (n = 252) was almost identical, while there were very few deaths among Hispanic people (n = 9) and people of other races (n = 4). In 4 cases race was undetermined. Since non-Hispanic Black and non-Hispanic White people have different age distributions in Chicago, it is important to take this into consideration when considering rates. . . . The rate for non-Hispanic Black people is almost twice as high as the rate for non-Hispanic White people for each age interval except the first" (Whitman 1995, 1). African Americans were five times more likely than whites to die in Missouri

heat waves between 1979 and 1988 (U.S. Centers for Disease Control and Prevention 1996), and elderly blacks have been identified as the group most vulnerable to heat-related health crises in several case studies (Applegate, et al. 1981; U.S. Centers for Disease Control and Prevention 1984). In recent years public health scholars have been inquiring into what they call the Latino paradox: the finding that, on a range of health outcomes, Latinos fare better than other groups who appear to have fewer risks of mortality or morbidity. See, among others, Abraido-Lanza, et al. (1999). Chapter 3 offers a social ecological perspective on this question.

11. Gibson 2000, 54.

12. Chicago's concept of a community area was established more than fifty years ago through the work of the Social Sciences Research Committee of the University of Chicago, with the cooperation of local agencies and the U.S. Bureau of the Census. According to the Chicago Fact Book Consortium (1995, xvii), the community areas were originally drawn on the basis of consideration such as "(1) the settlement, growth, and history of the area; (2) local identification with the area; (3) the local trade area; (4) distribution and membership of local institutions; and (5) natural and artificial barriers such as the Chicago River and its branches, railroad lines, local transportation systems, and parks and boulevards." The community areas do not correspond precisely with Chicago's neighborhood and community structure. In fact they are artificial constructions of social scientists and bureaucrats more than they are organic categories known and used by city residents. Community areas are useful for comparing sections of the city, mostly because statistical data for them goes back several decades, allowing comparative and historical analysis, and because census track data are sometimes too small to reveal trends and tendencies in aggregated communities. There are now seventy-seven community areas in the city of Chicago, with 1990 populations ranging from 6,828 (Near South Side) to 114,079 (Austin) and averaging about 36,000.

13. In the social sciences, the long tradition of social epidemiology established by Durkheim (1951) and applied to death in the United States by Evelyn Kitagawa and Philip Hauser (1973) has established considerable evidence that death and dying are eminently social and stratified processes. Yet given the current literature on the heat wave, which includes official reports issued by government agencies and scientific studies conducted by health scholars, it is important to illustrate the ways in which everyday inequalities in Chicago expressed themselves through the failing bodies of the city's most vulnerable residents.

14. Paul Farmer's *Infections and Inequalities: The Modern Plagues* (1999) is an exemplary model for a multilayered approach to social epidemiology that incorporates concern for the political economy of inequality into its analytic project.

15. The analysis blends the comprehensive approach to the study of social suffering established by Pierre Bourdieu in *The Weight of the World* (1999) with the model of disaster research developed by Amartya Sen (1981).

16. See Bourdieu's introductory essay in *The Weight of the World* (1999, 3) for a discussion of how bringing together diverse and divergent viewpoints into an account of social suffering helps to establish relationships among peo-

ple whose actions touch one another even when they do not make direct contact.

17. The project of exploring the relationships of different parts and people in the city was central to the early Chicago School sociologists, but subsequent generations of urban scholars tended to focus on particular neighborhoods or groups. As Richard Sennett explains, "The first members of the Chicago School . . . asked questions about the internal character of the city, about how the different parts of the city functioned in relation to each other, about the different kinds of experience to be had within the same city at the same point in time" (1969, 12).

18. See Bourdieu's *The State Nobility* (1996), and especially the preface by Loïc Wacquant, for an elaboration of the concept of symbolic power.

19. Mauss ([1916] 1979).

20. A variation of this position helped to found and motivate the Chicago tradition of urban sociology. In his classic essay, "The City: Suggestions for the Investigation of Human Behavior in the Urban Environment," Robert Park ([1916] 1969) drew on Durkheim's legacy to argue that the city is itself an extreme case that facilitates social research. "A great city," Park claimed, "tends to . . . lay bare to the public view in a massive manner all the human characters and traits which are ordinarily obscured and suppressed in smaller communities" (126). Michael Burawoy (1998) articulates the second principle in his theoretical explanation of the extended case method. "Institutions," he argues, "reveal much about themselves when under stress or in crisis, when they face the unexpected as well as the routine" (1998, 14).

21. Among the major statements in the debates about new forms of urban inequality are Peter Marcuse, "What's So New about Divided Cities?" (1993); Peter Marcuse, "The Enclave, the Citadel, and the Ghetto: What Has Changed in the Post-Fordist U.S. City" (1997); Loïc J. D. Wacquant, "The Rise of Advanced Marginality: Notes on Its Nature and Implications" (1996); Douglas Massey, "The Age of Extremes: Concentrated Affluence and Poverty in the Twenty-First Century" (1996); and Manuel Castells, *End of Millennium* (1998).

22. Nieves 2000.

23. Al Hunter's *Symbolic Communities* (1974) remains the best analysis of the symbolic construction of Chicago community areas, and of the myths of community that pervade the city.

24. Donoghue, et al. 1997, 11.

25. In *The Truly Disadvantaged* (1987) and *When Work Disappears* (1996), sociologist William Julius Wilson documents the extent of Chicago's devastation as the city lost hundreds of thousands of manufacturing jobs. Wilson's focus on the extreme impact of this decline on Chicago's poor African Americans should not obscure the broader consequences of de-industrialization on the city.

26. Fegelman 1995, 3.

27. Shen, et al. 1998.

28. Schreuder and Stein 1995, 1.

29. In a 1970 article published in the journal *Environmental Research*, Frank Oechsli and Robert Buechley (1970) used the excess mortality concept to assess the death tolls from Los Angeles heat waves in 1939, 1955, and 1963.

30. For a more complete description of the methodology Whitman and his colleagues used, see Whitman, et al. (1997).

31. No matter how vigorously health officials insisted that the dangers of the heat were not specific to Chicago, reporters repeatedly asked why Chicago had experienced so much more mortality than other cities. *Morbidity and Mortality Weekly Report* and the National Weather Service have published reviews of the deaths in Milwaukee (National Weather Service 1996; U.S. Centers for Disease Control and Prevention 1996), and a group of Wisconsin scholars have written an unpublished manuscript study of the crisis (Nashold, et al., n.d.), but the Milwaukee disaster has received little public attention. There is a similar history for a devastating Wisconsin fire in the town of Peshtigo in 1871. Although it proved to be far more deadly than Chicago's Great Fire in the same year, it has received far less attention.

See Paul Jargowksy, *Poverty and Place* (1997); and Douglas Massey and Nancy Denton, *American Apartheid* (1993) for data on segregation by race and class in Chicago and Milwaukee. Both cities have relatively high rates of concentrated poverty and racial segregation. The concentrations of deaths in the city provide good reason to think that conditions specific to the urban environment contributed to the vulnerability of Chicago and Milwaukee residents. Researchers from the Illinois Department of Public Health (1997) showed that although the heat wave affected the southern regions of Illinois, the Chicago mortality rate of 20 per 100,000 residents was ten times higher than the rate downstate, which was 2 per 100,000 residents.

32. Fegelman 1995, 3.

33. Ibid.

34. Illinois Department of Public Health 1997.

35. Marcel Mauss ([1916] 1979) proposes this kind of inquiry in his essay "Social Variations of the Eskimo: Social Cohesion in Polysegmentary Societies." Explaining the methodology of his ethnological research, Mauss writes that "the question arises at once, not only of institutions taken one at a time or of collective representations taken each on its own, but of the general agreement of all those things into a social system. How to describe this fact, which welds each society together and frames the individual, in terms that are not overly literary, too inaccurate, too little defined."

36. Though see "Living with the Dying," the provocative study by Robert Buckingham and colleagues (1976), in which the authors compare the experience of dying in a hospice to that of dying in a hospital. These are not cases of dying alone, for although the patients are relatively secluded in their institutional settings, they receive some attention and support from staff.

37. Most of the people who died alone in their homes were so isolated that it is difficult to trace what they did before they perished. The widespread belief that the heat wave victims had been largely abandoned by their families made it difficult to conduct reliable interviews with relatives of the decedents. Given the public discourse about the heat wave deaths, to ask a child or a sibling where they were when their relation died alone was also to accuse them of neglect.

My strategy for addressing these challenges involved using the tools of historians, such as archival research and interviews, to learn about the lived experiences of Chicago residents during the week. But in addition I conducted field-work to observe the conditions of seniors who lived alone as well as the social environments of key sites for my study, such as neighborhoods on the West Side, city government agencies, and a city newsroom where reporters wrote about the event. Places change in subtle ways from year to year, and the condi-tions of everyday life in these locations were no doubt somewhat different when I viewed them in the years immediately following the heat wave than they were during the crisis. I attempted to reproduce the conditions of the 1995 summer as much as possible in the residential areas where the climate has a clear impact on social life, so much of my fieldwork on the West Side and in the single room occupancy dwellings took place during subsequent summers. I was especially diligent about observing neighborhood conditions during extremely hot days, when the climate offered opportunities to revisit conditions that would be most similar to those prevalent in the heat wave.

38. This chapter aims to add an ethnographic perspective to current de-bates over what scholars of urban poverty call "neighborhood effects." See the articles in *Neighborhood Poverty: Context and Consequences for Children* (Brooks-Gunn, Duncan, and Aber 1997) for various discussions and debates over the question of whether neighborhoods, as social and spatial systems, have inde-pendent effects on the life chances or outcomes of residents.

CHAPTER ONE

1. See Nieves (2000, 10).

2. Studies of people who live alone show that the practice of surrounding oneself with stuff is quite common. See Rubinstein's (1986, 158–65) discussion of the activities of older men who live alone, especially the description of Mr. Cohen.

3. In focusing on the heat wave decedents the present text, too, fails to give a representative sample of older Americans who live on their own, but this is not its purpose. Instead, the story of the heat wave helps to deepen our knowl-edge of the isolated and reclusive seniors who have been largely excluded from academic studies and popular literature. There is little question that aging alone can be a rich personal and social experience, albeit one filled with chal-lenges. Social scientific work that documents the ways in which older people living alone make their lives meaningful has played a crucial role in upsetting unfounded myths about the impossibility of aging well.

In *The Unexpected Community,* for example, Arlie Hochschild (1973, xiv) doc-uments the active social lives of a group of Bay Area seniors who, as she emphat-ically states, "were not isolated and not lonely" but instead "were part of a com-munity I did not expect to find," one that worked together to solve the problem of loneliness that proves so troublesome for the elderly. There are vital commu-nities of older people, and Hochschild's research does the work of showing how these groups come into being and portraying them once they are made. But too often readers of Hochschild are so eager to celebrate the community she describes that they forget that she chose to study Merrill Court precisely because the residents there were an exceptional case. The opening lines of her epilogue explain the goal of her project much better than do many of her interpreters. She writes, "The most important point I am trying to make in this book concerns the people it does not discuss—the isolated. Merrill Court was an unexpected community, an exception. Living in ordinary apartments and houses, in shabby downtown hotels, sitting in parks and eating in cheap restaurants, are old people in various degrees and sorts of isolation" (Hochschild 1973, 137). Hochshild leaves it to others to render the social worlds of the isolated as explicit as she makes the world in Merrill Court.

The same could be said of Barbara Meyerhoff's renowned anthropological study, *Number Our Days* (1978), in which the focus is on the most integrated and socially active seniors who attend a community center for the elderly in Venice, California; and of Hamilton Gibson's *Loneliness in Later Life* (2000), in which the author makes a generalized argument about the low levels of loneliness among seniors on the basis of a sample comprising active elderly participants in a local university program.

4. Coles 1997, 4.

5. See Kearl (1996) for a discussion of the relationship between aging well and dying well. Kearl argues that "there is a curious silence in gerontological circles about death's bearing on the aging experience," but that recent controversies over euthanasia have helped to open debates about the good death (1996, 336). Sherwin Nuland (1993) is among the more recent writers to discuss the modern version of the *ars moriendi* as a necessarily collective process. Describing a man dying of AIDS, Nuland writes: "During his terminal weeks in the hospital, Kent was never alone. Whatever help they could or could not provide him at the final hours, there is no question that the constant presence of his friends eased him beyond what might have been achieved by the nursing staff, no matter the attentiveness of their care" (Nuland 1993, 196). In a British study of dying, Clive Seale (1995) found that in many cases dying in a hospital proved to be a more socially integrating experience than did dying at home when there were few sources of social support. Seale also assesses how communities are affected when one of their own dies alone.

6. Herbert Gans (1997) reports that the six best-selling sociology books in the United States are, in order, *The Lonely Crowd, Tally's Corner, Pursuit of Loneliness, Fall of Public Man, Blaming the Victim,* and *Habits of the Heart.* Of these, only *Blaming the Victim* does not explicitly address the issues of being alone, loneliness, or the collapse of community.

7. A cruel irony of the mortality among socially isolated Chicago residents is that Chicago, the birthplace and symbolic capital of U.S. urban sociology, is the living laboratory in which isolation was "discovered" in the American urban context and developed into a core category of social scientific analysis. Moreover, Chicago is the site through which William Julius Wilson (1987) reestablished social isolation as one of the primary issues in contemporary poverty research. If there is one place in the United States where sociological research would have made explicit the conditions as well as the causes and consequences of social isolation, it would surely be Chicago. Yet during and after the heat wave most everyone in the city, including social scientists and policy experts, expressed surprise and even disbelief at the extent of the condition. How, we should ask, could there be so much writing about social isolation in Chicago and yet so little knowledge about the status of the isolated?

Part of the answer is that the concept of isolation used by U.S. urban sociologists, beginning with Robert Park and continuing through the later generations of Chicago school social scientists, has not referred to the conventional meaning of the term: the literal disconnection of individuals from one another. Instead, sociologists have used the concept of isolation to describe the relationships among rather than within communities, a metaphor that draws upon the image of literally isolated individuals and extends it to the neighborhood or group level. With a few exceptions, sociologists have done little research on literal social isolation, leaving the matter to specialized researchers in epidemiology, social gerontology, and community psychology whose studies fail to explicate the social and historical contexts in which isolation occurs. Conceptually, however, the research on isolation has joined with social network studies to pave the way for a literal or relational definition of isolation. Since the 1970s a small number of social network analysts have constructed a relational category of isolation so that it refers to (1) a characteristic of a person's network, such as Claude Fischer and Susan Phillips's definition of *isolation* as "knowing relatively few people who are probable sources of rewarding exchanges" (1982, 22); (2) the behavior of a person in a network, such as the definition of *isolation* as "a lack of interaction or contact with individuals within one's social network" (LaVeist, et al. 1997, 723); or (3) some combination of the two (Krause 1993). William Julius Wilson (1996) also recognized a form of literal isolation, that of persons or groups who live in high-crime areas and restrict contact with neighbors or barricade themselves in their homes to be safe. Aware of the confusion that his terminology created, in his recent work Wilson cautions, "When speaking of social isolation, therefore, a distinction should be made between those families who deliberately isolate themselves from other families in dangerous neighborhoods and those who lack contact or sustained interaction with institutions, families, and individuals that represent mainstream society" (1996, 64). Elijah Anderson (1999) and Frank Furstenberg and his colleagues (1998) have also found that isolation and reclusion are survival strategies for residents of poor areas with high crime levels.

8. The focus on living and dying alone should not obscure the fact that isolation in the city remains a relatively uncommon condition. The majority of city dwellers, as Claude Fischer ([1976] 1984, 1982) has convincingly shown, are integrated into personal networks that provide them with support during normal times as well as times of crisis. There is, by now, compelling evidence that Wirth's general theory of urbanism—the thesis that city living will break down most forms of solidarity, destroying social groups and creating an anomic society and alienated, isolated individuals—is simply not true; nor is there evidence that city residents on the whole are any less socially integrated than residents of rural areas. On this matter, then, urban sociology is at odds with the lay perception that, as many of my informants put it, "big cities make isolation happen." Whether urbanites remain with their traditional ethnic groups (Drake and Cayton [1945] 1993; Gans 1962; Hannerz 1969; Kornblum 1974; Suttles 1968) or form new subcultural groups on the basis of shared interests and experiences (Fischer 1975, [1976] 1984), decades of research have shown that despite the common experience of feeling alone in crowded urban areas (Riesman, Glazer, and Denny 1950), in private life most city dwellers have rich and rewarding relationships and social networks (Fischer and Phillips 1982).

What I want to show here, however, is that literal social isolation arises in certain situations which, though historically unusual, are becoming more common in American cities today.

9. General population data are from the U.S. Bureau of the Census. Wuthnow (1998) reports the data on the increase in the total number of people living alone from 1970 to 1994; the Administration on Aging (1999, 4) reports that 9.9 million noninstitutionalized seniors lived alone in 1998. The number of women living alone doubled between 1970 and 1996, rising from 7.3 million to 14.6 million. The number of men living alone nearly tripled during the same period, going from 3.5 million to 10.2 million.

10. Two important studies of seniors who live alone are Clive Seale, "Living Alone towards the End of Life" (1996), and Robert Rubinstein, *Singular Paths: Old Men Living Alone* (1986).

11. This conception of social isolation departs from both sociological definitions of the term, which generally refer to relations between groups rather than people, and from conventional gerontological definitions of isolation, which define isolation as being single or living alone. There are an increasing number of social network studies and gerontological reports that classify social integration or isolation by relative levels of social contact. Rubinstein (1986, 172–79), for example, classifies social integration and activity on a scale ranging from "very low range" to "high range"; and Gibson (2000, 4–6) lists four types of loneliness: "physical aloneness," "loneliness as a state of mind," "the feeling of isolation due to a personal characteristic," and "solitude."

12. See Gibson (2000) for a review of studies showing that most seniors who live alone are not lonely. There are a number of epidemiological studies showing the significance of social integration for longevity and health, including articles written from extensive longitudinal studies in Alameda County, California; Tecumseh, Michigan; and Durham County, North Carolina (see Blazer 1982; House, Robbins, and Metzner 1982; Seeman, et al. 1987).

According to federal statistics, older people who live alone or with nonrelatives are more than three times more likely to be poor than are seniors who live with families (Administration on Aging 1999, 10). Thompson and Krause (1998, S356) find not only that people who live alone report more fear of crime than those who live with others, but also that "the greater sense of security among those who live with others appears to permeate beyond the home because they report less fear of crime than their counterparts."

A recent study in the *New England Journal of Medicine* (Gurley, et al. 1996) suggests that their solitary condition leaves them vulnerable in emergencies and times of illness. Researchers in San Francisco, a city about one-fourth the size of Chicago, report that in twelve weeks emergency medical workers found 367 people who lived alone and were discovered in their apartments to be either incapacitated or, in a quarter of the cases, dead. "Our results," they argue, "indicate that it is common for elderly people living alone to be found helpless or dead in their homes" (1996, 1714, 1716). The victims, as in the Chicago heat wave, were disproportionately old, white, and African American, with older black men most overrepresented. Many of them suffered tremendously while they waited to be discovered in their homes, suffering "that could (have been) reduced by earlier intervention," but that was exacerbated by the victims' isolation (1996, 1714, 1716). The success of mobile emergency call systems, or personal health alarms, is one indication of the extent to which we recognize the danger of living alone.

13. Gibson 2000.

14. Despite these difficulties, a small number of studies attempt to enumerate or characterize isolates within narrow demographic boundaries. One survey, for example, finds that 4.3 percent of elderly African-American women live alone and reported having no contact with family or friends in the two weeks prior to their interview (LaVeist, et al. 1997); a study of isolation in Atlanta reveals that poor people are less likely than others to live with another adult, have even one close social tie, or have a discussion partner outside the home (Tigges, Brown, and Green 1998); and another survey shows that elderly residents of deteriorated neighborhoods are more likely than seniors in nondeteriorated neighborhoods to have limited interaction with others (Krause 1993). All these data, however, are likely to underestimate the extent of literal isolation because the most isolated people would not have been accessible to researchers and would therefore have been excluded from the surveys.

Rubinstein's (1986) study of older men who live alone is also based on a sample of men who participate in senior centers and are therefore relatively integrated; yet Rubinstein classifies sixteen of his forty-seven informants as having a "very low range" or a "low range" of social contacts because they reported zero to two subjectively significant ties. According to Rubinstein, "Four men . . . were part of no active social circles or groups. Three of the four were limited in their ability to get out of the house due to physical disabilities. Two of the four had virtually no family, while the other two were estranged. . . . These men had no one they could identify as a close friend." Twelve other men "are associated with one or no social circles or activity groups. They rarely make or receive phone calls, nor do they often write or receive personal letters. Official contacts make up a large percentage of weekly contacts" (1986, 172–3).

15. In Milwaukee, which experienced a heat wave mortality rate comparable with Chicago in 1995, roughly 27 percent of the decedents were found alone in their homes more than one day after the estimated time of death, and roughly 75 percent of the victims were older than sixty years of age (Nashold n.d.).

16. See Semenza, et al. (1996, 86–87, 90).

17. City of Chicago 1995, 4.

18. Jacobs is quoted in Siewers 1995, 11. For thorough documentation of the trends toward isolation, see Robert Putnam's *Bowling Alone* (2000, pt. 1 and pp. 99–106). Despite the many criticisms of Putnam's analysis, I have yet to see compelling evidence to dispute his findings that in the 1990s Americans spent far less time socializing with friends, family, and neighbors than they did in the previous decades. I find Putnam's argument about the causes of this atomization less persuasive. "Generational change," which is his most important causal mechanism, is itself a condition—or even a stand-in for "history"—that needs a social explanation beyond what Putnam provides. Moreover, his account of the relative social integration of the elderly, whose "contribution to community life almost doubled" between the 1970s and 1990s, emphasizes the exceptional activity of younger, healthier seniors but says nothing about

the older and more isolated elderly (2000, chap. 14, esp. pp. 256–57). Social service workers for the elderly and gerontologists such as Rubinstein (1986), though, argue that there is bipolar distribution of highly active and mostly reclusive seniors. It is true that good health, robust pensions, and ample time allow some members of the oldest generation to participate vigorously in civic life; but illness, poverty, and constraints on mobility isolate many others. The question of whether there is a coherent, unified generational culture that explains this variation remains unclear.

19. In *The Culture of Fear,* Barry Glassner (1999) makes a similar argument about the ways in which widespread fear, particularly about security, has influenced a range of American cultural practices.

20. These trends are both national and international phenomena. According to a study by the U.S. Bureau of the Census, 12 percent of the population in the United Nations list of developed countries was sixty years of age or older in 1950, but the proportion grew to 19 percent by 1998 and is projected to reach 28 percent by 2025. The numbers of people aged 60 years or older is rising in developing countries as well, going from 100 million in 1950 to 355 million in 1998 and a projected 839 million by 2025 (Lawson 1998). The report also predicts a vast increase in the population of Americans aged 80 years or older, with the number of men projected to grow from 2,881,000 in 1998 to more than 5,600,000 by 2025, and the number of women from 5,835,000 to more than 8,750,000 in the same period. Although the increasing longevity of males means that fewer married women will experience long periods of living alone, the absolute number of seniors living alone is expected to rise. Authors of the U.S. Census report on caretaking show that in the United States in 1995, 17 percent of men and 42 percent of women older than 65 years of age lived alone (Lawson 1998). In another study Christopher Jencks and Barbara Boyle Torrey (1988) report that from 1960 to 1985, the percentage of all Americans 65 to 74 years of age who lived alone grew from 17 to 25, and for Americans aged 75 years or older the increase was even more dramatic, going from 21 percent to 39 percent in just twenty-five years. Of course, most people who live by themselves maintain social contacts with family and friends, and although some estimate that older people who live alone spend the overwhelming majority of their time without company, it is important to make an analytic and descriptive distinction between social isolation and living alone. Still, living alone, whether in a home, an apartment, or a hotel, is a necessary precondition for the kind of isolation that is of interest to us here.

21. In *Bowling Alone,* Robert Putnam (2000, 265) reports the connection between isolation and depression, but does not elaborate its implications for the social insecurity of seniors.

22. See the literature review on African Americans with living children in Wolf, et al. (1983, 465, 470) and the reviews of men and social networks in Patterson (1998) and Fischer and Phillips (1982).

23. See the review as well as the findings in Wolf, et al. (1983, 465, 469). The Indiana University study is reported in Fleming-Moran, Kenworthy-Bennett, and Harlow (1991).

24. Although it has a similar name, Little Brothers Friends of the Elderly is a secular organization and is not associated with Little Brothers of the Poor.

See any of the recent annual reports published by Little Brothers Friends of the Elderly. The passage here is quoted from the 1997 report.

25. Keigher 1991, 72.

26. Martin 1995, 2.

27. In an article showing the association between neighborhood deterioration and social isolation, Neal Krause (1993, 19) constructs a measure for deterioration that includes interviewers' and respondents' assessments of (1) the respondent's dwelling; (2) the physical condition of nearby houses, buildings, streets, and roads; and (3) other environmental stressors, including noise level, air quality, and safety from crime. See Thompson and Krause (1998, S354–S356) for an excellent review of the literature that shows a relationship between local social ecology and residents' social ties and fears about crime.

28. Just as city residents tend to be more concerned about crime than residents of suburban and rural areas, African Americans and other ethnic groups who live in areas with higher levels of crime are more likely than whites to report fear of crime in surveys (Joseph 1997; Miethe 1995, 19). Moreover, there is evidence that signs of neighborhood "disorder," such as abandoned buildings, vandalism, litter, and graffiti, instill fear in local residents, whereas, as Richard Taub and his colleagues (1984) found in Chicago, neighborhood resources, such as stores, safe public spaces, and active collective life, provide incentives for city dwellers to overcome their fears and participate in public life (see also Joseph 1997; Miethe 1995; Skogan 1990). Second, as Sally Engle Merry (1981) concluded from her study of a high-crime, multiethnic urban housing project, once residents of a particular area grow fearful of crime, a vicious cycle begins: Fear causes people to increase the amount of time they spend at home and reduces their willingness to socialize with their neighbors; reclusiveness increases the social distance between residents and their neighbors, creating a community of strangers who grow even more fearful of one another; heightened fear leads to heightened reclusiveness, and so on. Third, according to the National Crime Victimization Interview Survey (Federman, et al. 1996), people living in poverty are more likely than others to be "afraid to go out." In the survey conducted in 1992, 25 percent of families receiving welfare and 20 percent of poor families reported that they were afraid to go out, whereas only 9 percent of financially stable families reported the same. Fourth, survey research has shown that among the elderly, blacks are more likely than other groups to be fearful of crime, and that in opposition to the general trend black men are both more likely to be afraid of crime than black women and more likely to express feelings of vulnerability (Joseph 1997; Skogan 1993). Far from irrational, these concerns reflect the practical knowledge that black seniors in general, and elderly black men in particular, are more likely than other older people to be victimized by crime. Indeed, this condition helps explain why older African Americans were more likely than any other group in Chicago to die during the 1995 heat wave, and suggests that they were victims of the structures of urban violence and inequality before they became, in the city's logic, victims of their own fear.

29. Thompson and Krause 1998, S356.

30. Anderson's (1999) observations of social isolation and reclusion as forms of protection, especially for children in violent neighborhoods, stem

from his ethnographic research in Philadelphia. Furstenberg and his colleagues' (1998) findings about isolation are based on survey research of urban families with children in the school system. Wilson's (1996) discussion of isolation as a protection strategy appears in *When Work Disappears*. In *Our America*, an oral history of growing up in the projects on Chicago's Near South Side, teenage journalists LeAlan Jones and Lloyd Newman make avoiding violence and managing fear some of their central themes. "They used to shoot a lot in the summer," Jones begins. Newman answers ominously, "That's why I stayed in my house most of the time" (Jones, Newman, and Isay 1997, 31).

31. Relative to other comparable countries, Americans have good reason to be worried about crime: in a context where guns are easy to obtain and levels of gun-related violence are among the highest in the world, roughly one-fourth of U.S. households are touched by crime each year, and about one-half of the population will be victimized by a violent crime in their lifetime (Miethe 1995). Doing fieldwork in even the most objectively dangerous streets of Chicago makes it clear that the common depiction of city residents, particularly those who live in poor and violent areas, as constantly paranoid, so acutely concerned about proximate threats that they can hardly move, is a gross misrepresentation of how fear is managed and experienced. "It's caution, not fear, that guides me," Eugene Richards, a senior citizen living in North Lawndale explained during a discussion of managing danger in the area. Eugene will walk a few blocks during the day, but he refuses to go more than four blocks without a car. Alice Nelson, a woman in her seventies who lives in Little Village, walks during the day and carries small bags of groceries with her. "But I won't go out at night," she told me.

32. Secter 1995, 7.

33. Ehrenhalt 1995, 29.

34. In *Exotics at Home*, anthropologist Micaela di Leonardo (1999, 125) levels a strong criticism of social scientists who draw upon a nostalgic " 'world we have lost' vision of safe ghettos in which individuals could sleep on fire escapes in the summer, and in which the middle classes provided role models and leadership to the rest." She is right to caution against the historical fantasy that middle-class and poor African Americans were tightly bound in easy relations of affinity, yet there is historical basis for the argument that public spaces in the ghetto became less viable during the postwar period (Wacquant 1994). My older informants in North Lawndale and in other African-American neighborhoods insisted on the extent to which the public areas around them had become more dangerous and threatening, especially at night.

35. Glassner (1999) reports that Americans older than sixty-five years of age are sixteen times less likely than Americans under age twenty-five to be victimized by crime.

36. See Lawlor, et al. (1993, 9) for a discussion of poverty among the Chicago elderly.

37. Glassner 1999, 44. In a survey analyzing the impact of watching or listening to city news, researchers found that "people who more often listen to radio news or watch television news express significantly higher levels of fear," and that "the same effect appears for local TV" (Chiricos, Escholz, and Gertz 1997).

38. Glassner 1999, 45.

39. See James Jasper's *Restless Nation* (2000, 12, 132) for a discussion of the gendered character of America's culture of individualism. "American men have few ways of thinking about people in groups, or about factors that affect people as groups," he writes.

40. See the discussions of neighborhood watches and community policing programs in Davis (1998) and, in Chicago, Skogan and Hartnett (1997). For accounts of the new fortress architecture prevalent in U.S. cities, see the articles collected in *Architecture of Fear* (Ellin 1997), which include discussions of gated communities, walled cities, and private security systems. Much of this work was inspired by Mike Davis, whose treatise on Los Angeles, *City of Quartz* (1990), oriented critical attention toward the ways in which city residents and governments remake urban space to defend against feared minorities.

41. The set of problems in nursing homes are well documented in other studies, so here I focus on other crucial sources of housing for seniors that receive less public attention. For a historical account of single room occupancy dwellings, see Paul Groth's book *Living Downtown* (1994); and for a sociological study documenting the nature of social support networks in contemporary Chicago SROs, see Charles Hoch and Robert Slayton's *New Homeless and Old* (1989).

42. Steinberg 1995, 10.

43. Chicago Housing Authority 1995, 2.

44. Building Organization and Leadership Development 1995.

45. Hoch and Slayton 1989.

46. The data on lost units in Chicago is reported in Hoch and Slayton 1989, 121, and the national data is presented in Groth 1994, 283. See Jencks (1994) for a discussion of the debate over the number of SRO units destroyed. Drawing on evidence that he acknowledges to be "less than ideal," Jencks discounts the highest calculations of SRO units lost in the 1970s and 1980s, including the well-known study indicating that 1.1 million rooms were lost between 1970 and 1982, because they came from a study that included units with two rooms. Jencks also cites the Census Bureau American Housing Survey to show that the number of one-room rental units fell from 1,114,000 in 1973 to 789,000 in 1989.

47. Groth 1994, 271. Mental health researchers estimate that the total number of patients in state-funded institutions dropped by roughly five hundred thousand between 1955 and 1995, with SROs, prisons, and the streets picking up much of the load.

48. Urban historian Eric Monkkonen (1993, 345) argues that "[t]he sad practice of lumping together all sorts of people in need has diminished with the provision of broader aid to the elderly and the ill," but the current system of state programs for seniors, the mentally ill, and substance abusers has clearly failed to end the practice entirely.

49. Hoch and Slayton 1989, 164.

50. See the discussion of SROs and the interests of developers in Suttles (1990).

51. These are the words used by Frederick Engels ([1845] 1984) to describe the housing conditions of the Manchester working class in his classic account.

Engels's remark that "such a district exists in the heart of the second city of England, the first manufacturing city of the world" has an ironic resonance for the case of Chicago, America's own "Second City" and historic manufacturing center.

52. Most of the twenty-seven hotels surveyed by Keigher (1991, 52–53) "have a formal lobby or living room, but many show remarkably few signs of social life. Few hotels appear to have gone to any trouble to create sociable space and some evidently try to discourage it."

53. Keigher (1991) also found that SRO residents tended to be out of touch with social service workers and medical providers. Many of the residents in her study were interested in receiving support but did not know how and where to get it, and the health-care needs of the residents are "staggering" (Keigher 1991, 49–50).

54. The relationship between alcohol or drug consumption and heatstroke is reported in Kilbourne, et al. (1982). Herbert Simon (1994) found an association between neuroleptic drug consumption and hyperthermic disorders.

55. Rollinson 1990, 194–95. His claim is particularly striking in light of Rollinson's disclaimer that he likely undersampled the most deteriorated hotels, since six SROs refused to grant him access, as well as the most isolated residents, since they would be the most difficult to find and the least inclined to participate in his study.

56. Ibid.

57. Keigher 1991, 51.

58. Rollinson 1990, 200.

59. Hoch and Slayton 1989, 151.

60. Ibid., 161.

61. Keigher 1991, 49.

62. Rollinson 1990.

63. Keigher 1991, 47.

64. According to a *Chicago Sun-Times* list of 45 heat wave victims interred by the Cook County Medical Examiners Office, 33 of the 45 decedents, or roughly 75 percent, were men (*Chicago Sun-Times* 1995, 14).

65. Orloff 1993, chap. 3; Fischer 1982, 253; Hoch and Slayton 1989, 128.

66. Though, as Ann Orloff (1993) shows, it is important to note that men typically have better access to pensions because they have relatively longer and more continuous experience in the formal labor market.

67. See R. W. Connell's *Masculinities* (1995, 21–27) for a critical discussion of the literature on "sex roles." Robert Rubinstein (1986, 20–21) finds that two-thirds of the single elderly men in his sample who had no children also reported "no close family at all," whereas "seventeen of the 29 men with children had generally close relationships with all or some of their children." For an account of how men are excluded from various welfare state programs, see Susser (1993).

68. Rubinstein 1986, 1.

69. Liebow 1967, 214, 218–19. Two compelling anthropological studies that explore the relationships between male violence and hardship are Bourgois (1995) and Lancaster (1992).

70. Gurley, et al. 1996, 1710.

CHAPTER 2

1. Semenza, et al. 1996, 84.

2. The researchers explain that they "included deaths due to cardiovascular causes in the case definition because previous studies had demonstrated an excess of deaths from cardiovascular disease during periods of high heat" (ibid.).

3. Semenza explains that "many people were so isolated that we weren't able to include them in the study. Our estimate of the significance of social isolation in the study is in fact an underestimate because we eliminated the most isolated people from the sample."

4. According to Karen Smoyer (1998, 1813), "by focusing on population-related risk factors and by matching cases and controls by neighborhood of residence, [the design] cancelled out any observable effects of neighborhood characteristics and precluded the evaluation of environmental variables beyond the scale of the household."

5. For a useful review, see Ralph Catalano and Kate Pickett (1999), "A Taxonomy of Research Concerned with Place and Health."

6. Smoyer (1998, 1820) claims that, in general, "the differences between high-mortality and low-mortality tracts were more pronounced during heat waves." She finds that in some years the distribution of heat wave mortality in St. Louis census tracts was random, but that "the mean values of several census tract variables were significantly different between high- and low-mortality tracts" (p. 1820). The problem with these measures is that during less fatal heat waves the number of deaths is too small to generate reliable comparisons across neighborhoods. Smoyer warns that "if relatively few deaths occur, the variation in tract-level mortality rates will be small and tract-level patterns are unlikely to emerge" (ibid.). But the opposite is also true: small differences in the number of heat wave deaths across tracts or neighborhoods may generate exaggerated indicators of the relative risk levels.

Smoyer also notes that two previous studies of heat wave mortality in St. Louis and New York, one led by Henschel and the other by Schuman, found not only a spatial distribution of health risk, but a significant association between place-based conditions and heat wave mortality as well. In addition, Martinez and colleagues (1989) discovered geographical patterns in heat wave mortality among the elderly.

7. See note 12 of the introduction for a discussion of Chicago's community areas.

8. There is an enormous literature on the historical development and social conditions of Chicago's African-American regions. The classic study of the Black Belt is St. Clair Drake and Horace Cayton, *Black Metropolis* ([1945] 1993).

9. Despite significant reductions in the crime rates during the late 1990s, the levels of violent crime in poor black areas of the city remain comparatively high, making it difficult for residents to feel safe in the streets. A study by the Epidemiology Program at the Chicago Department of Public Health (1996) showed that in 1994 and 1995 the overall violent crime rate as reported to the Chicago Police Department, a clear underestimation of the true victimization level, showed that there were 19 violent crimes for every 100 residents of Fuller Park, the community area that had the highest mortality levels during the heat

wave. Other community areas with high heat wave mortalities had similar crime levels: Woodlawn, with the second-highest heat mortality rate, reported 13 violent crimes per 100 residents; Greater Grand Crossing reported 11 per 100; Washington Park, Grand Boulevard, and the Near South Side, all among the most deadly spots during the disaster, listed rates above 15 crimes per 100 residents as well, suggesting, as did the Illinois Department of Public Health, an association between the everyday precariousness of life in these neighborhoods and vulnerability during the heat wave. In contrast, Lincoln Park, the prosperous community on the Near North Side, reported two violent crimes for every 100 residents, and a heat wave mortality rate among the lowest in the city.

10. There is, however, an analytical danger in using community area data to document the spatial logic of the heat wave's effects. The large size and overall ethnoracial or class diversity of some of the community areas hide smaller pockets of poverty, crime, and even high heat wave deaths in neighborhoods within them. One cluster of streets in Uptown notorious for its dilapidated SRO dwellings, for example, was the spot of at least seven heat-related deaths, making it perhaps the most deadly location in the city; yet Uptown as a whole was not one of the fifteen areas with the highest general death rates.

11. As Laurence Kalkstein explains in *Lancet* (1995, 858), areas with "black roofs, red brick exteriors, and lack of ventilation . . . are especially unsuited to hot conditions."

12. Shen, et al. 1995.

13. Smoyer (1998, 1822) notes the lack of and need for such qualitative research projects. In her list of important future directions for place-based research on heat wave mortality, "first is to use qualitative methods to unravel the more complex relationships between place and heat wave mortality risk."

14. The best example of a comprehensive effort to use ethnographic research to assess a range of Chicago community areas is the Comparative Neighborhood Study, directed by William Julius Wilson and Richard Taub at the University of Chicago. The project, which began in 1993, employed roughly ten graduate students for several years and covered four community areas. By 2001, the project had produced several dissertations and books about individual areas (including Mary Pattillo-McCoy's *Black Picket Fences* [1999]), but not a broader set of findings based on cross-area comparisons.

15. For a review of methodological debates about the uses of case studies, see the edited volume by Charles Ragin and Howard Becker, *What Is a Case? Exploring the Foundations of Social Inquiry* (1992). In this comparative neighborhood study I follow convention by using Chicago community areas as the units of analysis. Although, as Sudhir Venkatesh (2001) and Al Hunter (1974) have argued, community areas are constructions of social scientists rather than indigenous expressions of neighborhood identities, the relatively large size of typical community areas made them useful for this study. The distribution of the seven-hundred-plus heat wave deaths in the seventy-seven Chicago community areas proved more meaningful than the distribution among the census tracts or the neighborhood units constructed by Robert Sampson and colleagues for the Harvard Public Health Study (1997). The two latter units are too small and numerous to generate reliable mortality rates for the acute event. The comparison here therefore borrows from Jennifer Platt's (1992) practice

of using conventional cases with uncertain theoretical status but unquestioned practical utility as scientifically constructed objects of scholastic and political importance. Yet after choosing the units of analysis I conducted the research in a style closer to John Walton's (1992) or Michel Wieviorka's (1992), constructing variables, categories, and theoretically grounded observations on the basis of evidence uncovered in the field.

16. Controlling for these conditions allowed me to guard against the possibility that compositional factors on key measures accounted for difference in mortality.

17. Whitman, et al. 1997, 1515–18. Note that the population of Latinos in South Lawndale was likely much higher than the official total, since the community area is a center for migrant workers who are often uncounted by census takers.

18. Some caution is warranted when interpreting the data on earnings in both Little Village and North Lawndale, since much of the local economic activity is in the informal labor market and is generally unreported by workers. Many studies have established that the official poverty line in the United States is a poor indicator of poverty (Citro and Michael, eds. 1995). See Ruggles (1990) for a review of the debates and Federman, et al. (1996) for a discussion of the consequences of being poor. In the American context, families earning significantly more than the official limit suffer from relative deprivations of primary goods such as health care, decent housing, energy, and food. Poverty researchers also debate the question of what counts as a "high-poverty" area at the census tract level. Paul Jargowsky (1997, 10–11) uses the 40 percent poverty rate at the census tract level as the criterion for ghettos, barrios, and slums, but he also reports that the 20 percent census tract poverty rate criterion would capture the bottom quintile of American census tracts.

19. Recent research led by Sampson (1997, 918) suggests that in addition to the proportion of residents who are poor, and the proportion of residents who are old and alone, the collective efficacy of the community—defined as the "social cohesion among neighbors combined with their willingness to intervene on behalf of the common good"—should affect the capacity of local residents to survive the disaster. In fact, bringing social cohesion into the equation makes the puzzle of why Little Village experienced such a relatively low death rate even more difficult to solve: according to the measure developed by Sampson and his colleagues, Little Village has a more negative collective efficacy rating than North Lawndale, and should therefore have had weaker social support systems during the disaster.

20. Conventional scholarly wisdom allows analysts to claim that characteristics of groups, as groups, explain the differences among groups. Yet, as Loïc Wacquant (1997a, 224) argues, " 'race' cannot be both object and tool of analysis, explanandum and explanans."

21. For a discussion and critique of analogous forms of racial reasoning, see Gould ([1981] 1996).

22. Angel, et al. 1996.

23. See Anderson (1999), Frazier (1939), Pattillo-McCoy (1999), and Stack (1974). Male "old-heads" and grandmothers have been focal subjects of Elijah Anderson's books on social relations in black communities in Philadelphia

(1990, 1999). Anderson (1999, 206) quotes E. Franklin Frazier's account of black families, in which he argues that "the oldest woman is regarded as the head of the family, it has been the grandmother who has held the generations together." Merril Silverstein and Linda Waite (1993) call these findings into question, arguing that there is little evidence for many of the claims about the intensity of social support activities in networks of black seniors.

24. With the exception of the recent inquiries into the effects of neighborhood environments on local residents (see Brooks-Gunn, Duncan, and Aber 1997 and Sampson, Raudenbush, and Earls 1997), much of the recent research on urban poverty has obscured the great variation in the social and spatial conditions in poor neighborhoods. As urban scholars including Herbert Gans (1995) and Michael Katz (1993) have shown, most of the social scientific research, policy reports, and journalistic writing on the putative urban underclass failed to specify the people or neighborhoods that count as members or representatives of the group. One effect of this flexible but slippery terminology is that both predominately black and Latino community areas with high rates of poverty, unemployment, crime, or other social problems have been lumped together into the same neighborhood category despite the significant variation among and within poor neighborhoods, and even among poor neighborhoods populated by the same ethnoracial group. When poor neighborhoods are differentiated, such as in Paul Jargowsky's *Poverty and Place* (1997), they are typically given labels such as *barrio, ghetto,* or *slum* that are exclusively based on the ethnoracial identity of the dominant local community and ignore the other social, economic, or spatial features of the local environment altogether. Jargowsky's scheme is an improvement over more homogeneous classifications, yet it, too, implicitly denies the salience of other social conditions.

25. McKenzie 1925, 64.; Mauss [1916] 1979.

26. In a recent article, Dingxin Zhao (1998, 153) makes an analogous argument by showing that the campus ecology of Beijing universities nurtured various forms of networking during normal times and consequently supported social activism during a crisis, the prodemocracy protests in 1989. Zhao claims that ecology determines the structure and strength of social networks as well as the spatial positions and routine activities of people in a community.

27. Many generations of Chicago school sociologists have called attention to the relationship between social ecology and the quality or organization of neighborhood social life. In recent decades urban scholars influenced by European social theorists such as Henri LeFebvre, Manuel Castells, and David Harvey have rediscovered the significance of the spatial life of cities. In the 1990s a number of U.S. social scientists initiated a series of studies to determine whether neighborhoods have independent effects on a range of social and educational outcomes. The early results of these quantitatively based neighborhood effects studies have shown that, although families are the key agents in promoting children's development, neighborhood conditions do matter for different age groups in ways that vary over the life course (Brooks-Gunn, Duncan, and Aber 1997).

28. Taub, et al. 1984.

29. Chicago Fact Book Consortium 1995.

30. Hirsch 1983, 192.

31. Ibid., 194.

32. See Sharon Zukin's chapter, "While the City Shops," in *The Cultures of Cities* (1995) for a discussion of how shopping plays a constitutive role in the process of society making. Zukin also explores the consequences of commercial flight and neighborhood decline in Brooklyn and Chicago.

33. Jacobs 1961, 36–37.

34. Skogan 1990, 13.

35. See the Introduction of *All Our Kin* (Stack 1974) for a discussion of the residential density and spatial concentration of the two extended family networks in Stack's study. Orlando Patterson (1998, xi) has criticized books such as *All Our Kin* for perpetuating "what may be called the myth of the 'hood,' the belief that viable informal friendship patterns and communities exist, compensating for the breakdown or absence of more formal institutions. Through sheer, baseless repetition, and through nonrepresentative case studies of a few Afro-American housing projects by urban anthropologists, it has become an accepted belief that large networks of support and natural neighborhood communities are out there waiting to be developed and built on."

36. Jacquelyn Wolf and colleagues (1983, 469) report that "distance from an older person's household is the strongest determinant of frequency of contact with family and friends of black elders, as has been previously demonstrated for white elders."

37. As Neil Krause (1993) reports, social gerontologists have shown that "higher overall neighborhood quality is related to increased contact with family members." In his own work, Krause (1993, 9–10) shows that "deteriorated neighborhoods . . . tend to promote distrust of others and older adults who are more distrustful of others tend to be more socially isolated [in the literal sense]." (It is worth noting that during a period of economic development in the late 1990s, though, a Walgreens with a pharmacy and a Dominick's grocery store opened on Roosevelt Road in North Lawndale.)

38. In *Paths of Neighborhood Change*, Richard Taub and colleagues (1984, 60) show the importance of commercial attractions in pulling people out of their homes and into the public places where social contact is more likely. Taub's group found that Chicago's African Americans prefer to shop outside of their own neighborhoods, partly because they believe that they cannot get high-quality products there.

39. My informants' complaints about the difficulty of finding nutritious food and basic goods in the area suggest that social ecology, and not simply cultural tastes and preferences, contributes to the high levels of obesity and diabetes in North Lawndale and other poor black communities similar to it. The elderly, who are often unable to drive or to pay to be driven out of the area to go shopping, have the most difficult time getting healthy foods. Many of the senior citizens I met stocked up on canned and packaged products so that they would always have something to eat, but did not have fresh foods in their homes as much as they would have liked.

The small stores in the area are full of sugary food with little nutritional value and seldom stock the foods that public health workers, concerned about the high levels of diabetes, obesity, and heart disease in the area, recommend. The products that local stores do carry are significantly more expensive than they are in larger stores outside the ghetto. "You've got to have a car to stretch your dollar around here," an elderly woman told me during one of my visits to a neighborhood park. "Or you've got to get some special fare cards from the city and take the bus. Stores in this area are expensive. And you're giving away your money if you shop here." "They sell liquor and this and that," a man in his sixties added, "but the prices are just sky high. I haven't been in those small stores other than for a paper."

40. Laurie Kaye Abraham (1993, 139–40) makes a similar argument about the difficulties for the elderly who try to maintain healthy daily routines in violent areas that lack sources of nutritional food. "Complying with health advice is harder for the poor than for the middle class, which has more choices. . . . Urban poverty may refuse to accommodate the simplest healthy habits. For example, during Tommy's second checkup at Lawndale Christian, Dr. Jones told him that he needed to walk regularly so he wouldn't lose his ability. 'I don't want to be no prey,' Tommy answered."

41. City of Chicago 1996.

42. Crime rates tend to go up in summer, when the heat pushes people to spend more time outdoors than they do during other seasons. But when the heat becomes too extreme, crime rates actually decrease because would-be criminals become too lethargic to engage in crime.

43. See, among others, Bourgois (1995) and Sanchez-Jankowski (1991).

44. This is why the major local social movements, such as "take back the street" marches, antidrug sit-ins (in which residents sit out on the streets with active drug markets), neighborhood garden projects, and efforts to board up abandoned buildings and fence in empty lots, focus on reclaiming physical and social space for residents.

45. Residents of nearby neighborhoods report similar concerns. In a survey conducted in May 1994, for example, residents of a public housing project on the West Side found that 40 percent of the residents in one set of buildings, and 11 percent in another, reported that bullets had been shot into their apartments in the previous year. The authors of *The Hidden War* report that "a majority of the residents (63 percent) we surveyed said they felt unsafe if they were outside alone at night, and some (33 percent) felt unsafe even inside their own apartment" (Popkin, et al. 2000, 100–102).

46. Anderson 1999, 118.

47. In his ethnographic study of an area with an active drug market, Elijah Anderson (1999) found that many parents in high-crime areas forced their children to stay at home so that they would not get involved in or be subjected to the dangers of the local street life. Children in these situations become alienated from their peers and their local communities. Protected from the streets, they become vulnerable to the psychological and developmental dangers of confinement and isolation.

48. According to Krause (1993, 16), "a neighborhood may contain physical barriers that tend to restrict contact with others. For example, dark hallways in apartments, broken steps, and crooked walkways may discourage older adults with physical limitations from visiting others."

49. Residents' practical knowledge of their neighbors stands in stark contrast with the social relations in Hampton, the affluent white suburb where

M. P. Baumgartner (1988) conducted ethnographic research. Baumgartner found that there was a "scarcity of social knowledge involved in the middle-class relationships" that typified neighborhood connections in Hampton. Residents of the suburb maintained their social distance by avoiding one another whenever possible and established only weak ties to the community.

50. Most but not all of the churches are technically within the North Lawndale community area. See North Lawndale Family Network (1998).

51. On the historical significance of black churches, see Frazier (1961) and Lincoln (1990). On black churches in Chicago, see Drake and Cayton ([1945] 1993), Pattillo-McCoy (1998), and Spear (1967). Despite the rhetorical use of the term the "black church," there is obviously no singular and unified black religious institution. As Omar McRoberts (2001, 8–11) writes, "There has never existed a homogeneous black community or a universal black church to defend it." During the time I spent in North Lawndale, I observed that the churches play several major roles there, including (1) serving as a site for people to congregate during regular days as well as on special occasions and rituals; (2) contributing to various forms of political organizing in the neighborhoods; (3) mediating relationships between residents and government agencies, such as the police and the Department of Health, both of which ran meetings or programs out of church buildings; (4) coordinating economic development programs by bringing residents together with planners, politicians, and developers; (5) organizing community service projects, such as clothing banks and antidrug marches, as well as secular community organizations; (6) providing key services, such as meals, rides to shopping areas, health care, and home visits, to people in need, as well as day care and summer camps for children; (7) helping with the construction and remodeling of local housing; (8) connecting local residents with employers; (9) hosting block club and other neighborhood meetings; (10) offering private educational alternatives to the local public schools; and (11) counseling and consoling residents after traumas as well as celebrating with residents during good times. Clearly, then, the local churches were and are key resources in North Lawndale, and their contributions extend far beyond the sacred realm.

52. Meares 1998.

53. City of Chicago 1995, 4.

54. Omar McRoberts makes similar observations in his research on church-based support services in Four Corners, an African-American region of Boston. For a synthesis of his study, see McRoberts (2001).

55. See Albert Hunter's *Symbolic Communities* (1974, 187) for a discussion of block clubs. Hunter found that the clubs "appear to be more prevalent within the black communities of Chicago."

56. See *From Abandonment to Hope* for one powerful study of neighborhood revitalization (Leavitt and Saegert 1990).

57. With important exceptions, scholars of urban poverty have been insufficiently attentive to the variation in neighborhoods or blocks within larger community areas, and it is important to note that there are some well-organized communities with strong social bonds in areas such as North Lawndale. Some of the best organized communities exist adjacent to some of the most dangerous streets in Chicago.

58. See Sampson, et al. (1997) for a discussion of the significance of residential stability. But in a recent article, Catherine Ross and colleagues (2000, 581) argue that "[i]n affluent neighborhoods, stability is associated with low levels of distress; under conditions of poverty the opposite is true. . . . Stability does not reduce perceived disorder under conditions of poverty, as it does in more affluent neighborhoods."

59. Spergel and Grossman 1997.

60. City of Chicago 1996.

61. In *Primitive Classification,* Emile Durkheim and Marcel Mauss ([1903] 1963) argue that classification systems represent social formations, although they were not as interested in the political construction of symbolic differences as later sociologists, such as Albert Hunter (1974), who used their theories to analyze symbolic communities.

62. Hunter 1974, 74.

63. Chicago Fact Book Consortium 1995, 110; Pugh 1997.

64. Chicago Fact Book Consortium 1995, 110.

65. Wirth and Bernert, eds. 1949.

66. Pugh 1997.

67. Massey and Denton 1993, 137.

68. In "Three Pernicious Premises in the Study of the American Ghetto," Loïc Wacquant (1997b, 343) argues that a ghetto is an institutional form of "ethnoracial closure and control. In ideal-typical terms, a ghetto may be characterized as a bounded, racially and/or culturally uniform socio-spatial formation based on (1) the forcible relegation of (2) a 'negatively typed' population . . . to a (3) reserved, 'frontier territory,' in which this population (4) develops under duress a set of parallel institutions" that (5) duplicate dominant institutions "at an incomplete and inferior level while (6) maintaining those who rely on them in a state of structural dependency." According to Wacquant, in U.S. cities only African-Americans have been subjected to unmatched levels of each of the five "elementary forms of racial domination: prejudice, discrimination, segregation, ghettoization, and violence."

69. According to 2000 figures from the U.S. Bureau if the Census, the official Hispanic population in Chicago grew by more than 200,000 between 1990 and 2000, while the number of whites fell by 150,000 and the African-American population fell by 20,000. Hispanics also accounted for 69 percent of the new residents in the six-county metropolitan region.

70. McMurray 1995, 33.

71. Suttles 1968, 73.

72. The socially generative role of the social ecology of Little Village operates similarly to the campus ecology in Beijing analyzed by Zhao (1998).

73. Daniel Dohan (1997) has documented some of the ways in which Latino families, particularly immigrants, are strained by labor markets that demand long working days and pay little in return.

74. Jacobs 1961, 34–35.

75. As of 1990, there were 98,554 residents in the Eleventh Police District and 131,852 residents in the Tenth Police District.

76. Residents were particularly worried about the meager resources available to local youths. The only large public park in the area was in the southwest-

ern corner of Little Village, too far away for most kids to reach by foot and too dangerous for youths associated with the wrong gangs. The local schools were severely overcrowded, though several new facilities had opened or were about to open by the time I left in 1999.

77. According to one recent news article, the Archdiocese of Chicago claims that it has roughly eight hundred thousand Hispanic parishioners, about one-third of its total membership (Irvine 2001).

78. Angel, et al. 1996.

79. In this process, the ethnographic research helps to identify the kinds of information that are relevant to solving the analytic problem at hand. Without close observation of local conditions, survey researchers interested in the same issues might not locate the significant conditions.

80. Two areas with high crime rates but low population decline, Riverdale and Auburn Gresham, were among the lowest heat mortality areas. Future research could assess whether population stability buffers the social impacts of high crime on collective life.

81. Shen, et al. 1995; Smoyer 1998.

82. See Paul Jargowsky's *Poverty and Place* (1997), which describes the increasing numbers of such concentrated poverty regions in Chicago during the later decades of the twentieth century.

CHAPTER THREE

1. The Police Department investigates unusual deaths and produces official knowledge about conditions at the scene. The police death report, which contains information about the body, the place of death, any signs of foul play, and the whereabouts of next of kin and neighbors, becomes a crucial part of the decedent's record. Police officers are also in charge of transporting the dead to the morgue when an autopsy is required and coordinating their work with the Medical Examiner's staff.

2. Emergency Net News Service 1995.

3. See the commissioned report on the Fire Department's resources and conducted by TriData Corporation in 1998 and 1999. Motivated by the report, new Fire Department commissioner James T. Joyce added twelve new basic life support ambulances to the city's fleet in 1999.

4. The tensions between firefighters and paramedics date to the early 1970s, when Richard J. Daley upgraded the emergency medical services that firefighters and civilian employees had staffed through the Comprehensive Employment and Training Act. Paramedics were excluded from the firefighters' union until the 1980 firefighters' strike, when the union tried to expand its ranks from within. But they continue to receive less furlough time and lower salaries than firefighters, and divisions within the department are legendary. In 1995 the city lost an arbitration dispute with paramedics, who won millions of dollars in back pay for overtime. Firefighters remain the dominant members of the department, particularly at the administrative level.

5. Dematte, et al. 1998 and Semenza, et al. 1999.

6. Raika 1995.

7. Spielman and Mitchell 1995b, 9.

8. Mitchell and Jimenez 1995, 12.

9. Ibid.

10. Dematte, et al. 1998.

11. Semenza, et al. 1996, 87. Chicago also had not implemented the new hot weather-health watch/warning system that is based on synoptic weather variables rather than simply the heat index. According to Laurence Kalkstein and colleagues (1996, 1519), heat warning systems that are attentive to a more comprehensive set of conditions provide "greater public awareness of excessive heat conditions, [and] may have played an important role in reducing Philadelphia's total heat-related deaths during the summer of 1995."

12. *Chicago Sun-Times* columnist Michael Sneed (1995, 4) reported that Daley spent part of the weekend in his Grand Beach, Michigan, home, and several other city officials I interviewed confirmed this report.

13. Spielman and Mitchell 1995a, 1.

14. In accusing the city of committing "murder by public policy," Scates joined a long line of critics who have levied similar charges against governments that contribute to the vulnerability of citizens during crises. In *Late Victorian Holocausts,* Mike Davis (2001) chronicles the dissenting voices of officials and journalists who viewed the state as responsible for the deaths of millions of Indians in famines. As Robert Knight, editor of the *Indian Economist and Statesman,* wrote: "We and our contemporaries must speak without reserve or be partakers in the guilt of multitudinous murders committed by men blinded to the real nature of what we are doing in this country" (quoted in Davis 2001, 53–54).

15. National Weather Service 1996, viii.

16. Raika 1995.

17. Raika 1995, 2.

18. The manifesto for the new governmental ethos of efficiency and entrepreneurialism is David Osborne and Ted Gaebler's *Reinventing Government* (1992). The book was celebrated by public officials from both major U.S. political parties, and President Bill Clinton made it a blueprint for his political reforms. On efficiency in quality management, see Beinart (1997), Eig (1999), and Glastris (1992); on outsourcing see Seidenstat (1996); on citizens as consumers see Osborne and Gaebler (1992); on rewarding consumers who have access to information, see Gilbert (1995); on punishing people with weak skills and limited resources, see Halpern (1999); on media scrutiny and managing public opinion, see Cook (1998); and on the role of public relations professionals in government agencies, see Kaniss (1991).

19. For accounts of disaster which represent the government primarily as a reactive institution, see Erikson (1976) and Larson (1999). See Esping-Anderson's *The Three Worlds of Welfare Capitalism* (1990, 23) for a concise argument that the welfare state is a stratifying institution. "The welfare state," he explains, "is not just a mechanism that intervenes in, and possibly corrects, the structure of inequality; it is, in its own right, a system of stratification. It is an active force in the ordering of social relations." For discussions of the role of the state in producing vulnerability to urban disasters, see the essays collected in *Crucibles of Hazard: Mega-Cities and Disasters in Transition* (Mitchell, ed. 1999). Davis has made this point in two of his recent books. He documents the role of the state in producing vulnerability to extreme climatic events in

nineteenth-century India, China, and Brazil in *Late Victorian Holocausts* (2001), and for contemporary Los Angeles in *Ecology of Fear* (1998).

20. See *American Pharaoh* for a discussion of Richard J. Daley's passion for city beautification programs (Cohen and Taylor 2000, 166–67).

21. The *Tribune*'s stories on failure in the Chicago public school system were published in *Chicago Tribune* (1992). The account of Chicago's improved bond rating is reported in *Economist* (1995).

22. See Alexander (1998, ix) for the Policy Research Action Group report; Jargowsky (1997, 78) for the data on concentrated poverty in Chicago; and Greenwich, Leavy, and Jones (1996, 3) for the account of economic development plans in Chicago. The massive increase in incarceration of poor city residents, especially African Americans and Latinos, was the most powerful of the many strategies for regulating inequality by removing poor people from the public.

23. National Weather Service 1996, ix. Chicago had experienced dangerous heat before the summer of 1995. In 1983, 1986, and 1988, severe heat spells had been associated with the excess deaths of 208, 167, and 294 Chicago residents, respectively (Whitman, et al. 1997, 1517); local media had done substantial reporting on the events. "1988 was a dress rehearsal for the 1995 disaster," local public health leader Quentin Young told me. "But the city wasn't ready for the real performance."

24. Although some accounts depict the formal structure and spirit of the reinvented government in purely organizational terms, it is in fact an eminently political form.

25. See Goetz (1997) for an insightful organizational study of an urban fire department.

26. In *Normal Accidents,* sociologist Charles Perrow (1984, 4, 9) documents the risks of tight coupling in organizations that use advanced technology to *produce* hazardous materials, since the complex chains of causality make it difficult to predict the impact of any particular problem. Political organizations, which often have to *react* to crises, often suffer from the opposite problem, because loose coupling slows their responsiveness. Karl Weick has made the most comprehensive assessments of the organizational problems stemming from loose coupling. For a relatively recent reconceptualization of the loose coupling literature, see Orton and Weick (1990).

27. In the 1990s a number of structural changes altered the conditions for city service delivery. While cuts in federal social support and public assistance programs and the declining political power of cities left urban centers like Chicago with meager resources for addressing concentrated and advancing poverty and deprivation (Jargowsky 1997; Wacquant 1996; Weir 1998), the professionalization of city government workers and the importation of flexible managerial strategies from the private sector (Eig 1999; Hambleton 1990; Seidenstat 1996), the outsourcing and privatization of state programs (Seidenstat 1996), the increasing political competition for and reliance on grants from private foundations to support public assistance programs (Alexander 1998), and the transformation of citizens into consumers of public goods (Osborne and Gaebler 1992) imposed a new set of pressures on government administrators, employees, and the people they serve.

28. Esping-Anderson (1999, chap. 8) argues that "old welfare states" are out of sync with the "new social risks" posed by today's labor markets and failing families. Contemporary labor markets demand flexibility and force many workers to rearrange their lives, by migrating or working odd hours, in order to work; millions of workers, especially in the United States, fail to earn a living wage for their labor; and unemployment rates in many European countries are stubbornly high. Families, he argues, were long a source of social support when markets collapsed, but contemporary marriages are unstable and are unreliable sources of protection.

29. Spielman and Mitchell 1995a, 6.

30. Kass 1995c. In *Acts of God* (2000), historian Ted Steinberg shows that in the aftermath of great disasters that devastate the most poor and vulnerable populations, elite journalists and political officials have consistently argued that the government should not be held accountable for the purportedly uncontrollable consequences of natural forces.

31. Richards 1995, 29.

32. See Perrow (1984).

33. Metro Seniors in Action 1995, 4.

34. Ibid., 1.

35. See Monkkonen (1993). Political scientist Michael Lipsky (1980) also lists police officers as among the main "street-level bureaucrats" who recreate and enact public policy in their interactions with citizens.

36. Flock 1995.

37. Skogan and Hartnett 1997; Skogan, et al. 1999. See Crank (1994) for a discussion of how the myth of the police officer as neighborhood watchman has been used in community policing campaigns. The authors of *Reinventing Government* quote former Houston police chief and U.S. Drug Czar Lee Brown defining the community policing movement as follows: "We're redefining the role of the patrol officer—we want him to be a community organizer, community activist, a problem solver" (Osborne and Gaebler 1992, 49). Although there is great variation among urban community policing programs, according to political scientists Wesley Skogan and Susan Hartnett (1997, 5) the fundamental characteristics of community policing include (1) *reformed decision making processes* that gives discretion to officers in the field and *organizational decentralization* that allows for increased communication between the police and the citizenry; (2) *problem-oriented policing strategies;* (3) *responsiveness to public demands;* and (4) *a commitment to helping local communities develop their own strategies* for managing crime problems.

38. Skogan and Hartnett 1997, 100, 231.

39. Skogan and Hartnett (1997, 81–84) made the same conclusion after their survey established that 72 percent of Chicago officers reported that that they thought "CAPS would generate 'unreasonable demands on police by community groups,'" and a similar proportion felt that the program placed a "greater burden on the police to solve all community problems," including those that, one officer said, "'are out of our hands.'"

40. Skogan, et al. 1999, 120.

41. *Chicago Weekend* 1995, 1.

42. Starks 1995.

43. In the entrepreneurial government of the 1990s, the optimal condition for promoting state support was when the local government could steer its constituents to state, federal, or private resources. These are precisely the conditions that a group of resourceful state employees at the Department on Aging identified when, in 1992, they received a grant from a local private foundation to help them develop the Benefits Eligibility Checklist program. Initiated in 1993, BEC was built around a short and simple form on which Chicago seniors could report their income and assets and then check the benefits they were receiving from a long list of entitlements. The Department on Aging would distribute the forms to seniors throughout the city and, when they returned the completed copy, BEC workers would run the information through a simple computer program that determined whether the seniors were eligible for any benefits that they were not receiving. If they were, BEC workers would contact them and help the seniors enroll.

BEC was funded mainly by private foundations and designed to tap into public money that lay primarily outside the city budget (of the benefit programs listed on the checklist, twenty-eight were funded by county, state, federal, and private sources, and fourteen were funded by the city of Chicago). Not long after initiating BEC, the city hired an advertising agency to generate a marketing campaign promoting the program. In addition to the advertisements placed on buses and billboards throughout Chicago, the city distributed brochures explaining that Mayor Daley's question, "Are seniors receiving all the benefits they are entitled?" inspired the Department on Aging to create BEC. From 1993 to 1997 the program would process fifty-eight thousand applications and help seniors apply for some fifty-seven thousand benefits—impressive figures for a period in which cities were working aggressively to push people off of public assistance programs.

After the first few years of private funding, the grant ended and the city decided to integrate BEC into the corporate budget, albeit with a substantially reduced allocation and a skeleton staff. Following the heat wave, the Department on Aging used BEC workers to go door to door, searching for isolated elderly to integrate into the city's service delivery system in neighborhoods that had high numbers of seniors living alone. By the late 1990s, BEC's staff of roughly twelve street workers in Chicago represented the front lines of the city's efforts to identify residents who were old and alone. The street workers, whom I shadowed for several weeks, were part-time employees who were in the streets for less than forty hours a month. Identifying isolated seniors is inherently difficult and time-consuming work, but Department on Aging administrators had used BEC to implement at least some formal programs accomplishing the task. Chicago learned from the heat wave that its emerging population of homebound seniors would need special forms of social assistance on a regular basis as well as in emergencies. So long as it was supported by and operationalized through external funds, the BEC program was an effective vehicle for initiating a policy response. The question that remains is whether BEC, and similar social support programs, will survive if and when private support streams dry up.

44. Alexander 1998, x.

45. Osborne and Gaebler 1992, 19.

46. See Loïc Wacquant (1997b) for a discussion of how governmental agencies, policy makers, and scholars have avoided U.S. ghettos while continuing to propose remedies and introduce programs that impact the lives of ghetto dwellers.

47. During his mayoral campaign against Richard M. Daley in 2000, U.S. Representative Bobby Rush surprised Chicago voters by restating criticisms of Daley's heat wave response. A mayoral aide summarily dismissed Rush's charges, and the congressman lost the election in a landslide.

48. For the argument that governments should enable rather than provide for their citizens, see Neil Gilbert's *Welfare Justice: Restoring Social Equity* (1995, 148) and Osborne and Gaebler's *Reinventing Government* (1992).

49. See, for example, Charles Perrow and Mauro Guillen, *The AIDS Disaster* (1990), for a compelling analysis of how organizations managing the AIDS crisis in Philadelphia marginalized poor minorities and intravenous drug users from support networks and programs.

50. Halpern 1999, 14.

51. Internal pressures within state agencies and advocacy organizations push social workers and organizers to reward the most entrepreneurial clients with special attention. Overwhelmed with problem cases but, in an environment when agencies must show successful outcome measures to garner resources from external funders, expected to produce tangible results, the social workers I observed engaged in what Lipsky called "creaming," the practice of favoring and working intensively on the cases of people "who seem likely to succeed in terms of bureaucratic success criteria" (Lipsky 1980, 107).

52. Pearson (1995). According to one public health study reported by Ted Steinberg (2000, 193–94), heating bills in the early 1990s were so expensive that "poor parents tended to withhold food from their kids to pay the heating bills."

53. Semenza, et al. 1996, 87. Some environmentalists have criticized programs that provide air-conditioning to the poor on the grounds that such policies provide short-term assistance but heighten the risks of pollution and long-term climatic crises.

54. See Levitan's *Programs in Aid of the Poor* (1991 98–99) for a review of LIHEAP.

55. Steinberg 2000, 195. See Pearson 1995 for the report on the cuts to LIHEAP.

56. Hartstein 1995.

57. This strategy had proved effective for the Chicago Department of Revenue, which had helped win Mayor Daley considerable public and political acclaim when it outsourced its parking ticket enforcement programs to Electronic Data Systems, a private firm that buckled down on delinquent violators and generated millions of dollars of revenue for the city. One key to the parking program's success was the agency's widespread use of the Denver boot, which the city used to force residents to either pay their fees or give up their cars. See *Economist* (1995).

58. Wallace 1993, 233.

CHAPTER FOUR

1. See Kleppner (1985) for a compelling account of the Bilandic blizzard crisis. Kleppner argues that Bilandic's mismanagement of the crisis was probably not the reason he lost his campaign, yet the popular impression that the blizzard sealed his downfall remains strong.

2. Squires, et al. 1987, 85–86.

3. At a 1998 conference on community policing, for example, Chicago sponsored a major session on how police departments could use public relations and marketing programs to increase awareness of police projects.

4. Cook 1998, 122. Some of the best accounts of the role of symbolic politics in governing regimes are Kaniss 1991, Schudson 1978, and Suttles 1990.

5. Cater 1959.

6. Linsky, O' Donnell, and Moore 1986, 203.

7. Habermas 1989, 193–95.

8. See Lee (1999) for a discussion of how entrepreneurial work on the part of government officials and bureaucrats shapes public issues.

9. Neal 1995, 25.

10. Kass 1995a, 1.

11. Spielman and Mitchell 1995a, 7.

12. Jimenez and Rodriguez 1995, 6; Kass 1995a, 1; Spielman and Mitchell 1995b, 1.

13. Jimenez and Rodriguez 1995, 6.

14. Spielman and Mitchell 1995a, 6.

15. In his classic essay, " Regions and Region Behavior," Erving Goffman (1959, chap. 3) argues that backstage regions are spaces for informality and inappropriate social conduct, whereas front-stage or public regions require more careful self-regulation and control. The charged press conference during the heat wave was a literal front-stage moment, and Lyne's blunt assessment that the city had mishandled the crisis would have been inadmissible anywhere other than the literal backstage.

16. Spielman and Mitchell 1995a, 7.

17. Kass 1995a, 4.

18. One alderman I interviewed explained that although she was furious about the city' s weak emergency response she did not make any critical public statements about the problems because she did not want to distract the Mayor's Office from the urgent public health work before it.

19. Cotliar 1995, 8; Kaplan and Stein 1995, 10.

20. Cotliar 1995, 8; Kaplan and Stein 1995, 1, 10.

21. On Friday, 28 July, the *Chicago Tribune* published an article with the headline "Donoghue is Backed on Heat-Wave Toll" on page 3 of the Metro ection (Kass 1995a).

22. Kass and Kaplan 1995, 1.

23. Ibid.

24. Metro Seniors in Action (1995). After the heat wave, some environmentalists did argue that governments had contributed to the production of a deadly climate by directly manufacturing or tolerating the manufacture and emission of dangerous pollutants. Most environmental scientists argue that global warming increases the frequency of heat waves and other extreme

weather events, and some argue that elevated levels of carbon monoxide in the hot air make contemporary summers more dangerous.

25. Stone 1997, 181–83.

26. Kass 1995d, 3.

27. See Arendt (1963, 84–86) for the classic discussion of how governments and societies develop euphemistic language as a method for disguising violence they commit but are unwilling to face. In *States of Denial*, Stanley Cohen (2001, chap. 4) reviews the language games involved in denial.

28. In the chapter entitled "Reaching Those at Risk," for example, the commission warns that cultural and linguistic isolation among seniors who have aged in place while their neighborhood has changed and their friends and families have fled the city has left 48 percent of city seniors who live alone with "no one available to help them" (City of Chicago 1995, 19).

29. Ibid., 3, 12.

30. Ibid., 3.

31. Ibid., 4 (italics added).

32. Ibid., 4. The commission interpreted the underutilization of city cooling centers and the refusal of some seniors to open their doors to strangers offering their assistance as evidence that seniors do not want assistance from the government.

33. Ibid., 3–4.

34. Pierre Bourdieu (1991, 1996) has shown that governments have a unique capacity to establish not merely the official accounts of major events and social processes, but also the terms and categories that organize the debate. Bourdieu calls this political work the "legitimate symbolic violence" that structures the way we see and do not see the social world.

35. Cohen 1996, 2001.

36. Cohen 1996; 2001, 7, 8, 80, 109, 113, 134.

37. Official arguments that victims of extreme events deserve or cause their own demise are so common in cases of disaster that Daniel Alvarez, who levied the charge in Chicago, could have taken his words from a script. Medical anthropologist Veena Das (1995) shows that medical scientists and state bureaucrats in India attributed deaths from the Bhopal chemical disaster to the individual behavior of local residents. In the official language and reporting on the event, Das argues, "it is not the character of the methyl isocyanate that seems to be at issue but the behavior of the people who tried to run when faced with this inexplicable phenomenon" (1995, 151). Amartya Sen (1981) and Mike Davis (2001) also document the techniques through which officials in India and China respectively blamed victims of famines for their own starvation.

38. Two city officials who had departed in the early and mid-1990s reported that the St. Louis heat plan that national health experts regard as the model intervention program was, in fact, developed from Chicago's original plan.

Of course, we can never know all the risks we face, and the process through which governments determine which forms of protection they will provide is deeply political. Mary Douglas and Aaron Wildavsky (1983, 7) argue that modern societies entrust governments and policy makers with the responsibility of protecting them from a set of dangers selected "according to the strength and direction of social criticism." And, as we have seen, national public health agencies not only have a long history of documenting the human costs of heat waves, but also have shown which groups are most vulnerable to heat-related crises and outlined preventive strategies.

Faced with a broad range of potential health dangers, city administrators decided that the risk of future heat disasters was not severe enough and the condition of vulnerable residents was not dire enough to merit an elaborate plan. Several of my informants told me that the emergency response system had been cast aside when the Fire Department streamlined its operations and "cut the fat" to gain organizational efficiency. In Douglas and Wildavsky's framework (1983, 4), the Fire Department did not blind itself to the danger of heat disasters so much as it *accepted this risk* and *compromised its knowledge* of how to manage it. This was an eminently political decision, though one whose human implications far outweighed its political consequences in Chicago.

39. Lee 1999, 455.

40. According to political scientist Murray Edelman (1988, 102), "dramatic incidents involving individuals in the limelight displace attention from the larger configurations that explain the incidents and much else as well."

41. Herbert Gans's *Deciding What's News* (1979) remains the best account of the organizational and social conditions in which journalists decide what is newsworthy.

CHAPTER FIVE

1. In *Television: Technology and Cultural Form,* Raymond Williams ([1974] 1992, 98–99) analyzes several sequences of televised evening news broadcasts in which "a number of important matters are included, [but] the connections between them are as it were deliberately not made." Williams argues that the odd combination of inchoate images and jumbled stories does the cultural work of effacing relationships among issues and events broadcast on television.

2. Gaye Tuchman (1973) has studied the ways in which journalists "routinize the unexpected" by placing even unanticipated events into familiar narrative frames and story types.

3. Gans 1979, 52–55.

4. Molotch and Lester 1974, 109.

5. Ibid., 109–10.

6. Fallows 1996, 7.

7. Rosen 1999, 281.

8. Boorstin 1961, 8.

9. Michael Schudson (1978, 6) argues that the media "[tend] to subordinate news values to commercial values, and critics from various persuasions rightly worry about what CBS news anchor Dan Rather termed the 'showbizification' of news."

10. For a study of investigative journalism focusing on best practices and featuring a *Chicago Tribune* reporter, see Ettema and Glasser (1998, 37–39, 171–72).

11. Philip Schlesinger, quoted in Gans (1979, 81).

12. According to Herbert Gans (1979), Leon Sigal (1986), and several of the other leading sociologists who study the media, officials, elites, and other

key sources are often able to use the media to project their perspectives into the public and to define the major issues of the time.

13. This is an issue of great significance because once a story is selected for coverage its placement in the news medium influences its impact and dissemination. Yet sociologists have paid little attention to the process of determining how stories are treated once they are produced. Studies of media representations that survey journalistic accounts often fail to distinguish among different pieces based on their location within a news medium, and therefore ignore the context and the hierarchical order in which the reports were published.

14. In an influential article about news and accidents published in 1975, Harvey Molotch and Marilyn Lester (1975) found that after an oil spill in Santa Barbara, California, the local media produced stories that were more comprehensive and substantive than the national accounts. Propinquity, they argue, is a key determinant of coverage.

15. The content analysis was conducted independently by two researchers, sociology graduate students Ellen Berrey (Northwestern University) and Scott Leon Washington (Princeton University), whose findings were then averaged. The researchers determined two dominant frames for each text (including news article, feature, editorial, and letter), headline, and graphic image published in the *Tribune* and *Sun-Times*. There were 143 texts and 100 graphics from the *Tribune*, as well as 159 texts and 47 graphics from the *Sun-Times*, included in the analysis.

16. The Metro desk is the editorial desk for the Metro section of the paper as well as for the stories about Chicago that make section 1.

17. Like other social collectives and organizations, there is a patterned rhythm in the life of news agencies; they operate differently in different seasons, days, and times, with periods of intense activity as well as of relatively light work.

18. The City News Bureau of Chicago, which closed in 1999, was a wire service for local news that operated in the city for 108 years and served as the training ground for generations of city reporters.

19. AP is the acronym for the Associated Press, one of the oldest and largest news organizations in the world.

20. Le and Kates 1995, 1.

21. For a more complete account of the twenty-four hour local news station, see Lieberman (1998).

22. Sociologists who studied news organizations in the 1970s found that journalists established a set of conventional categories that they used to routinize their work and assert control over the production process. Stories typically fit into one of the predetermined categories that organize news content, and the nature of the story largely determines the resources, labor, and attention given to its coverage. Frames, therefore, help to define problems, diagnose causes, make moral judgments, and suggest remedies, to determine not only whether people notice something but how they see and evaluate it. See Gamson (1992), Goffman (1974), and Entman (1993).

23. Castells 1996, 333. James Fallows (1996), Michael Schudson (1995), and Pierre Bourdieu (1998) have made similar points about the increasingly segregated cultural world of journalists. "No one," Bourdieu claims, "reads as many

papers as journalists, who tend to think that everybody reads all the newspapers. . . . To know what to say, you have to know what everyone else has said" (1998, 24). On the other hand, some journalists report that the challenge of working inside such a professional echo chamber is precisely that they have to come up with an original voice and a personal contribution. This is more possible in magazines than it is in daily publications and broadcasts, which require fast production.

24. Bourdieu 1998, 23–25.

25. Among many recent insider critiques, see James Squires, *Read All About It!* (1993), James Fallows, *Breaking the News* (1996), and Michael Janeway, *Republic of Denial* (1999).

26. Michael Schudson (1978, 11) argues that "news is as much a product of sources as of journalists; indeed, most analysts agree that sources have the upper hand."

27. Kaniss 1991, 176.

28. See Gaye Tuchman's classic article, "Objectivity As Strategic Ritual: An Examination of Newsmen's Notions of Objectivity" (1972), for a discussion of how journalists treat regular official sources with less skepticism than they do other sources of information.

29. Other studies have shown that officials play a particularly influential role as sources during disasters, when centralized and public agencies have special access to information about human and property damage (Sood, Stockdale, and Rogers 1987; Vaughan 1996).

30. Royko 1995; Schreuder and Gorner 1995.

31. Kass 1995b, 3.

32. Schreuder and Gorner 1995, 6.

33. Semenza 1995.

34. The *Tribune* story is Callahan (1995). The *Sun-Times* report is Rodriguez and Brown (1995, 1, 8).

35. Pierre Bourdieu (1998) argues that this is but one of the journalistic conventions that has the effect of hiding the very perspectives and stories that it shows, of conjuring the appearance of openness when in fact the channels for directing coverage are generally closed. For more thorough accounts of the construction and function of the journalistic "myth of objectivity," see Gans (1979), Schudson (1978), and Tuchman (1972).

36. Spielman and Mitchell 1995b, 1, 9.

37. Kass 1995a, 4.

38. Bryant 1995; McSherry 1995b.

39. See Gans (1979: 131–38) for a thorough discussion of beat reporters and general reporters.

40. Stein 1995a, 1995b.

41. Kiernan and Zielinski 1995, 1.

42. Ibid.

43. Ibid., p. 6 (italics added).

44. This practice is part of the reason that there is a professional distance between the copy editors and the reporters at the *Tribune*, a gulf sufficiently wide to convince one copy editor that there is "a weird animosity between us." "We're such strangers," she explained, because they work at different desks

and have vastly different responsibilities, as well as because the work of copy editors, such as trimming articles for space if they are too long, can dramatically alter reporters' stories. Recently, *Tribune* editors tried to reduce this gap and defuse reporters' concerns about the accuracy of headlines by instituting an experimental program in which reporters were asked to submit headline suggestions to copy editors along with their articles. Despite their frequent frustrations with the headlines, reporters largely refused to participate in the program. More concerned about taking on additional work than about the quality of the headlines accompanying their stories, they ended the experiment before it affected the production routine.

Some reporters, however, remain sensitive to the copyediting on their articles, and they try to foster relationships with the copy desk that increase their control over the process. Schreuder's method for reducing the possibility that her stories will not fare well with the copy editors is to get to know them personally and reward them for good work. "I try to develop a regular relationship with the copy desk, because I feel like a lot of times they look fast at something," she said. "Sometimes when they catch a factual error or something I bring a roll of Life Savers to them. Because they have a very difficult task." Nonetheless, Schreuder as well as most other reporters recalled several cases in which bad copyediting had sabotaged their writing, either gutting its key contents or cutting straight from the bottom and ruining the ending. In these cases, Shreuder pointed out, "you just want to crawl under your desk because . . . it's your name that's on the story, and . . . it's you the public calls, it's you who has to take them and the sources on the line." For several reporters, their fears of the changes made by copy editors are so strong that they often refuse to read their stories until long after they are published. "It's too late anyway," one explained, and another admitted, "I just can't handle it."

45. In *Constructing the Political Spectacle,* Murray Edelman (1988, 120) argues that spectacular news coverage of public happenings "helps erase history, social structure, economic inequalities, and discourse from the schemas that account for well-being and privations. . . . By definition a spectacle highlights obtrusive current news that captures its audience and seems to have a self-evident meaning. The meaning and the development itself are typically expressions and vivid reinforcements of the dominant ideology that justified extant inequality." Edelman's argument bears the marks of Guy Dubord's classic text, *Society of the Spectacle* ([1967] 1983). Dubord argues that "[t]he spectacle is ideology par excellence, because it exposes and manifests in its fullness the essence of all ideological systems: the impoverishment, servitude, and negation of real life. The spectacle is materially 'the expression of the separation and estrangement between man and man'" ([1967] 1983, 215).

46. In *Deciding What's News,* Herbert Gans (1979, 82 and chap. 3) identifies seven key considerations in the process of selecting newsworthy stories: "source, substantive, product, and value considerations; and commercial, audience, and political considerations."

47. The *Chicago Tribune* has produced zoned newspapers for decades, but only recently did advanced publishing technologies allow the company to swap front-page stories and graphics with ease. In 1995 the paper used this technique frequently, but managers and editors subsequently determined that

readers preferred a more consistent front page and the swapped stories became less common. In *Making Local News,* Phyllis Kaniss (1991) discusses the *Tribune*'s early experiments with zoning, and she also found that central cities provided more compelling news for metropolitan readers.

These changes are now part of the daily routine for news production at the *Chicago Tribune.* While they enable the paper to increase its market share by attracting readers who are mostly interested in local issues, they also contribute to the social and symbolic fragmentation of the metropolis, dividing readers among various news communities based on their place of residence. The city paper, then, loses some of its capacity to integrate urban communities through at least a common text that represents the life of the city, a function attributed to it by Benedict Anderson (1983) and some Durkheim-influenced sociologists of the media (e.g., Chaney [1986]). Instead, the paper helps to fracture the symbolic metropolitan community along borders built according to marketing principles (Klinenberg 2000).

A technological leader in the field, the *Tribune* is on the cutting edge of production and distribution techniques for organizing the paper for specific markets. Other major papers, such as the *New York Times* and the *Washington Post,* produce several regional editions daily, but only the *Los Angeles Times,* which covers a more sprawling and less coherent urban space, and the *Orlando Sentinel,* which like the *Los Angeles Times* is owned by the Tribune Company, compare with the *Chicago Tribune* in its marketing to different communities within the same metropolitan area. Facing increasing competition from other news providers, such as cable television and the Internet, more and more newspapers have adopted the *Tribune* model and begun producing zoned editions based on the interests of hyperlocal markets.

48. Tennison 1995.

CONCLUSION

1. *Chicago Tribune* 1995, 8.

2. Palecki, Changnon, and Kunkel 2001, 8.

3. Ibid., p. 15.

4. Ibid., pp. 19–21.

5. Ibid., pp. 13–14.

6. Ibid., p. 8.

7. Laurence Kalkstein and his colleagues (1996) have produced the most thorough set of studies showing that sophisticated advance warning systems and strong public health strategies can reduce the impact of heat waves.

8. Manier 1999, 6.

9. See the draft report, *Climate Change 2001: Impacts, Adaptation, and Vulnerability,* from the Intergovernmental Panel on Climate Change (2001, 15).

10. There is a growing public health literature on the negative health consequences of extreme inequality. Among many important studies, see Kaplan, et al. (1996) and Kennedy, Kawachi, and Prothrow-Stith (1996).

11. Massey 1996, 399.

12. Squires 1993; Bagdikian 1997.

13. See Joseph Turow, *Breaking Up America: Advertisers and the New Media World* (1997) for the most comprehensive account of how the advertising indus-

try has contributed to the specialization of news products and the segmentation of media audiences.

14. Reporters I interviewed made this same point, as does Phyllis Kaniss in *Making Local News* (1991).

15. Pierre Bourdieu (1999, 629) eloquently explains the scientific as well as the political reasons to conduct such biosocial investigations: "Producing awareness of those mechanisms that make life painful, even unlivable, does not neutralize them; bringing contradictions to light does not resolve them. But, as skeptical as we may be about the social efficacy of the sociological message, one has to acknowledge the effect it can have in allowing those who suffer to find out that their suffering can be imputed to social causes and thus to feel exonerated, and in making generally known the social origin, collectively hidden, of unhappiness in all its forms, including the most intimate, the most secret. Contrary to appearances, this observation is not a cause for despair; what the social world has done, it can, armed with this knowledge, undo."

EPILOGUE

1. See the excellent discussions of mythology and history in Ross Miller, *American Apocalypse: The Great Fire and the Myth of Chicago* (1990); and Karen Sawislak, *Smoldering City: Chicagoans and the Great Fire, 1871-1874* (Sawislak 1995).

2. See Marshall Sahlins, "The Return of the Event, Again," in Sahlins 2000, 293-351) for a rich account of the debates over evenemential history, and an attempt to forge a synthesis between structural and evenemential approaches.

3. Quoted in McSherry 1995.

4. Quoted in Jimenez 1995, 8.

Bibliography

Abraham, Laurie Kaye. 1993. *Mama might be better off dead.* Chicago: University of Chicago Press.

Abraido-Lanza, Ana, Bruce Dohrenwend, Daisy Ng-Mak, and J. Blake Turner. 1999. The Latino mortality paradox: A test of the 'salmon bias' and healthy migrant hypotheses. *American Journal of Public Health* 89:1543–48.

Administration on Aging. 1999. Profile of older Americans: 1999. Washington, D.C.: United States Administration on Aging.

Alexander, Stephen. 1998. Public resource allocation in Chicago: Impact of the city's budget process on low and moderate-income communities. Chicago: Policy Research Action Group.

Anderson, Benedict. 1983. *Imagined communities.* New York: Verso.

Anderson, Elijah. 1990. *Streetwise: Race, class, and change in an urban community.* Chicago: University of Chicago Press.

———. 1999. *Code of the street: Decency, violence, and the moral life of the inner-city.* New York: W. W. Norton.

Angel, Jacqueline, R. Angel, J. McClellan, and K. Markides. 1996. Nativity, declining health, and preferences in living arrangements among elderly Mexican Americans: Implications for long-term care. *The Gerontologist* 36:464–73.

Applegate, William, John Runyan, Linda Brasfield, Mary Lynn Williams, Charles Konigsberg, and Cheryl Fouche. 1981. Analysis of the 1980 heat wave in Memphis. *American Geriatrics Society* 29:337–42.

Arendt, Hannah. 1963. *Eichman in Jerusalem: A report on the banality of evil.* New York: Viking Press.

Bachelard, Gaston. [1934] 1984. *The New Scientific Spirit.* Boston: Beacon Press. Originally published under the title *Le Nouvel Esprit Scientifique* (Paris: Presses Universitaires de France, 1934).

Bagdikian, Ben. 1997. *The media monopoly.* Boston: Beacon Press.

Baumgartner, M. P. 1988. *The moral order of a suburb.* New York: Oxford University Press.

Beck, Ulrich. 1992. *Risk society: Towards a new modernity.* London: Sage.

Beinart, Peter. 1997. The pride of the cities. *The New Republic,* 30 June, 16–24.

Biel, Steven. 1996. *Down with the old canoe: A cultural history of the Titanic disaster.* New York: W. W. Norton.

Blazer, Dan. 1982. Social support and mortality in an elderly community population. *American Journal of Epidemiology* 115:684–94.

Boorstin, Daniel. 1961. *The image: a guide to pseudo-events in America.* New York: Harper Colophon Books.

Bourdieu, Pierre. 1991. *Language and symbolic power.* Cambridge, Mass.: Harvard University Press.

————. 1996. *The state nobility.* Stanford, Calif.: Stanford University Press.

————. 1998. *On television.* New York: The New Press.

Bourdieu, Pierre, et al. 1999. *The weight of the world: Social suffering in contemporary society.* Stanford, Calif.: Stanford University Press.

Bourgois, Philippe. 1995. *In search of respect: Selling crack in El Barrio.* Cambridge: Cambridge University Press.

Brooks-Gunn, Jeanne, Greg Duncan, and J. Lawrence Aber. 1997. Neighborhood poverty: Context and consequences for children. New York: Russell Sage Foundation.

Bryant, Rick. 1995. Experts: Daley won't feel the heat for long. *The Daily (Chicago) Southtown,* 23 July.

Buckingham, Robert, S. A. Lack, B. M. Mount, L. D. Maclean, and J. T. Collins. 1976. Living with the dying: Use of the technique of participant observation. *Canadian Medical Association Journal* 115:1211–15.

Building Organization and Leadership Development (BOLD). 1995. BOLD group endorses CHAPS police unit. Press release. Chicago: BOLD.

Burawoy, Michael. 1998. The extended case method. *Sociological Theory* 16:4–33.

Callahan, Patricia. 1995. Residents leave cooling centers in cold. *Chicago Tribune,* 17 July, sec. 2, pp. 1, 4.

Castells, Manuel. 1996. *The rise of the network society.* Oxford: Blackwell Publishers.

————. 1998. *End of millennium.* Oxford: Blackwell Publishers.

Catalano, Ralph, and Kate Pickett. 1999. A taxonomy of research concerned with place and health. In *Handbook of social studies in health and medicine,* edited by Gary Albrecht, Ray Fitzpatrick, and Susan Scrimshaw. London: Sage.

Cater, Douglass. 1959. *The fourth branch of government.* Boston: Houghton Mifflin.

Chaney, David. 1986. The symbolic mirror of ourselves: Civic ritual in mass society. In *Media, culture, and society: A critical reader,* edited by Richard Collins. Beverly Hills: Sage.

Chicago Fact Book Consortium. 1995. Local community fact book: Chicago metropolitan area. Chicago: Academy Chicago Publishers.

Chicago Housing Authority. 1995. Elderly receive needed security through Chicago Housing Authority protection of seniors program. Press release. Chicago: Chicago Housing Authority.

Chicago Sun-Times. 1995. List of those who died alone. 25 August, p. 14.

Chicago Tribune. 1992. *The worst schools in America.* Chicago: Contemporary Press.

Chicago Weekend. 1995. Daley, city guilty of negligence, says Rush. 23 July, p. 1.

Chiricos, Ted, Sarah Escholz, and Marc Gertz. 1997. Crime, news, and fear of crime: Toward an identification of audience effects. *Social Problems* 44:342–57.

Citro, Constance, and Robert Michael. 1995. *Measuring poverty: A new approach.* Washington D.C.: National Academy Press.

City of Chicago. 1995. Final report: Mayor's commission on extreme weather conditions. November.

City of Chicago, Department of Public Health. 1996. An epidemiological overview of violent crimes in Chicago, 1995.

Cohen, Adam, and Elizabeth Taylor. 2000. *American pharaoh: Mayor Richard J. Daley: his battle for Chicago and the nation.* Boston: Little, Brown, and Company.

Cohen, Stanley. 1996. Government responses to human rights reports: Claims, denials, and counterclaims. *Human Rights Quarterly* 18:517–43.

———. 2001. *States of denial: Knowing about atrocities and suffering.* Cambridge: Polity Press.

Coles, Robert. 1997. *Old and on their own.* New York: DoubleTake Books.

Comerio, Mary. 1998. *Disaster hits home: New policy for urban housing recovery.* Berkeley and Los Angeles: University of California Press.

Connell, R. W. 1995. *Masculinities.* Berkeley and Los Angeles: University of California Press.

Cook, Timothy. 1998. *Governing with the news: The news media as a political institution.* Chicago: University of Chicago Press.

Cotliar, Sharon. 1995. Count isn't overblown, medical examiner insists. *Chicago Sun-Times,* 19 July, p. 8.

Crank, John. 1994. Watchman and community: Myth and institutionalization in policing. *Law and Society Review* 28:325–51.

Cronon, William. 1995. Introduction: In search of nature. In *Uncommon ground: Toward reinventing nature,* edited by William Cronon. New York: W. W. Norton.

Das, Veena. 1995. *Critical events: An anthropological perspective on contemporary India.* Oxford: Oxford University Press.

Davis, Mike. 1990. *City of quartz: Excavating the future in Los Angeles.* London: Verso.

———. 1998. *Ecology of fear: Los Angeles and the imagination of disaster.* New York: Metropolitan Books.

———. 2001. *Late Victorian holocausts: El Nino famines and the making of the Third World.* London: Verso.

Dematte, Jane, Karen O'Mara, Jennifer Buescher, Cynthia Whitney, Sean Forsythe, Turi McNamee, Raghavendra B. Adiga, and I. Maurice Ndukwu. 1998. Near-fatal heat stroke during the 1995 heat wave in Chicago. *Annals of Internal Medicine* 129:173–81.

di Leonardo, Micaela. 1999. *Exotics at home: Anthropologists, others, American modernity.* Chicago: University of Chicago Press.

Dohan, Daniel. 1997. Culture, poverty, and economic order in two inner-city areas. Ph.D. diss., University of California, Berkeley.

Donoghue, Edmund, Michael Graham, Jeffrey Jentzen, Barry Lifchultz, James Luke, and Haresh Michandani. 1997. Criteria for the diagnosis of heat-related deaths: National Association of Medical Examiners. *The American Journal of Forensic Medicine and Pathology* 18:11–14.

Douglas, Mary, and Aaron Wildavsky. 1983. *Risk and culture: An essay on the selec-*

tion of technological and environmental dangers. Berkeley and Los Angeles: University of California Press.

Drake, St. Clair, and Horace Cayton. [1945] 1993. *Black metropolis: A study of Negro life in the northern city.* New York: Harcourt, Brace and Company. Reprint, Chicago: University of Chicago Press.

Dubord, Guy. [1967] 1983. *The society of the spectacle.* Detroit: Black and Red. Originally published under the title *La Société du Spectacle* (Paris: Editions Burchet-Chastel, 1967).

Durkheim, Emile. 1951. *Suicide: A study in sociology.* Translated by John A. Spaulding and George Simpson; edited with an introduction by George Simpson. New York: Free Press.

Durkheim, Emile, and Marcel Mauss. [1903] 1963. *Primitive classification.* Chicago: University of Chicago Press. Originally published under the title *De quelques formes primitives de classification* (*Année sociologique,* 1901–2).

Economist. 1995. Da manager: City government. 4 March, pp. A25–26.

Edelman, Murray. 1988. *Constructing the political spectacle.* Chicago: University of Chicago Press.

Ehrenhalt, Alan. 1995. *The lost city: The forgotten virtues of community in America.* New York: Basic Books.

Eig, Jonathan 1999. Da rules. *Chicago Magazine,* November, pp. 114–25.

Ellin, Nan, ed. 1997. *Architecture of Fear.* Princeton, N.J.: Princeton Architectural Press.

Emergency Net News Service. 1995. Caution urged during heat wave. <www.emergency.com.heatwave.htm>. Accessed 13 December 2000.

Engels, Frederick. [1845] 1984. *The condition of the working class in England.* Chicago: Academy Chicago Publishers. Originally published under the title *Die Lage der Arbeitenden Klasse in England* (Leipzig: O. Wigand, 1845).

Entman, Robert. 1993. Framing: Toward clarification of a fractured paradigm. *Journal of Communication* 43:51–58.

Erikson, Kai. 1976. *Everything in its path: Destruction of community in the Buffalo Creek flood.* New York: Simon and Schuster.

———. 1994. *A new species of trouble: The human experience of modern disasters.* New York: W. W. Norton.

Esping-Anderson, Gøsta. 1990. *The three worlds of welfare capitalism.* Princeton, N.J.: Princeton University Press.

———. 1999. *Social foundations of postindustrial economies.* Oxford: Oxford University Press.

Ettema, James, and Theodore Glasser. 1998. *Custodians of conscience.* New York: Columbia University Press.

Fallows, James. 1996. *Breaking the news: How the media undermine American democracy.* New York: Vintage.

Farmer, Paul. 1999. *Infections and inequalities: The modern plagues.* Berkeley and Los Angeles: University of California Press.

Federman, Maya, Thesia Garner, Kathleen Short, W. Boman Cutter IV, John Kiely, David Levine, Duane McGough, and Marilyn McMillen. 1996. What does it mean to be poor in America? *Monthly Labor Review,* 17 May, pp. 3–17.

Fegelman, Andrew. 1995. Medical examiner takes the heat. *Chicago Tribune,* 25 July, sec. 2, p. 3.

Fischer, Claude S. 1975. Toward a subcultural theory of urbanism. *American Journal of Sociology* 80:1319–41.

———. [1976] 1984. *The urban experience.* New York: Harcourt, Brace, Jovanovich. Reprint, San Diego: Harcourt, Brace, Jovanovich.

———. 1982. *To dwell among friends: Personal networks in town and city.* Chicago: University of Chicago Press.

Fischer, Claude, and Susan Phillips. 1982. Who is alone? Social characteristics of people with small networks. In *Loneliness: A sourcebook on current theory, research, and therapy,* edited by Leticia Anne Peplau and Daniel Perlman. New York: Wiley.

Fleming-Moran, M., T. Kenworthy-Bennett, and K. Harlow. 1991. Illinois state needs assessment survey of elders aged 55 and over. Bloomington: Heartland Center on Aging, Disability, and Long Term Care, School of Public Health and Environmental Affairs, Indiana University; and the National Center for Senior Living, South Bend.

Flock, Jeff. 1995. Chicago morgue struggle to keep up with heat deaths. 16 July, Cable Network News (CNN).

Fornek, Scott, and Neil Steinberg. 1995. Death was the only equalizer for varied victims. *Chicago Sun-Times,* 17 July, p. 10.

Frazier, E. Franklin. 1939. *The Negro family in the United States.* Chicago: University of Chicago Press.

———. 1961. *The Negro church in America.* Liverpool, England: Liverpool University Press.

Freudenburg, W. R. 1988. Perceived risk, real risk: social science and the art of probabilistics risk assessment. *Science* 242:44-49.

Furstenberg, Frank, Thomas Cook, Jacqueline Eccles, and Arnold Sameroff. 1998. *Managing to make it: Urban families and adolescent success.* Chicago: University of Chicago Press.

Gamson, William. 1992. *Talking politics.* New York: Cambridge University Press.

Gans, Herbert. 1962. *The urban villagers: Group and class in the life of Italian-Americans.* Glencoe, Ill.: Free Press.

———. 1979. *Deciding what's news.* New York: Pantheon.

———. 1995. *The war against the poor: The underclass and antipoverty policy.* New York: Basic Books.

———. 1997. Best-sellers by sociologists: An exploratory study. *Contemporary Sociology* 26:131–35.

Gibson, Hamilton. 2000. *Loneliness in later life.* London: Macmillan Press.

Gilbert, Neil. 1995. *Welfare justice: Restoring social equity.* New Haven, Conn.: Yale University Press.

Glassner, Barry. 1999. *The culture of fear: Why Americans are afraid of the wrong things: crime, drugs, minorities, teen moms, killer kids, mutant microbes, plane crashes, road rage, and so much more.* New York: Basic Books.

Glastris, Paul 1992. Reinventing da mayor. *U.S. News and World Report,* 23 March, pp. 40–42.

Goetz, Barry. 1997. State theory and fire control: selection mechanisms in local government. *Critical Sociology* 23:32–62.

Goffman, Erving. 1959. *The presentation of self in everyday life.* New York: Anchor Books.

———. 1974. *Frame analysis.* New York: Harper Colophon.

Gould, Stephen Jay. [1981] 1996. *The mismeasure of man.* New York: W. W. Norton. Reprint, New York: W. W. Norton.

Greenwich, Howard, Jacqueline Leavy, and John Jones. 1996. *Moving beyond the basics: Building Chicago for the next century.* Chicago: Neighborhood Capital Budget Group.

Groth, Paul. 1994. *Living Downtown.* Berkeley and Los Angeles: University of California Press.

Gurley, Jan, Nancy Lum, Merle Sande, Bernard Lo, and Mitchell Katz. 1996. Persons found in their homes helpless or dead. *New England Journal of Medicine* 334:1710–16.

Habermas, Jurgen. 1989. *The structural transformation of the public sphere.* Cambridge, Mass.: MIT Press.

Halpern, Robert. 1999. *Fragile families, fragile solutions: A history of supportive services for families in poverty.* New York: Columbia University Press.

Hambleton, Robin. 1990. Future directions for urban government in Britain and America. *Journal of Urban Affairs* 12:75–94.

Hannerz, Ulf. 1969. *Soulside: Inquiries into ghetto culture and community.* New York: Columbia University Press.

Hartstein, Larry. 1995. Hydrant-closing crews pelted with bullets. *Chicago Tribune,* 17 July, sec. 2, p. 4.

Hirsch, Arnold. 1983. *Making the second ghetto: Race and housing in Chicago, 1940–1960.* Cambridge: Cambridge University Press.

Hoch, Charles, and Robert Slayton. 1989. *New homeless and old: Community and the skid row hotel.* Philadelphia: Temple University Press.

Hochschild, Arlie Russell. 1973. *The unexpected community: Portrait of an old age subculture.* Berkeley and Los Angeles: University of California Press.

House, James, Cynthia Robbins, and Helen Metzner. 1982. The association of social relationships and activities with mortality: Prospective evidence from the Tecumseh Community Health Study. *American Journal of Epidemiology* 116:123–40.

Hunter, Albert. 1974. *Symbolic communities: The persistence and change of Chicago's local communities.* Chicago: University of Chicago Press.

Illinois Department of Public Health. 1997. Vital Statistics Basic Research Series 1/3. Springfield.

Intergovernmental Panel on Climate Change. 2001. Summary for policymakers: Climate change 2001: impacts, adaptation, and vulnerability. Geneva.

Irvine, Martha. 2001. Hispanic influx shaping Chicago. *Chicago Sun-Times,* 11 March, p. 1.

Jacobs, Jane. 1961. *The death and life of great American cities.* New York: Vintage.

Janeway, Michael. 1999. *Republic of denial: Press, politics, and public life.* New Haven, Conn.: Yale University Press.

Jargowsky, Paul. 1997. *Poverty and place: Ghettos, barrios, and the American city.* New York: Russell Sage Foundation.

Jasper, James. 2000. *Restless nation: Starting over in America.* Chicago: University of Chicago Press.

Jencks, Christopher. 1994. *The homeless.* Cambridge, Mass.: Harvard University Press.

Jencks, Christopher, and Barbara Boyle Torrey. 1988. Beyond income and poverty: Trends in social welfare among children and the elderly since 1960. In *The vulnerable*, edited by John Palmer, Timothy Smeeding, and Barbara Boye Torrey. Washington D.C.: The Urban Institute Press.

Jimenez, Gilbert. 1995. Strangers bid heat victims sad farewell. *Chicago Sun-Times*, 26 August, pp. 1–8.

Jimenez, Gilbert and Alex Rodriguez. 1995. Death toll climbs to 179. *Chicago Sun-Times*, 18 July, p. 6.

Jones, LeAlan, Lloyd Newman, and David Isay. 1997. *Our America: Life and death on the South Side of Chicago*. New York: Washington Square Press.

Jones, T. Stephen, Arthur Liang, Edwin Kilbourne, Marie Griffin, Peter Patriarca, Steven G. File Wassilak, Robert Mullan, Robert Herrick, H. Denny Donnell Jr., Keewhan Choi, and Stephen Thacker. 1982. Morbidity and mortality associated with the July 1980 heat wave in St. Louis and Kansas City, Mo. *Journal of the American Medical Association* 247:3327–31.

Joseph, Janice. 1997. Fear of crime among black elderly. *Journal of Black Studies* 27:698–717.

Kalkstein, Laurence. 1995. Lessons from a very hot summer. *Lancet* 346:857–59.

Kalkstein, Laurence, Paul Jamason, J. Scott Greene, Jerry Libby, and Lawrence Robinson. 1996. The Philadelphia hot weather—health watch/warning system: Development and application, summer 1995. *Bulletin of the American Meteorological Society* 77:1519–28.

Kaniss, Phyllis. 1991. *Making local news*. Chicago: University of Chicago Press.

Kaplan, George, Elsie Pamuk, John Lynch, Richard Cohen, and Jennifer Balfour. 1996. Inequality in income and mortality in the United States: Analysis of mortality and potential pathways. *British Medical Journal* 312:999–1003.

Kaplan, Joel, and Sharman Stein. 1995. City deaths in heat wave triple normal. *Chicago Tribune*, 20 July, sec. 1, pp. 1, 10.

Kasper, Judith. 1988. Aging alone: Profiles and projections. New York: The Commonwealth Fund.

Kass, John. 1995a. Daley, aides try to deflect heat criticism. *Chicago Tribune*, 18 July, sec. 2, p. 1.

———. 1995b. Donoghue is backed on heat-wave toll. *Chicago Tribune*, 28 July, Chicago, sec. 2, p. 3.

———. 1995c. In the heat, government shouldn't take beating. *Chicago Tribune*, 23 July, sec. 4, p. 1.

———. 1995d. Rambunctious aldermen sideline dog law, heat-wave probe. *Chicago Tribune*, 2 August, sec. 2, p.3.

Kass, John, and Joel Kaplan. 1995. Heat plan is launched. *Chicago Tribune*, 21 July, sec. 2, pp.1, 6.

Katz, Michael. 1993. *The "underclass" debate*. Princeton, N.J.: Princeton University Press.

Kearl, Michael. 1996. Dying well: The unspoken dimension of aging well. *The American Behavioral Scientist* 39:336–60.

Keigher, Sharon. 1991. *Housing risks and homelessness among the urban elderly*. New York: Haworth Press.

Kennedy, Bruce, Ichiro Kawachi, and Deborah Prothrow-Stith. 1996. Income distribution and mortality: Cross-Sectional ecological study of the Robin Hood Index in the United States. *British Medical Journal* 312:1004–7.

Kiernan, Louise, and Graeme Zielinski. 1995. Casualties of heat just like most of us: Many rejected any kind of help. *Chicago Tribune,* 18 July, sec. 1, pp. 1, 6.

Kilbourne, E., K. Choi, T. Jones, and S. Thacker. 1982. Risk factors for heat-stroke. *Journal of the American Medical Association* 247:3332–36.

Kitagawa, Evelyn, and Philip Hauser. 1973. *Differential mortality in the United States: A study in socioeconomic epidemiology.* Cambridge, Mass.: Harvard University Press.

Kleppner, Paul. 1985. *Chicago divided: The making of a black mayor.* DeKalb: Northern Illinois University Press.

Klinenberg, Eric. 2000. Information et production numerique. *Actes de la Recherche en Sciences Sociales* 134:66–75.

Kornblum, William. 1974. *Blue collar community.* Chicago: University of Chicago Press.

Krause, Neal. 1993. Neighborhood deterioration and social isolation in later life. *International Journal of Aging and Human Development* 36:9–38.

Lancaster, Roger. 1992. *Life is hard: Machismo, danger, and the intimacy of power in Nicaragua.* Berkeley and Los Angeles: University of California Press.

Larson, Erik. 1999. *Isaac's storm: A man, a time, and the deadliest hurricane in history.* New York: Crown.

LaVeist, Thomas, Robert Sellers, Karin Elliot Brown, and Kim Nickerson. 1997. Extreme social isolation, use of community-based support services, and mortality among African American elderly women. *American Journal of Community Psychology* 25:721–32.

Lawlor, Edward, Gunnar Almgren, and Mary Gomberg. 1993. Aging in Chicago: Demography. Chicago: Chicago Community Trust.

Le, Phuong, and Joan Giangrasse Kates. 1995. If you can stand the heat, you must be out-of-towner. *Chicago Tribune,* 13 July, sec. 2, pp. 1, 6.

Leavitt, Jacqueline, and Susan Saegert. 1990. *From abandonment to hope: Community-households in Harlem.* New York: Columbia University Press.

Lee, Mordecai. 1999. Reporters and bureaucrats: Public relations counter-strategies by public administrators in an era of media disinterest in government. *Public Relations Review* 25:451–563.

Lev, Michael. 1995. Alone in life, unclaimed in death. *Chicago Tribune,* 30 July, sec. 1, pp. 1, 12.

Levitan, Sar A. 1991. *Programs in aid of the poor.* Baltimore: Johns Hopkins University Press.

Lieberman, David. 1998. The rise and rise of 24-hour local news. *Columbia Journalism Review,* no. 37 (November/December): 54–57.

Liebow, Elliot. 1967. *Tally's corner: A study of Negro streetcorner men.* Boston: Back Bay Books.

Lincoln, C. Eric, and Lawrence Mamiya. 1990. *The black church in the African-American experience.* Durham, N.C.: Duke University Press.

Linsky, Martin, Wendy O'Donnell, and Jonathan Moore. 1986. *Impact: How the press affects federal policymaking.* New York: W. W. Norton.

Lipsky, Michael. 1980. *Street-level bureaucracy: Dilemmas of the individual in public services.* New York: Russell Sage Foundation.

Little Brothers Friends of the Elderly. 1997. Annual report: Little Brothers is about relationships. Chicago: Little Brothers Friends of the Elderly.

Lowry, William. 1967. The climate of cities. *Scientific American* 217:15–23.

Manier, Jeremy. 1999. Lessons of '95 helped keep heat toll down. *Chicago Tribune,* 3 August, sec. 1, p. 6.

Marcuse, Peter. 1993. What's so new about divided cities? *International Journal of Urban and Regional Research* 17:355–65.

———. 1997. The enclave, the citadel, and the ghetto: What has changed in the post-Fordist U.S. city. *Urban Affairs Review* 33:228–64.

Martin, Andrew. 1995. City murders on rise along with thermometer. *Chicago Tribune,* 14 July, sec. 2, p. 3.

Martinez, Beverly, Joseph Annest, Edwin Kilbourne, Marilyn Kirk, Kung-Jong Lui, and Suzanne Smith. 1989. Geographic distribution of heat-related deaths among elderly persons. *Journal of the American Medical Association* 262:2246–50.

Massey, Douglas. 1996. The age of extremes: Concentrated affluence and poverty in the twenty-first century. *Demography* 33:395–412.

Massey, Douglas, and Nancy Denton. 1993. *American apartheid: Segregation and the making of the underclass.* Cambridge, Mass.: Harvard University Press.

Mauss, Marcel. [1916] 1979. Seasonal variations of the Eskimo: A study in social morphology (in collaboration with Henri Beuchat). London and Boston: Routledge & Kegan Paul. Orignally published under the title *Essai sur les variations saisonnièrs des sociétés Eskimos: étude de morphologie sociale* (Paris, 1916).

McKenzie, R. D. 1925. The ecological approach to the study of the human community. In *The city: Suggestions for investigation of human behavior in the urban environment,* edited by Robert Park and Ernest Burgess. Chicago: University of Chicago Press.

McMurray, Scott. 1995. Little Village hits big. *Chicago,* October 1995, pp. 33–35.

McRoberts, Omar, 2001. Black churches, community and development. *Shelterforce,* January/February, pp. 8–11.

McSherry, Meg. 1995a. Burying the forgotten. *The Daily (Chicago) Southtown,* 26 August, pp. A1–A5.

———. 1995b. Staying ahead of heat. *The Daily (Chicago) Southtown,* 23 July, pp. A1–A8.

Meares, Tracey. 1998. Peace and crime. *Chicago Kent Law Review* 73:669–705.

Merry, Sally Engle. 1981. *Urban danger: Life in a neighborhood of strangers.* Philadelphia: Temple University Press.

Metro Seniors in Action. 1995. Heat wave ravages seniors, Daley passes buck. *Metro Senior,* pp. 1, 3.

Meyerhoff, Barbara. 1978. *Number our days.* New York: Touchstone Books.

Miethe, Terance. 1995. Fear and withdrawal. *The Annals of the American Academy* 539:14–29.

Miller, Ross. 1990. *American apocalypse: The Great Fire and the myth of Chicago.* Chicago: University of Chicago Press.

Mitchell, James, ed. 1999. *Crucibles of hazard: Mega-cities and disasters in transition.* Tokyo: United Nations University Press.

Mitchell, Mary, and Gilbert Jimenez. 1995. CDC endorses county coroner's heat findings. *Chicago Sun-Times,* 28 July, p. 12.

Molotch, Harvey, and Marilyn Lester. 1974. News as purposive behavior: On the strategic use of routine events, accidents, and scandals. *American Sociological Review* 39:101–12.

———. 1975. Accidental news: The great oil spill as local occurrence and national event. *American Journal of Sociology* 81:235–60.

Monkkonen, Eric. 1993. Nineteenth century institutions. In *The "underclass" debate,* edited by Michael Katz. Princeton, N.J.: Princeton University Press.

Nashold, Raymond, Jeffrey Jentzen, Patrick Remington, and Peggy Peterson. N.d. Excessive heat deaths, Wisconsin, June 20–August 19, 1995. Unpublished manuscript.

National Weather Service. 1996. Natural disaster survey report: July 1995 heat wave. Silver Spring, Md.: U.S. Department of Commerce, National Oceanic and Atmosphere Administration, National Weather Service.

Neal, Steve. 1995. Daley's leadership wilted in heat crisis. *Chicago Sun-Times,* 25 July, p. 25.

Nieves, Evelyn. 2000. In San Francisco, more live alone, and die alone, too. *New York Times,* 25 June, p. 10A.

North Lawndale Family Network. 1998. Community assets: A North Lawndale directory of services 1998–99. Chicago: North Lawndale Family Network.

Nuland, Sherwin. 1993. *How we die: Reflections on life's final chapter.* New York: Vintage.

Oechsli, Frank, and Robert Buechley. 1970. Excess mortality associated with three Los Angeles September heat spells." *Environmental Research* 3:277–84.

Orloff, Ann Shola. 1993. *The politics of pensions: A comparative analysis of Britain, Canada, and the United States, 1880–1940.* Madison: University of Wisconsin Press.

Orton, J. Douglas, and Karl Weick. 1990. Loosely coupled systems: A reconceptualization. *Academy of Management Review* 15:203–23.

Osborne, David, and Ted Gaebler. 1992. *Reinventing government: How the entrepreneurial spirit is transforming the public sector.* New York: Plume.

Palecki, Michael, Stanley Changnon, and Kenneth Kunkel. 2001. The nature and impacts of the July 1999 heat wave in the Midwestern U.S.: Learning from the lessons of 1995. *Bulletin of the American Meteorological Society* 82, no. 7:1353–67.

Park, Robert. [1916] 1969. The city: Suggestions for the investigation of human behavior in the urban environment. In *Classic essays on the culture of cities,* edited by Richard Sennett. Englewood Cliffs, N.J.: Prentice-Hall. Originally published in *American Journal of Sociology* 20:577–612.

Patterson, Orlando. 1998. *Rituals of blood.* Boston: Beacon.

Pattillo-McCoy, Mary. 1998. Church culture as a strategy of action in the black community. *American Sociological Review* 63:767–84.

———. 1999. *Black picket fences: Privilege and peril among the black middle class.* Chicago: University of Chicago Press.

Pearson, Rick. 1995. Funding to help poor pay heating bills evaporating. *Chicago Tribune*, 20 July, sec. 2, p. 6.

Perrow, Charles. 1984. *Normal accidents*. New York: Basic Books.

Perrow, Charles, and Mauro Guillen. 1990. *The AIDS disaster: The failure of organizations in New York and the nation*. New Haven, Conn.: Yale University Press.

Platt, Jennifer. 1992. Cases of cases . . . of cases. In *What is a case? Exploring the foundations of social inquiry*, edited by Charles Ragin and Howard Becker. Cambridge, Mass.: Cambridge University Press.

Popkin, Susan, Victoria Gwiasda, Lynn Olson, Dennis Rosenbaum, and Larry Buron. 2000. *The hidden war: Crime and the tragedy of public housing in Chicago*. New Brunswick, N.J.: Rutgers University Press.

Pugh, Ralph. 1997. Pilsen/Little Village. *Chicago History* 26, no. 1 (spring):40–61.

Putnam, Robert. 2000. *Bowling alone: The collapse and revival of American community*. New York: Simon and Schuster.

Ragin, Charles, and Howard Becker, eds. 1992. *What is a case? Exploring the foundations of social inquiry*. Cambridge, Mass.: Cambridge University Press.

Raika, Robert. 1995. *Report of the heat related deaths in Cook County*. Illinois State Senate, Springfield.

Richards, Cindy. 1995. Less government? Not if it costs me. *Chicago Sun-Times*, 21 July, p. 23.

Riesman, David, Nathan Glazer, and Reuel Denny. 1950. *The lonely crowd: A study of the changing American character*. New Haven, Conn.: Yale University Press.

Rodriguez, Alex, and Mark Brown. 1995. 116 die; few using city cooling centers. *Chicago Sun-Times*, 17 July, pp. 1, 8.

Rollinson, Paul. 1990. The story of Edward: The everyday geography of elderly single room occupancy (SRO) hotel tenants. *Journal of Contemporary Ethnography* 19:188–206.

Rosen, Jay. 1999. *What are journalists for?* New Haven, Conn.: Yale University Press.

Ross, Catherine, John Reynolds, and Karlyn Geis. 2000. The contingent meaning of neighborhood stability for residents' psychological well-being. *American Sociological Review* 65:581–97.

Royko, Mike. 1995. Killer heat wave or media event? *Chicago Tribune*, 18 July, sec. 1, p. 3.

Rubinstein, Robert. 1986. *Singular paths: Old men living alone*. New York: Columbia University Press.

Ruggles, Patricia. 1990. *Drawing the line: Alternative poverty measures and their implications for public policy*. Washington, D.C.: Urban Institute Press.

Sahlins, Marshall. 2000. *Culture in practice*. New York: Zone Books.

Sampson, Robert, Stephen Raudenbush, and Felton Earls. 1997. Neighborhood and violent crime: A multivariate study of collective efficacy. *Science* 277:918–24.

Sanchez-Jankowski, Martin. 1991. *Islands in the streets: Gangs and American society*. Berkeley and Los Angeles: University of California Press.

Sawislak, Karen. 1995. *Smoldering city: Chicagoans and the Great Fire, 1871–1874*. Chicago: University of Chicago Press.

Schreuder, Cindy, and Peter Gorner. 1995. Coroners don't always agree on when heat kills. *Chicago Tribune,* 18 July, sec. 1, pp. 1, 6.

Schreuder, Cindy, and Sharman Stein. 1995. Cities learn lessons from killer heat. *Chicago Tribune,* 20 July, sec. 2, p. 1.

Schudson, Michael. 1978. *Discovering the news.* New York: Basic.

———. 1995. *The power of news.* Cambridge, Mass.: Harvard University Press.

Seale, Clive. 1995. Dying alone. *Sociology of Health and Illness* 17:376–92.

———. 1996. Living alone towards the end of life. *Aging and Society* 16:75–91.

Secter, Bob. 1995. People forget how to beat the heat. *Chicago Sun-Times,* 18 July, p. 7.

Seeman, Teresa, George Kaplan, Lisa Knudson, Richard Cohen, and Jack Guralnik. 1987. Social network ties and mortality among the elderly in the Alameda County study. *American Journal of Epidemiology* 126:714–23.

Seidenstat, Paul. 1996. Privatization: Trends, interplay of forces, and lessons learned. *Policy Studies Journal* 24:464–77.

Semenza, Jan. 1995. Letter to Chicago Department of Public Health, 20 July. Atlanta.

Semenza, Jan, Joel McCullough, W. Dana Flanders, Michael McGeehin, and John Lumpkin. 1999. Excess hospital admissions during the July 1995 heat wave in Chicago. *American Journal of Preventive Medicine* 16:269–77.

Semenza, Jan, Carol Rubin, Kenneth Falter, Joel Selanikio, W. Dana Flanders, Holly Howe, and John Wilhelm. 1996. Heat-related deaths during the July 1995 heat wave in Chicago. *New England Journal of Medicine* 335:84–90.

Sen, Amartya. 1981. *Poverty and famines: An essay on entitlement and deprivation.* Oxford: Oxford University Press.

Sennett, Richard. 1969. An introduction. In *Classic essays on the culture of cities,* edited by Richard Sennett. Englewood Cliffs, N.J.: Prentice Hall.

Shen, Tiefu, Holly Howe, Celan Alo, and Ronald Moolenaar. 1998. Toward a broader definition of heat-related death: Comparison of mortality estimates from medical examiners' classification with those from total death differentials during the July 1995 Chicago heat wave. *The American Journal of Forensic Medicine and Pathology* 19:113–18.

Shen, Tiefu, Holly Howe, Ruth Ann Tobias, and Chandrima Roy. 1995. Executive summary: Community characteristics correlated with heat-related mortality. Chicago, Illinois, July 1995. Illinois Department of Public Health, Springfield.

Siewers, Alf. 1995. Isolated times may have fed heat wave toll. *Chicago Sun-Times,* 23 July, p. 11.

Sigal, Leon. 1986. Sources make the news. In *Reading the news,* edited by Robert Karl Manoff and Michael Schudson. New York: Pantheon.

Silverstein, Merrill, and Linda Waite. 1993. Are blacks more likely than whites to receive and provide social support in middle and old age? Yes, no, and maybe so. *Journal of Gerontology* 48:S212–22.

Simon, Herbert. 1994. Hyperthermia and heatstroke. *Hospital Practitioner* 8: 65–80.

Singer, Eleanor. 1987. Reporting hazards: Their benefits and costs. *Journal of Communication* 37:10–26.

Skogan, Wesley. 1990. *Disorder and decline: Crime and the spiral of decay in American neighborhoods.* Berkeley and Los Angeles: University of California Press.

———. 1993. The various meanings of fear. In *Fear of crime and criminal victimization,* edited by Wolfgang Bilsky, Christian Pfeiffer, and Peter Wetzels. Stuttgart: Ferdinand Enke Verlag.

Skogan, Wesley, and Susan Hartnett. 1997. *Community policing, Chicago style.* New York: Oxford University Press.

Skogan, Wesley, Susan Hartnett, Jill DuBois, Jennifer Comey, Marianne Kaiser, and Justine Lovig. 1999. *On the beat: Police and community problem solving.* Boulder, Colo.: Westview.

Slater, Philip. 1990. *The pursuit of loneliness.* Boston: Beacon Press.

Smoyer, Karen. 1998. Putting risk in its place: Methodological considerations for investigating extreme event health risk. *Social Science Medicine* 47:1809–24.

Sneed, Michael. 1995. Michael Sneed's column. *Chicago Sun-Times,* 20 July, p. 4.

Sood, Rahul, Geoffrey Stockdale, and Everett M. Rogers. 1987. How the news media operate in natural disasters. *Journal of Communication* 37:27–41.

Spear, Allan. 1967. *Black Chicago: The making of a Negro ghetto 1890–1920.* Chicago: University of Chicago Press.

Spergel, Irving, and Susan Grossman. 1997. The Little Village project: A community approach to the gang problem. *Social Work* 42:456–70.

Spielman, Fran, and Mary Mitchell. 1995a. City ignored emergency plan. *Chicago Sun-Times,* 18 July, p. 1.

———. 1995b. The shocking toll: 376. *Chicago Sun-Times,* 19 July, pp. 1, 9.

Squires, Gregory, Larry Bennett, Kathleen McCourt, and Philip Nyden. 1987. *Chicago: Race, class, and the response to urban decline.* Philadelphia: Temple University Press.

Squires, James. 1993. *Read all about it! The corporate takeover of America's newspapers.* New York: Times Books.

Stack, Carol. 1974. *All our kin: Strategies for survival in a black community.* New York: Harper Torchbook.

Starks, Robert. 1995. The black community demands the firing of the superintendent of Fire and other department heads in the wake of heat disaster. *Chicago Standard News,* 20 July.

Stein, Sharmon. 1995. Exceptionally high humidity proved to be the real culprit. *Chicago Tribune,* 18 July, sec. 2, pp. 1, 4.

Steinberg, Neil. 1995. Seniors suffer and endure in sweltering CHA high-rise. *Chicago Sun-Times,* 17 July, p. 10.

Steinberg, Ted. 2000. *Acts of God: The unnatural history of natural disaster in America.* New York: Oxford University Press.

Stone, Deborah. 1997. *Policy paradox: The art of political decision making.* New York: W. W. Norton.

Susser, Ida. 1993. Creating family forms: The exclusion of men and teenage boys from families in the New York City shelter system. *Critique of Anthropology* 13:267–85.

Suttles, Gerald. 1968. *The social order of the slum: Ethnicity and territory in the inner city.* Chicago: University of Chicago Press.

———. 1990. *The man-made city: The land use confidence game in Chicago.* Chicago: University of Chicago Press.

Szasz, Andrew, and Michael Meuser. 1997. Environmental inequalities: Literature review and proposals for new directions in research and theory. *Current
Sociology* 45:99–120.

Taub, Richard, D. Garth Taylor, and Jan Durham. 1984. *Paths of neighborhood
change: Race and crime in urban America.* Chicago: University of Chicago Press.

Tennison, Patricia. 1995. Finding the mane attraction." *Chicago Tribune,* 20 July,
Metro-McHenry, p. 1.

Thompson, Estina, and Neal Krause. 1998. Living alone and neighborhood
characteristics as predictors of social support in later life. *Journal of Gerontology* 53B:S354–64.

Tigges, Leann, Irene Brown, and Gary Green. 1998. Social isolation of the urban poor: Race, class, and neighborhood effects. *Sociological Quarterly* 39:
53–77.

TriData Corporation. 1999. *Comprehensive review of Chicago Fire Department.* Ar-
lington, Va. June.

Tuchman, Gaye. 1972. Objectivity as strategic ritual: An examination of newsmen's notions of objectivity. *American Journal of Sociology* 77:660–79.

———. 1973. Making news by doing work: Routinizing the unexpected. *American Journal of Sociology* 79:110–31.

Turow, Joseph. 1997. *Breaking up America: Advertisers and the new media world.*
Chicago: University of Chicago Press.

U.S. Centers for Disease Control and Prevention. 1984. Epidemiologic notes
and reports illness and death due to environmental heat—Georgia and St.
Louis, Missouri, 1983. *Morbidity and Mortality Weekly Report* 33, no. 23:325–6.

———. 1995a. Heat-related illnesses and deaths—United States, 1994–1995.
Morbidity and Mortality Weekly Report 44:465–68.

———. 1995b. Heat-related mortality—Chicago, July 1995. *Morbidity and Mortality Weekly Report* 44:577–79.

———. 1996. Heat-related mortality—Milwaukee, Wisconsin, July 1995. *Morbidity and Mortality Weekly Report* 45:505–7.

U.S. Department of Commerce, Bureau of the Census. 1995. *Statistical Abstract
of the United States.* Washington, D.C.

Vaughan, Diane. 1996. *The Challenger launch decision: Risky technology, culture,
and deviance at NASA.* Chicago: University of Chicago Press.

Velkoff, Victoria, and Valerie Lawson. 1998. International brief: Gender and
aging: caregiving. Washington, D.C.: U.S. Department of Commerce, Bureau of the Census.

Venkatesh, Sudhir. 2001. Chicago's pragmatic planners: American sociology
and the myth of community. *Social Science History* 25, no. 2:276–317.

Wacquant, Loïc. 1994. The new urban color line: The state and fate of the
ghetto in PostFordist America. In *Social theory and the politics of identity,* edited
by Craig Calhoun. Oxford: Basil Blackwell.

———. 1996. The rise of advanced marginality: Notes on its nature and implications. *Acta Sociologica* 39:121–39.

———. 1997a. For an analytic of racial domination. *Political Power and Social
Theory* 2:221–34.

———. 1997b. Three pernicious premises in the study of the U.S. ghetto. *International Journal of Urban and Regional Research* 21:341–53.

Wallace, Roderick. 1993. Recurrent collapse of the fire system in New York City: The failure of paramilitary systems as a phase change. *Environment and Planning A* 25:233–44.

Walton, John. 1992. Making the theoretical case. In *What is a case? Exploring the foundations of social inquiry*, edited by Charles Ragin and Howard Becker. Cambridge: Cambridge University Press.

Weir, Margaret. 1998. Big cities confront the new federalism. In *Big cities in the welfare transition*, edited by Alfred Kahn and Sheila. Kammerman. New York: Columbia University School of Social Work.

Whitman, Steve. 1995. Comments on the report of the Morbidity and Mortality Analysis Committee. 6 September, Chicago Department of Health, Chicago.

Whitman, Steven, Glenn Good, Edmund Donoghue, Nanette Benbow, Wen-yuan Shou, and Shanxuan Mou. 1997. Mortality in Chicago attributed to the July 1995 heat wave. *American Journal of Public Health* 87:1515–18.

Wieviorka, Michel. 1992. Case studies: History or sociology. In *What is a case? Exploring the foundations of social inquiry*, edited by Charles Ragin and Howard Becker. Cambridge: Cambridge University Press.

Williams, Raymond. [1974] 1992. *Television: Technology and Cultural Form*. London: Fontana. Reprint, Middleton, Conn.: Wesleyan University Press.

Wilson, William Julius. 1987. *The truly disadvantaged: The inner city, the underclass, and public policy*. Chicago: University of Chicago Press.

———. 1996. *When work disappears: The world of the new urban poor*. New York: Alfred Knopf.

Wirth, Louis, and Eleanor Bernert. 1949. *Local community fact book of Chicago*. Chicago: University of Chicago Press.

Wolf, Jacquelyn, Naomi Breslau, Amasa Ford, Henry Ziegler, and Anna Ward. 1983. Distance and contacts: Interactions of black urban elderly adults with family and friends. *Journal of Gerontology* 38:465–71.

Wuthnow, Robert. 1998. *Loose connections: Joining together in America's fragmented communities*. Cambridge, Mass.: Harvard University Press.

Zhao, Dingxin. 1998. Ecologies of social movements: Student mobilization during the 1989 prodemocracy movement in Beijing. *American Journal of Sociology* 103:1493–1529.

Zukin, Sharon. 1995. *The cultures of cities*. Oxford and Malden, Mass.: Blackwell Publishers.

Index